Praise for Dennis Kimbro's previous book,
Think And Grow Rich: A Black Choice
(coauthored with Napoleon Hill)

"Dennis Kimbro has taken Napoleon Hill's masterpiece and set it on the cutting edge. By combining ideas for achievement with his own innate wisdom, Dennis Kimbro has, in fact, redefined success—not just for Black America, but for anyone lucky enough to read a copy of this book. . . . It will long stand as the definitive guide for *anyone* in search of success. *Think and Grow Rich: A Black Choice* is a triumph, not only for the writer, but also for the reader."

—HARVEY MACKAY
Author of
Beware the Naked Man Who Offers You His Shirt
and
Swim With the Sharks Without Being Eaten Alive

"*Think and Grow Rich: A Black Choice* is the perfect updating of a classic, a must-read for Black America. Kimbro and Hill have created a sensible and powerful guide to getting ahead that will long stand as the guide not only to *reaching,* but also *explaining,* success."

—AHMAD RASHAD
Network Host

"This book should be required reading for all African Americans truly committed to the pursuit of happiness and fulfillment."

—*Black Enterprise*

Also by Dennis Kimbro
Published by The Random House Publishing Group:

THINK AND GROW RICH: A BLACK CHOICE

DAILY MOTIVATIONS FOR AFRICAN-AMERICAN SUCCESS

Dennis Kimbro

THE RANDOM HOUSE PUBLISHING GROUP • NEW YORK

A Fawcett Book
Published by The Random House Publishing Group
Copyright © 1993 by Dennis Kimbro

Published in the United States by Fawcett Books, an imprint of The Random House Publishing Group, a division of Random House, Inc., New York, and simultaneously in Canada by Random House of Canada Limited, Toronto.

Fawcett Books and colophon are trademarks of Random House, Inc.

www.ballantinebooks.com

Library of Congress Catalog Card Number: 93-90037

ISBN 0-449-22325-6

Manufactured in the United States of America

First Hardcover Edition: November 1993
First Mass Market Edition: November 1994

OPM 29 28 27 26 25 24 23 22 21 20

Who Are We?

*"We're a special people, We're the best and the
brightest our ancestors ever produced!"*
—JAMES WELDON JOHNSON, WRITER

Who are we? We're African Americans, and we are achievers!
We are mothers, fathers, sons, daughters, nieces, and nephews. We are doctors, lawyers, teachers, writers, and entrepreneurs. *We're African Americans, and we are achievers!*

We are jet black, blue black, dark brown, brown-skinned, medium brown, yellow, high yellow, light-skinned, fair skinned, light, bright, almost white, redbone, but Afro-American to the bone. *We're African Americans, and we are achievers!*

We have climbed the highest mountains, scaled the highest heights. We are visionaries, innovators, dreamers, creators, leaders, builders, and doers. *We're African Americans, and we are achievers!*

We made it past slavery. We've been hurried and hassled; discouraged and downtrodden. We've provided an unpaid service to this country by serving others first and ourselves last. Yet we are survivors, overcomers, those who have endured. Though we're the last hired and the first fired, we know the meaning of perseverance. We know a setback is a setup for a comeback. We've survived the end of the world, and now handle miracles by appointment only.

On a scale from one to ten, we are one hundred! *We're African Americans, and we are achievers!*

I am an African-American Achiever.

Designed for Success

"I know who my real Father is."
—REVEREND CECIL "CHIP" MURRAY,
A.M.E. CHURCH, LOS ANGELES

Former heavyweight boxing champion Joe Frazier once said, "Prayer is just as important as roadwork." The ex-champ beat the odds by utilizing hard work, self-confidence, and unshakable faith—the power within.

Dr. Georgia L. McMurray, who has been stricken with Charcot-Marie-Tooth atrophy, a congenital degenerative disease that has left her completely paralyzed, is one of the nation's top educators. From her motorized wheelchair she continues her research and remains committed to championing the causes of young adults, particularly teenage mothers. Dr. McMurray's remarkable life proves that a physical challenge of any kind—whether an early pregnancy or a rare disease—need not be a limitation to excellence. Much in demand, she closes her speeches with a prayer: "I ask God for strength to continue the journey."

The Archbishop Desmond Tutu continues to fight the greatest enemy known to mankind: ignorance. Armed with nothing more than an unconquerable faith, Bishop Tutu refuses to bend or bow. On more than one occasion he has mentioned that "God will see me through."

Joe Frazier, Dr. Georgia McMurray, and Bishop Tutu understand the Universal Law of Spiritual Power that governs their lives. They know that the vitality of the Creator—the designer of the universe—permeates every fiber of our being. Infinite Intelligence guides us to health, happiness, and prosperity. Chase your dreams! Climb the highest mountain. Call upon the spiritual power that rests within.

I know who my Father is. Today I will step out boldly and conquer new worlds.

An Identity Crisis

*"We've been called colored, Negro, black,
everything.... Why can't we just be free?"*
—PAUL MOONEY, COMEDIAN

Most people haven't the slightest idea of who they are and what they are. When questioned about their *true* identity many are equally confused. *Who are you?*

Historically we were called "nigger" before we had the right to vote, "nigras" when just a few of us went to the polls, "colored folk" when our numbers began to swell, and "Negroes" when we began the great migration north in the forties and fifties. *But who are you?* With power in the 1960s came self-respect. "Black," it seemed, was the final step on the road to dignity and equality. Not so, say many leaders and social activists of the day. "African American," it has been said, is the proper term. But again, I ask, *who are you?*

Each of us sooner or later will search for our true identity. For example, "wetbacks" became "illegal aliens" and then "undocumented workers." The "old" became the "elderly" and now "senior citizens"; the "crippled" became "handicapped," "disabled," and now "physically challenged."

If any of the above labels—*African American*, *black*, *Negro*, or *colored*—seems symbolically out of place, then of course it should and must go. But if you told me that you are a "mind with a body," a "spiritual being," a part of the great "I AM," you would be closer to the truth. You would be in line with the African proverb that states, "If you don't know who you are, anyone can name you; and if anyone can name you, you will answer to anything."

I know who I am: a child of God. And I can do anything!

The Home Field Advantage

*"There are some countries so backward that their
people don't spend money until they have saved it."*
—A. G. GASTON, ENTREPRENEUR

There's an old fable about a man who was riding across the desert at night. As he crossed a riverbed, a voice came out of the darkness ordering him to halt. The voice then said, "Now, get off your camel." The man did so. The voice then said, "Pick up some gravel from the riverbed." The man complied. Finally the voice said, "Now mount and ride on. In the morning you'll be both glad and sorry."

As the sun rose, the rider looked at what he had picked up and discovered it was not gravel at all but a handful of precious gems! As the voice had said, he was both glad and sorry. Glad he had picked up a few and sorry he had not carried more. Like most fables, this one is based on human nature and has specific meaning for those fortunate to live in this land of opportunity.

We live in the richest country the world has ever known. We, African Americans, possess just about everything the wealthy possess—only in smaller amounts. We have homes, cars, stereos, televisions, and savings accounts—only in smaller quantities. Our food is just as tasty and plentiful; our homes are just as cozy. With only a fraction of the world's population, Black America possesses nearly 10 percent of the free worlds' total income.

But most of us are like the man in the fable. We are glad we have such a high standard of living but still have some regrets. Regrets because many never realize that financial independence has nothing to do with the amount of money you can earn, but only with what you do with the funds you possess.

Riches, in all its forms, are within my reach. I will reach for and receive my share.

You Know, I've Been Doing Some Thinking . . .

"If you could pray for only one thing, let it be for an idea."
—PERCY SUTTON, CEO AND PRESIDENT,
INNER CITY BROADCASTING

The United Negro College Fund professes that "a mind is a terrible thing to waste." Latch onto this thought. It's the first step on the road to freedom and prosperity. Mind is cause, and experience is effect.

Everything happens to us twice in life. First the inner, and then the outer. First the mental, then the physical. First the thought, then the thing. All causation is mental.

Harmonious living tells of harmonious thinking. A turbulent life reveals some kind of inner turmoil. We may believe that we are positive, settled people, but if we notice troubles or conflicts in our outer conditions, we must look within to see what inner negativity has surfaced. If you want to know what's in your subconscious, you don't have to go to a psychiatrist. Just look at the condition of your home, your car, your health, your relationships. Outer events are simply skin and bones of inner thoughts.

Whatever you experience in life is really the outpicturing of your thoughts up to this point. Change your thoughts and beliefs, and the outer picture must change also. Judge not according to appearances, but according to your mind's eye.

I am in complete control. My thoughts are in accord with my desires.

I Think I'll Pass

"In the darkest moments I can still find peace."
—MARIAN ANDERSON, OPERA STAR

Long ago a king, plagued by many worries, harassed on every side, called his wise men together. He asked them to invent a motto, a few magic words that would help him in time of trial or distress. "It must be brief enough to be engraved on a ring," he instructed, "so I can see it every day. It must be appropriate to every situation, as useful in prosperity as in adversity. It must be a motto wise and true and endlessly enduring, words by which a person could be guided for his or her life, in every circumstance, no matter what happens."

The wise men thought and thought, and finally came to the monarch with their magic words. These were words for every change or chance of fortune, declared the wise men. Words to fit every situation, good or bad. Words to ease the heart and mind in every circumstance. The words they offered to the king were: "This, too, shall pass."

Century after century this old legend has survived. Whether or not the motto was invented for a troubled king, no one really knows. But this much is certain: The words are wise and true and endlessly enduring. They have proved their power down through the ages, to uncounted men and women, in every land and every conceivable situation. These magic words will give comfort to the afflicted, courage to the frightened, and hope to the depressed. As we climb the ladder of success and encounter life's tougher moments, we can find solace in these words of wisdom: *This, too, shall pass.*

I can overcome any difficulty. Come what may, I know: This, too, shall pass.

Baby, My Feet Are Killing Me!

*"I'm no martyr. I just had a hard day at work.
My feet were hurting, and I was too tired
to give up my seat."*
—ROSA PARKS, MOTHER OF THE CIVIL RIGHTS MOVEMENT

It is often within oppressive circumstances that one gathers hope. Hope is the father of achievement. It reinforces ability, redoubles energy, fortifies existing talent, and increases faith. Armed with the power of hope, Rosa Parks sat down so that an entire race could stand up.

Hope places everything within perspective. It was hope that rescued the spirits of W. E. B. DuBois as he overcame racism and abuse at Harvard University and became the school's first African-American Phi Beta Kappa. It was hope that propelled Naylor Fitzhugh through Harvard's radically charged atmosphere nearly forty years later when he became the first African American to earn a master's degree in business administration. And it was HOPE that enabled a shy farm girl named Annie Mae Bullock to endure hardship, an abusive marriage, and the roller-coaster ride of the music industry. Today Tina Turner fills concert halls as millions jam to watch her strut her stuff.

As our ancestors toiled within the cotton fields of the South, hope was born. As they worked, they composed songs, "sorrow songs," out of their environment. With eyes of faith, they could look beyond their immediate enslavement and translate hope out of their existing circumstances.

Remember, life may not always run smoothly. Life sometimes travels in a downward spiral. Sometimes on the road to success we get weary. Our feet hurt. It is during these trying moments that we must fill our hearts with hope.

I've read the last chapter. I've read the last page. I know with hope I win!

There Should Be a Law

"God's laws last longer than those who break them."
——CHARLOTTE E. RAY,
FIRST AFRICAN-AMERICAN FEMALE LAWYER

In his return match with the great German boxer Max Schmeling, Joe Louis told his challenger during a prefight news conference, "You can run, but you can't hide. There is no hiding place in this ring." So it is with life and the principles of success. Nobody breaks the rules of success and prosperity. The laws of success are the laws of destiny.

Our Creator has clearly defined mental guidelines to direct our path: The laws of attraction, cause and effect, substitution, belief, habit, use or lose, and correspondence are only a few. Each guideline leads us to the safest and most fruitful path to travel. There is law and order in the universe. These rules for the road plant our feet on firm ground. They are words of reality that can provide light and uplift for our immediate pathways, and they can offer a beam of light down the corridors of our uncertain tomorrows.

No law has ever been passed that will keep an individual from acting like a fool. But obey these laws and prosper, disregard them and fail. Some say, "Look what I created!" but the truly successful say, "Look what I attracted."

I am a living magnet. I attract the circumstances that I desire.

Let the Truth Be Told

*"The best way to live in this world is to live
above it."*
—SONIA SANCHEZ, POET AND LECTURER

The question "What is Truth?" is the cry of every person's soul at some time in his or her life. Truth is the state in which spirit dwells, a state of perfection that is eternally, creatively active. Truth may be defined as the action of spirit.

For example, most of us think of ourselves as standing wearily and helplessly at the center of a circle bristling with tasks, burdens, problems, annoyances, and responsibilities that are rushing in upon us. At every moment we have a dozen different things to do, a host of problems to solve, a dozen challenges to endure. We see ourselves as overridden, overburdened, and overworked.

This is a common picture—but it is not the *truth*. No one, however crowded his or her life, has such an existence. What is the true picture of life? Imagine sands passing through an hourglass, one at a time. This is the true picture of your life, even on a very busy day. The crowded hours always come to you one moment at a time. *This is the only way they can come.* The day may bring many tasks and problems, but invariably they come in single file. They just trickle down one by one. And how do we handle them? One at a time.

Beware of half-truths. You might get hold of the wrong half. Truth is something that must be known in the heart, accepted in the mind, and enacted in life.

Knowing the Truth will set me free. I will become a seeker of Truth.

Baby on Board

"There aren't really enough crutches in the world for all the lame excuses."
—BILL DEMBY, PHYSICALLY CHALLENGED ATHLETE AND MOTIVATIONAL SPEAKER

The bottom line is always "Are you happy doing what you are doing?" Imagine the individual who works at a job that he hates, earning less than he wants, missing out on holidays and trips that he would love to take. He is lonely, depressed, and has never mastered the skills he needs to learn. Like a child, this immature soul has never stood on his own two feet and put forth the effort to justify his short stay on this planet. But he has all the reasons for why he is where he is! He blames the government, his wife, his children, his horoscope, his boss, the economy, his bad back, his lack of education, and his bad luck. Somehow he has arrived at the idea that if he has enough excuses and circumstances to blame, he's allowed to be miserable.

Life offers reasons or results. Some people get the idea that they both weigh the same. They don't. If you're not living the life you wish to live, doing the things you want to do, no excuse will do. Look around. You can find all kinds of people beating the odds. We see men and women succeeding and experiencing happiness with little education and even less money. These are achievers who point out that results are the only things that matter. They have made the same discovery as the man who said, "I used to blame the weather until I discovered that it rains on rich people too!"

The enjoyment we derive from life is inversely proportional to how much we blame our circumstances.

I blame no one for my conditions. Today I choose to be happy.

Pro Choice

"It's pretty hard for the Lord to guide you if you haven't made up your mind which way you want to go."
—MADAME C. J. WALKER, ENTREPRENEUR AND PHILANTHROPIST

It is not inconceivable that a few generations from now historians may record this age as the period of mankind's greatest folly. In the midst of the greatest abundance the world has ever seen, far too many suffer because of negative mental attitudes. These poor souls remain enmeshed in the jaws of despair and hopelessness when happiness is within their reach.

They are like a sculptor having both the training and the tools with which to work, standing before a huge block of marble, admiring its beauty yet never turning a hand. Or like the man who despises the darkness but sits alone in his modern home refusing to turn on the light switch. Will it be strange if future generations call them foolish? How many among us really believe that all good is ours right now? Not one in a thousand. For too long we have formed the habit of thinking a thing "too good to be true." *Nothing is too good to be true!*

The world is full of people who believe that choice is dead and freedom is a thing of the past. But we must continue to make choices—choices that will eventually determine our destiny. *Your greatest gift is the power of choice.*

Maggie L. Walker, America's first black female bank president, gave a rousing speech in which she said, "When it comes to success, the choice is simple. *You can either stand up and be counted, or lie down and be counted out!*" Choosing the right mental attitude is basic to all achievement.

I am aware of the power of choice and I choose success!

Silence of the Lambs

"Most people search high and wide for the key to success. If they only knew the key to their dreams lies within."
—GEORGE WASHINGTON CARVER, INVENTOR AND EDUCATOR

There is a way out of limitation that never fails, and it's shockingly simple. It calls for no formalities, no money, no effort, and little risk. It is obvious enough when you realize it, but so many overlook it. Here's a clue: *Be still, be quiet, and listen to your spirit.* If you will listen to your spirit, you will be amazed at the quick and striking results you will obtain. When you align yourself with this force—the inner voice—you are always in divine order. Everything about you will have meaning and purpose, and though the inner voice can be suppressed, it can never be silenced.

The Creator uses every aspect of our being—spiritual, physical, emotional, and intellectual—to communicate with us. When we learn to look for answers inwardly rather than outwardly, we no longer give people, institutions, or traditions authority to define who we are or what we can become. Although this transformation will cost nothing, it will not be free. As a matter of fact it will cost you a great deal, because the price of success always requires some type of payment.

And what exactly is the price? *None other than your life!* If you are prepared to render this sum, your results will be automatic and the answers you seek will not be very far. During the recent presidential inauguration Reverend William DeVeaux, pastor of Washington, D.C.'s, A.M.E. church, told President Clinton, "It takes great listening as well as great preaching to make a great sermon." God speaks to those who take the time to listen.

The key is within. I will search inward until I find it.

Hide and Seek

*"The best way to fight poverty is with a weapon
loaded with ambition."*
—SEPTIMA CLARK, EDUCATOR

According to ancient legend, there was an African tribe that was always at war with other tribes. They caused great destruction and pillaged at will. They had no morals, love, or compassion. A concerned elder of a nearby tribe moved quickly to try to save his people. He called together members from neighboring tribes in an attempt to right the wrongs. After much discussion the wise and insightful elder decided to take the key to his tribe's potential and hide it where the warring tribe could never find it. Where to hide this power became the question of huge importance.

Some suggested he bury it deep into the earth. Others said to place it on top of the highest mountain. Still others thought it best to sink it deep into the ocean. There was no agreement until the elder who had gathered them together said, "Here is what we will do. We will hide mankind's omnipotent power deep within man himself, for he will never think to look for it there."

Since this tale was told, Black America has traveled the globe, climbing, digging, probing, exploring, and constantly searching for something that it already possesses. Nearly a century ago, Marcus Garvey discovered it. Sixty years later, both A. Philip Randolph and Roy Wilkins found it and shared its secret with those who would listen. But as the story goes, our inexhaustible potential—our greatest gift—has been the best-kept secret of the ages.

I am now aware of my potential. I will use it wisely.

Hey, That Was My Idea

*"It's not what the dream is,
it's what the dream does."*
—JOHN H. JOHNSON, FOUNDER,
JOHNSON PUBLISHING COMPANY

During his campaign to become Seattle's first black mayor, Norman Rice told a frenzied crowd, "There's nothing more powerful than an idea. No weapon can destroy it; no power can conquer it!" An idea is power. Ideas rule the world. An idea even built the universe. A single idea—the sudden flash of thought—may be worth millions of dollars, and one trained mind can be the sponsor of a momentous plan. The real ideas of power are in your consciousness just waiting for the miracle of birth.

One idea can change the world. Johnnie Colemon changed the world in her lifetime by presenting humanity with the idea of a higher spiritual existence. Nelson Mandela changed the world by forcing a nation to adhere to the principle of personal freedom. The Reverend Barbara Harris changed the world with the idea that peace and harmony conquers all. Mary McLeod Bethune changed the world by transforming a world of ignorance and poverty into one of self-respect, personal excellence, and achievement. Martin Luther King and Malcolm X changed the world as they forced a nation to come to grips with its commitment to freedom. *And you, too, can change the world by giving birth to the many ideas that you harbor within.*

Dare what no person will dare. Seek to accomplish what no individual will attempt. Open up the channels between your mind and the creative force, and there is no limit to the good that will come pouring in. Concentrate your thoughts and ideas, and abundance will come flooding down. What you need, what mankind needs, is one good idea!

Today I will record all of my ideas. My ideas are power.

Equal Rights

*"Each of us is born free and equal. The tough job
is to outgrow it."*
—GUION STEWART BLUFORD, ASTRONAUT AND PHYSICIST

In reality all of us are born free and equal. But how many truly find meaning within these words? When one child is born into the lap of luxury with servants to attend his every whim and fancy, how can he be said to be born equal to the child who has difficulty securing many of life's simplest needs—adequate food, shelter, and clothing? How do we account for the great inequality among men and women? The following tale may provide a clue.

As a preacher and a soapmaker took a walk together, the soapmaker turned to the preacher and asked, "What good is religion? Look at all the trouble and misery within the world after thousands of years of teaching about goodness, truth, and peace—after all the prayers and sermons. If religion is so good for people, why should this be?"

The preacher said nothing. They continued to walk until they noticed a child playing in the gutter. Then the preacher said, "Look at that child. You say that soap makes people clean, but see the dirt on that little child? Of what good is soap? With all the soap in the world, that child is still filthy. I wonder how effective soap is after all?"

The soapmaker protested the analogy and said, "But, Preacher, that's not fair. You know soap is useless unless it is used."

"Exactly," replied the preacher. "So it is with religion." Each of us *is* equal in what counts most: We have *equal* access to the great Mind of the universe that governs all and knows all. Each of us can draw upon this Life Force for whatever our needs may be, but this power lies dormant unless we use it.

I am the master of my fate. I am equal to all men and women before God.

That's What Friends Are For

"Friendship is the only cement that will hold the world together."
—DUKE ELLINGTON, COMPOSER AND JAZZ GREAT

According to an old Eastern parable, two beggars formed a symbiotic relationship: one was blind and the other was born without legs. The blind man was strong enough to carry the legless man on his back. He became the legs for the lame man. In return, the lame man became the eyes for the blind one. Clinging to each other, they both benefited.

Dr. Alvin Pouissant, the noted psychiatrist, was asked what he would do if he felt a nervous breakdown coming on. He answered, "I would go down the street and find someone needy and immediately seek to help him." General Fred A. Gorden, commandant of cadets, United States Military Academy at West Point, concurred. He stated, "We are on the wrong track when we think of friendship as something to get, rather than something to give. *The world needs more warm hearts and fewer hot heads.*"

"To love others makes us happy," says Kenny "Babyface" Edmonds, one-half of Black America's hottest song-writing duo. His equally talented partner, Antonio "L.A." Reid, couldn't agree more. "Love is the glue," he replies, "that holds friendship together." Friendship is built upon love. You can say that a true and loyal friendship is an exceedingly rare and wonderful thing—like a happy marriage or a successful partnership. It needs attention, care, guarding, and above all, it needs to be needed.

Today I will plant the seeds of friendship by helping another.

As the World Turns

"The secret to success is to learn to accept the impossible, to do without the indispensable, and to bear the intolerable."
—NELSON MANDELA, SOUTH AFRICAN HUMAN RIGHTS ACTIVIST

There is an old saying that goes, It is impossible to succeed without suffering. Failure becomes the final test of persistence. He who has never failed has never succeeded.

Success of any kind is like a universal college degree. It can be earned only by following a certain course that exposes the achiever to life's adversities. It is impossible for success to be easy. Success is difficult; it's gut-wrenching, pain-inducing. It's built upon inconvenience. Success is a marathon, not a sprint. Success seems to follow a kind of natural selection process. Only those individuals who are willing to rally again after their failures, those who refuse to let defeat keep them down, those who seem to know that success can be theirs if they just stay with it long enough, finally win the fruits of life.

After failing many times in her bid for political office, former congresswoman Shirley Chisholm gave a clue to her secret of success: "The thing to try when all else fails is *again*." Most men and women who have hit their mark will admit that just as they felt they were finally reaching the point in life on which they had set their hearts, the rug was pulled out from under them and they found themselves back at the beginning. Only those of patient persistence are rewarded. Only those who can hang in there long after the crowd has left drink from the victor's cup. Repeated victories over your problems are the rungs on your ladder of success. Make your breaking point your turning point.

I can move any mountain, endure any valley, swim any river. I can do anything!

It All Adds Up

"A hand up is better than a hand out."
——SYBIL MOBLEY, DEAN, FLORIDA A & M SCHOOL OF
BUSINESS

Most of us normally perform far below our capabilities simply because we lack faith in ourselves. This can be changed. When we talk about faith and belief, we have to refer to the greatest book ever written and the greatest teacher of the ages. He summed it up when he said, "Go thy way; and as thou believed, so be it done unto thee."

This simple statement cuts both ways, like a two-edged sword. Faith is your key to unlock the door of success. Or it is the lock that imprisons and keeps you from experiencing success and achievement. "Faith keeps the man who keeps his faith," says the award-winning actor Lou Gossett. "Genuine faith," writes Dr. King, "is *assuring, insuring, and enduring.*" And singer Patti LaBelle captures the essence of faith. She says, "Faith gives us the courage to endure the present as we anticipate the future."

As a positive power, faith is the promise of the realization of things hoped for and unseen. Faith only comes by doing. We learn by doing. For example, we learn to walk not by reading books on walking or watching others walk, *but by walking.* We learn to talk not by listening to others talk, *but by talking.* We learn to love not by discussing love, *but by loving;* we learn to hope *by hoping.* And likewise we learn to add to our faith by expressing faith. In order for faith to be effective, it cannot exist in the passive state. Faith must be applied. *So add to your faith.*

I will add to my faith by expressing faith in those things that mean the most to me.

Step Back, Jack!

"No one can figure out your worth but you."
—PEARL BAILEY, SINGER AND ACTRESS

Our success, our wealth, and our abundance do not come from technology, or from our vast mineral resources, or from our production lines within our factories. They do not come from our manipulation of markets or our political and economic systems, science, or military might. Whence, then, you ask, do they emanate? Where can you find the key to the twenty-first century? It can be found where it has always been located—in you, the individual.

We have all read news stories telling of almost superhuman feats performed by people under the pressure of a strong emotional stimulus. For example, a twelve-year-old boy lifts an unmovable log off the legs of his father; or a slender housewife frees her husband trapped beneath the family car. People with a burning desire to accomplish an ambitious goal do accomplish it, while others, without realizing their full potential, fall by the wayside.

Watch an artist painting a picture and see how he occasionally steps back to gain perspective on what he is painting. Likewise, you might benefit from such an approach. Step back and evaluate—how much of your full potential are you using? Are you exercising your unique talents? Are you utilizing your precious gifts? It is altogether in your hands.

From this day forward I will live up to my full potential in every area of my life.

A Dime a Dozen

"Excellence is to do a common thing in an uncommon way."
—BOOKER T. WASHINGTON, EDUCATOR

There's so much talk about excellence today. Ours is a society obsessed with excellence. Are you striving to be your best? Are you committed to excellence or are you average? Though each of us is average in different areas of our lives, how great it is to be excellent! And make no mistake about it, we can all be excellent! Successful individuals like the famed educator Booker T. Washington encourage us to do our best.

"Success may involve talent," explained the celebrated choreographer Alvin Ailey. "But excellence involves *YOU*."

"If we are to move ahead as a people," warned former U.S. congresswoman Shirley Chisholm, "we must strive for the highest standards." Achievers know the difference between average and excellence. Excellence means standing up to life; living your life for a cause greater than yourself so future generations will know that YOU played a role. The successful are remembered for their contributions, and the failures are remembered because they tried, but the average are just forgotten.

Strive to make excellence your standard. A commitment to excellence is the antidote to mediocrity. You need only to stand up and choose personal excellence. This act alone will guarantee your success.

I will strive for and accept nothing less than excellence.

Make Up Your Mind

"Mix a conviction with a man and something happens."
—ADAM CLAYTON POWELL, FORMER CONGRESSMAN

A very wise man once said, "If you can tell me what you want, I can tell you how to get it." He was a wise man because he knew that each of us has the capability to achieve whatever we desire. The great majority of people who are dissatisfied with their lives suffer from not having decided upon what they want.

A young pianist visited Eubie Blake, the father of ragtime music, and said, "I want to write a musical score. Will you tell me how to go about it?"

"You're too young," replied the great black musician. "Wait until you are a few years older."

"But," objected the struggling artist, "you composed when you were barely in your teens."

"Yes," agreed Blake, "but I didn't have to ask anyone how to do it."

The question that begs asking is, How do I know I have the ability to achieve what I want? The answer is self-evident. We do not seriously want things that we do not have the ability to achieve. We all seem to have a built-in governor that keeps us from wanting what is beyond our capabilities. The wide spectrum of occupations and accomplishments shows us the diversity of human desires.

So what is the master formula for attainment? Simple. Make up your mind—know exactly what you want, and then DO IT!

I will make it my goal to find a goal.

What Makes the Great, Great?

"Destiny lies not in the stars, but in our hearts."
—WILLIAM W. BROWN, EX-SLAVE AND FIRST
AFRICAN-AMERICAN NOVELIST

Dr. Benjamin E. Mays, president emeritus of Morehouse College, explained that each of us can reach our level of true greatness—if we know what greatness is. Dr. Mays said, "Wealth, position, or power are no measure of greatness. Greatness is defined by what we have become and what we might have been. The people who close this gap we call great."

What makes the great, great? Dr. Mays found the answer. *Have you?*

What makes the great, great? Ask Alice Walker. After graduating from high school as valedictorian, young Alice was so poor that her neighbors took a collection to purchase her seventy-five-dollar bus ticket to Atlanta's Spelman College. But poverty proved to be no match. Today Alice Walker lives in a manner in which few do because her books are read by millions.

What makes the great, great? "I know the bitter taste of poverty," said Bessie Smith. "I've gone to bed with the gnawing pain of hunger." Though barefoot and dirt poor, she single-handedly created the musical expression that became known as the blues.

What makes the great, great? Though criticized, ridiculed, and told that colored players would never be allowed to compete, Andrew Rube Foster stayed true to his aim. In 1921 Foster formed the Negro League, professional baseball's first all-black organization.

What makes the great, great? After attending college in New York, Edith Sampson returned to her tiny Pittsburgh, Pennsylvania, home and saw her mother weeping. "Mother, why are you crying?" Edith asked. "We may not be able to keep you in school," her mother replied.

"Don't worry," her daughter responded. "I'll find a way. I'll study at home, at night, and every chance I get. Mother, you'll be proud, and *I will finish*!" Edith Sampson consequently became the first black female elected judge in the United States.

What makes the great, great? The answer lies within your heart. Begin now to close the gap and realize your destiny.

Today I will listen to the beatings of my heart. I will become what I am destined to become.

I Know Where You Are Coming From

"I don't care where you come from, I want to know where you're going."
—ANDREW YOUNG, FORMER U.S. AMBASSADOR

One of our most common and worst mistakes is to cover up our own abilities and potentialities by trying to be something we are not. A person could spend a lifetime studying the writings of Toni Morrison and never be able to write like her. The same would apply to sports, singing, acting, or anything else. If the person trying to write like this famed author would write naturally, he or she would have a much better chance of succeeding.

In doing what we most enjoy, we will probably make our greatest contribution to society, and the contribution we make to society will determine our rewards, both in real and in psychological terms. *As you sow, so shall you reap—there are no exceptions to this rule.*

Finding our real abilities that we usually keep buried is like prospecting for gold. It's not necessarily easy, but we don't mind the digging so much when we know the gold is really there. Unless we can find our true selves, we will never really know what it means to be fulfilled—to wake up in the morning eager for the day to begin. Finding the best work that we are suited for is the number-one responsibility of adult life. We can all do hundreds of things well, but one of those things we can do with uncommon ease and facility. When that happens, our work becomes our play. We are truly successful.

I will make my work my play, and my play my work.

Green with Envy

*"Some of us aren't prepared to accept success—
especially someone else's."*
—SARAH VAUGHAN, JAZZ LEGEND

Once upon a time there were two shopkeepers who were bitter rivals. Their stores were across the street from each other, and they would spend the better part of each day sitting in the doorway, each keeping an eye on the other's business. One night an angel appeared to one of the shopkeepers in a dream and said, "God has sent me to teach you a lesson. He will give you anything you ask for, but I want you to know that whatever you get, your competitor across the street will receive twice as much.

"Would you like to be wealthy? You can be very wealthy, but your neighbor will be twice as rich. Do you want to lead a long and healthy life? This you can have, but your neighbor's life will be longer and healthier. You can be famous, have children you will be proud of, whatever you desire. But whatever is granted to you, your competitor will be granted twice as much."

The man frowned, thought for a moment, and said, "All right, my request is this: Strike me blind in one eye."

We tend to be cruel and vent our rage against those we secretly envy. If a man has a better garden, he is envied by his neighbors; if he gains a promotion, he is envied by his fellow workers; if he is able to cope with events so that he lives happily, he is envied by failures. Yet in the end we only hurt ourselves with envy.

I am comfortable with who I am. There is no need for me to be envious of anyone.

Give the Sister Her Due

"Dipped in chocolate, bronzed with elegance,
enameled with grace, toasted with beauty. My Lord,
she is a Black woman!"
—YOSEF BEN-JOCHANNAN, HISTORIAN

Our struggle has always demanded great courage and conviction. Out of it have emerged women—sisters of undaunted spirit. *"SHE"roes!* Black women who perform deeds that ensure our survival and enrich our lives. Often their efforts are unsung but we know who they are. They're a mother, a daughter, an aunt, a niece, a grandmother, but all are sisters. Sheroes who have made a difference and propel us forward. Stand up and clap, and give the sisters their due!

Ladies and gentlemen, clap your hands for Aretha Franklin—the "Queen of Soul!" Trained in the church, gifted with a voice whose range and power have become her trademarks, she is for many the best gospel and rhythm and blues singer ever to stand before a microphone. Let's hear it for Carol Moseley Braun, who possesses a winning smile and a persuasive manner and became the first African-American woman elected to the U.S. Senate. Put your hands together for Corla Wilson-Hawkins, the nation's preeminent teacher. Each day she stands before children who have been labeled "disruptive" and "learning disabled" and tells them, "In spite of the problems, you're going to make it!"

Applaud loudly for trailblazer Oprah Winfrey, one of the first black women to host a nationally syndicated talk show, and the first of her race and gender to own a television and movie production studio complex. And what about Dorothy Brunson, owner of three successful radio stations, and arguably the wealthiest black woman in radio? Let's show some appreciation for pioneer journalist Ethel Payne, one of the first black women to travel with the White House press corps. And to Emmy award–winning broadcast journalist Charlayne Hunter-Gault. Let's salute Lillian Roberts, who rose from the post of shop steward at a Chicago hospital to organizer for the American Federation of State, County, and Municipal Employees. She has fought against the tide to become the most powerful African American in organized labor.

All rise for these and other unsung black women whose dedication and hard work inspire us to excel.

Today I salute the best thing ever given to the race—the black woman.

How May I Serve?

*"Success is not defined by the number of servants
you have, but by how many people you serve."*
—RALPH D. ABERNATHY, FORMER EXECUTIVE DIRECTOR,
SOUTHERN CHRISTIAN LEADERSHIP CONFERENCE

"Why are we here?" Dr. Martin Luther King was asked. "Life
requires our service," was his reply. Service is the key. Throw
yourself into this idea. How can I be of service, or how best
can I serve? And keep serving? The greatest thing in the world
is the opportunity to be of service to others. There is an entire
world crying out for our help, our ideas, our endless products
and services.

There is much to be said for the old cliché "service with a
smile." If your attitude is positive, and you go the extra mile,
giving added service over and above that which is required,
then you are well on your way to becoming a fulfilled person. The habit of giving more and better service brings rewards in many forms—both in the heart and in the pocketbook. Bread cast upon the water will return to sustain and
strengthen the individual who is rendering more service and
better service than is expected.

Kill 'em with service! That's the key to success in life. Give
your very best, and work at making it better, and give others
more than they expect. When you give freely, you *receive*
abundantly. Service is the answer—service to everyone who is
important to you. By serving mankind first, you can in turn be
provided with everything you could possibly want or desire.

I will center my thoughts on how I may be of service to others.

Don't Be a Know-it-all

*"No one knows less than the person
who knows it all."*
—HUGH GLOSTER, FORMER PRESIDENT,
MOREHOUSE COLLEGE

Do you belong to that body of individuals who seems to believe they already know enough? If success is your goal, you must become a storehouse for new information. You must avoid the pitfalls of becoming someone who is comfortable with his level of knowledge in the field of his choosing. In other words, don't be a know-it-all.

There's an eye-opening story abut three men who were sentenced to be guillotined—a priest, a doctor, and a college professor. Each was allowed to make one last statement prior to his execution. The priest was the first to approach the bench. His final words were, "Keep the faith!" The blade dropped on the priest, came within two inches of his neck, and mysteriously stopped. Everybody thought it was a miracle from above, and the priest was set free.

The doctor was next. He held his head high and uttered, "Physician, heal thyself!" Once again the guillotine mysteriously stopped inches from its destination. Thinking this was a message that the doctor was innocent, he, too, was liberated.

Finally the professor approached the chopping block and with a poor sense of timing said, "If you tighten the two bolts on the left, the guillotine will work as intended."

You see, some people think they have all the answers. Education is a lifelong process and should end only when you do. Every day is commencement day because education is cumulative.

I will take in new information as the first step to my growth and development.

Have You Written Your Will?

"The will to win, the desire to succeed, the urge to reach your full potential ... these are the keys that will unlock the door to personal excellence."
—EDDIE ROBINSON, GRAMBLING UNIVERSITY FOOTBALL
COACH

"How can I better my condition?" That is the question that will haunt you every day of your life. But you must first ask yourself if you have the will—the belief and the faith—to answer it.

You have seen men and women, inwardly no more capable than yourself, accomplish the seemingly impossible. You have seen others, after years of hopeless struggle, suddenly win their most cherished dreams. And you've wondered, "What is the power that gives new life to their dying ambitions, that motivates their jaded desires, that gives them a new start on the road to achievement?"

It is the *"I will"* power. The *I will* power gives them a new belief and a new faith in their power to win—as they leap forward and wrest success from seemingly certain defeat. What *will* you do? What *will* you accomplish? Have you written your *will*?

Start right now, where you stand, and begin to work on all the things you desire. Ask permission of no one. Concentrate your thoughts upon any proper undertaking, and achievement will be yours. Your *will* that you can succeed gives you personal power. Fortune waits for you—seize it boldly!

Today I will write my goals. I will write my will.

Soul Train

*"All our dreams come true— if we have the
courage to pursue them."*
—ALEXA CANADY, FIRST BLACK FEMALE NEUROSURGEON

Thoughts are, most assuredly, things. They are conceived in the mind, and they travel through time and space like ripples on a pond, affecting all that they touch. Thoughts are the building blocks of our experience. Writer and poet Paul Laurence Dunbar wrote, "The actions of men are the best interpreters of their thoughts." We think a thought, attach a feeling to it, and a circumstance in our life is attracted to it. If we want to see how we got to be where we are in life, we need only to trace our experience back to our thoughts.

We hear a great deal about the creative power of thought. Correctly speaking, it is the mind that is creative, and thought is its action. We often speak of a train of thought. It's a good metaphor. A train is a vehicle that delivers something or somebody to a certain destination. A train of thought, on the other hand, is a vehicle of mind that delivers its creative power into manifestation.

If we direct a train of thought to a mental image of lack, it will always arrive at its destination and unload creative power into this false image. The result: We build our own poverty station. Every train of thought we direct toward it delivers its load of creative power, and this poverty station bustles with activity. The way to bypass this poverty station is to stop making mental images of lack and deliver trains of thought to a new station. We should practice using the creative power of mind—the very essence of our soul—to construct only images of the good we desire to see made manifest.

I will think only abundant thoughts.

Who's the Boss?

"Learn to see, listen, and think for yourself."
—MALCOLM X, PAN-AFRICANIST AND HUMAN RIGHTS
ACTIVIST

One thing you must put aside in order to fulfill your unique possibilities is conformity. We all conform in hundreds of ways. Even those of us who feel we have gone our own separate ways in the world, who have lived more or less as independent spirits, are conformists to an extent that would surprise us if we became aware of our actions.

I once heard an amusing story that epitomizes the idea of conformity. It's about a small-town jeweler who, every morning, noticed a man stopping in front of his jewelry store to set his gold watch to the time of the large clock in his store window. The stranger did this without fail, day after day, month after month, year after year. One morning, as the jeweler was sweeping the sidewalk in front of his store, the man stopped to set his watch. On impulse the jeweler spoke to him. He said, "For years you've set your watch by my big clock each morning. Why?"

The man finished winding his watch, placed it in his pocket, and replied, "I'm the timekeeper at the factory down the street. Every day at noon my job is to blow the noon whistle, which tells everyone that it's time to break for lunch."

The jeweler stood aghast and then said, "That's odd. I've been setting my clock in the window for all these years by your noon whistle!" Each of us should realize that what others do, the way others conduct themselves, is not necessarily what we should do or how we should behave. We are all unique.

Success requires a degree of individualism. I am unique.

New and Improved

*"I know no great men or women, only those
striving to be. We are measured by what we do, not
by what we possess."*
—L. DOUGLAS WILDER, GOVERNOR OF VIRGINIA

"The true test of civilization," counseled Mary McLeod Bethune, the famed educator, "cannot be found in its census nor the size of its cities, nor its accomplishments. *The truest test is the quality of citizen it produces. Character is success, and there is no other.*"

The world, it is said, is in constant search for men and women who are not for sale; individuals who are honest, who promote the highest degree of integrity; who are sound from center to circumference, true to the heart's core. Courageous men and women who neither blink nor flinch at the first sign of adversity; bold individuals who know their places and fill them. If there is any power that can reverse the fortunes of a race, it is *character*! There may be little culture, sparse abilities, and fewer resources. Yet if there be a character of sterling excellence, it will demand influence and command respect.

Picture, if you will, Harriet Tubman without the thirst for freedom. How about the march toward equality without Martin Luther King? Or Kenya without Jomo Kenyatta, or Nelson Mandela without the will to hold on?

Every thought that enters your mind, every word you utter, makes its impression upon the innermost fiber of your being, and the result of these impressions is your character. You are, right now, in the place that belongs to you—for it is the one that you have earned by your consciousness. It is always a good place because you are in the right position to learn the lessons that you need to propel yourself to a *new and improved* stage of personal growth.

When my thoughts are right, I will always be in my right place.

Almost Finished

"I've made mistakes; we all do. But I don't believe that you have to have done it before to do it well. You only have to be smart and talented to do it well."
—SUZANNE DE PASSE, PRESIDENT, GORDY/DE PASSE
PRODUCTIONS

A young man armed with letters of introduction from many successful men presented himself before the president of a large corporation as a candidate for a position. "What can you do?" asked the chief executive. "Do you have any specialty?"

"I can do almost anything," answered the young man.

"Well," remarked the president, rising to end the interview, "I have no use for anyone who can do 'almost' anything. I prefer someone who can do one thing to perfection."

There is a great crowd of human beings just outside the door of proficiency. They can half-do many things, but can't do one thing to excellence. How many people have almost mastered another language that they can neither read nor write? How many are familiar with another science or discipline whose rudiments they have attempted but have yet to comprehend?

Everywhere we meet men and women who are almost successful. Here is a man who is almost a lawyer, but not quite. Here is another who is almost a physician but didn't quite complete his task. More than once I have read the story of a young woman who desired to become a skillful teacher. In all walks of life there are well-meaning men and women who are almost successful but have managed to fall short of their mark. The world is full of well-intentioned attempts, half-finished work. What a blessing to civilization are those who can do something to perfection.

The road to success is a destination and I will finish the journey.

Very Impressive

*"The key to success is to keep growing in all areas
of life— mental, emotional, spiritual, as well as
physical."*
—JULIUS ERVING, BASKETBALL LEGEND

Each day our subconscious is bombarded with thousands of impressions—both positive and negative. They come from the outsides as well as from within. Impressions flow in a constant stream, oftentimes uninvited. But the kinds of impressions admitted to our minds defines the scope of our lives.

When a higher truth and a pleasing thought sink into your mind and heart, you no longer suffer the penalty of not knowing that truth. You enjoy its radiating warmth. For example:

By seeing the real meaning of life, we destroy the painful feelings of futility.

By refusing to limit ourselves, we expand far beyond our fondest dreams.

By allowing love to be the perfect guide, we walk lightly.

By realizing our true potential, we never suffer from a poor self-image.

By staying focused on our goals, we bring into reality that which we desire most.

By understanding the power of thoughts, we are less concerned about outer circumstances.

By knowing our true identity, we fear not and experience quiet dominion.

By being receptive to positive impressions only, we replenish our spirit.

There are millions of beautiful impressions that you can receive each day.

I receive and accept only healthy, positive impressions into my mind.

There's a Reason for Everything

"I am now on the road to success, happiness and abundance. All traffic goes my way."
—JOHNNIE COLEMON, PASTOR,
CHRIST UNIVERSAL TRUTH CENTER

Do you ever wonder what you are doing here? Have you ever pondered if you have a purpose for living? Do you believe in destiny? And if there is a plan for your life, where did it come from?

You *do* have a purpose here, and it is a good one. Your sojourn has not been cast upon you by some outside agent who dispassionately chooses your fate. You choose your mission in life, and you will live it. Gwendolyn Brooks, the widely read educator and poet, wrote words that would give anyone pause: "I believe the purpose of life is to give us a greater realization of spiritual consciousness; something broader and more meaningful than materialism. None of us knows what lies ahead. The important thing is to use today as wisely as possible, and face tomorrow eagerly and cheerfully knowing that we will be equal to the task."

The goal of life is to find your life's purpose and thus light a path for future generations that would guide men and women toward the treasures that really matter—peace of mind, health and energy, loving relationships, financial independence, sense of personal fulfillment, and worthy goals and ideals.

We cannot help but notice the two parallel themes that border all of life. The first is that you can achieve as much success as you desire, providing you are willing to combine your natural God-given talents with newly acquired knowledge and are determined to pay the price for success. The second is that there will be no success without a purpose.

I will be pleased with what I accomplish today and be mindful of my goals.

Can You Feel the Spirit?

"This is the secret of life: being able to feed off the spirit."
—TREMAINE HAWKINS, GOSPEL SINGER

A story is told of an estate auction where some of the finest china, linens, and other items of great value were being sold. All of the items sold rapidly. But at the end of the auction the auctioneer offered an old, weather-beaten violin. Upon first notice, those in attendance laughed at the out-of-place object.

"What's the bid?" the auctioneer asked. Someone said, "I'll give you two dollars." Still another yelled, "I'll take it off your hands for fifty dollars."

Just then an elderly man got up, walked slowly to the front, and picked up the relic. He pulled out a handkerchief from his pocket and began to rub the instrument. As he rubbed, the violin began to shine. He then began to pluck the strings and turn the pegs to tune it. He placed the violin in position and began to play the familiar spiritual "Amazing Grace."

When he finished playing, the man gave the violin back to the auctioneer and walked slowly back to his seat. There wasn't a dry eye in the place. Finally the auctioneer composed himself and reopened the bidding. Someone bid five thousand dollars, another bid ten thousand. That violin sold that day for fifty thousand dollars! Someone who had been half asleep in the back room throughout the proceedings asked what made the difference. A frail woman answered that when the old man played he put everyone in the spirit.

When we place ourselves in tune with the spirit, we give our lives new meaning.

I give thanks that I now move with the spirit.

Waffle House

"The longer I live, the more deeply I'm convinced that the difference between the successful person and the failure, between the strong and weak, is a decision."
—WILLIE E. GARY, LAWYER WHO GAVE $10 MILLION TO SHAW UNIVERSITY

Making decisions can be tough. Making the right decision can be tougher. Take notice of those about you and you will observe the obvious: *Successful men and women reach decisions quickly and change them rarely. Unsuccessful men and women reach decisions slowly and change them often.* Entrepreneur and business advocate Percy Sutton told a group of entrepreneurial hopefuls, "Whenever you see a successful business, somebody is making tough decisions."

If you are in the habit of making up your mind today and changing it tomorrow, you are doomed to fail. If you are not sure which way to move, it is better to shut your eyes and move in the dark than to remain still and make no move at all. The world will forgive you if you make mistakes, but it will never forgive you if you waffle back and forth.

You are using time. Move with quick decision and time will favor you. Stand still and time will wipe you out. You cannot always make the right move, but if you make enough moves, you will learn about the special inner power that can keep you working for and with success. "There's only one thing worse than a bad decision," General Colin Powell emphasized to a group of combat troops, "and that's making *no decision*. Straddling the fence has driven many individuals to failure." The ability to arrive at complex decisions is the hallmark of the successful person.

Today I will form the habit of making decisions.

Slim and None

"It doesn't matter what you're trying to accomplish. It's all a matter of discipline. . . . I was determined to discover what life held for me beyond the inner-city streets."
—WILMA RUDOLPH, OLYMPIC CHAMPION

There is a breathtaking statue in Mexico that bears the unusual title "In Spite Of." The name was given to honor the sculptor rather than the subject in stone. During the time the sculptor was carving the statue, he suffered a tragic accident and lost his right hand. Nonetheless, he was so determined to finish the project that he learned how to chisel with his left hand. Appropriately enough, the statue was entitled "In Spite Of," because in spite of his handicap the sculptor managed to complete a moving work of art.

In spite of their blindness Ray Charles and Stevie Wonder sing and continue to entertain millions. In spite of a difficult childhood Oprah Winfrey has become television's number-one talk-show host. Despite lack of contacts or connections both Spike Lee and Robert Townsend persevered to produce numerous box office hits. In spite of losing his legs in Vietnam, Bill Demby overcame a host of physical challenges and motivates others to do their best. In spite of racism and bitter poverty, both Mary McLeod Bethune and Marva Collins transformed a world of ignorance and illiteracy into one of academic excellence and self-respect.

In spite of being blind, abused, orphaned, poor, uneducated, others have overcome, excelled, and triumphed. *And so can you!*

I will reach for my goals in spite of the obstacles.

The Fabric of Our Lives

"Remember, it's the little things that count."
—GEORGE JOHNSON, ENTREPRENEUR

Most of us will never receive an Oscar or a Nobel Prize or the Congressional Medal of Honor or an Emmy. These awards are reserved for an elite few. Let's face it, there's only one Michael—either Jordan or Jackson. Although every child born in these United States has the same right to become president, the simple fact remains that only a handful will ever occupy the Oval Office.

Nevertheless, we can all enjoy many of life's simplest pleasures, the little things that so many take for granted. Anyone can appreciate a pat on the back, a hug, a birthday kiss, a walk in the park, a get-well card, and sincere praise for a job well done. These small pleasures can also include a cozy fireplace on a cold winter's night, breakfast in bed, or taking in a beautiful sunset. Even greater enjoyments are available, such as freedom of speech, the right to vote for the candidate of your choice, and the freedom to worship. All of these, as well as many other simple pleasures, give us added enjoyment. There are so many things to be thankful for.

If life's greatest awards come your way, fine. Be grateful. But if they pass you by, don't fret. Just look around and begin to enjoy the small things. These things we will long cherish. Today may not be full of great pleasures, but it is full of little ones. You need only open your eyes. *It's the small things that comprise the true fabric of our lives.*

I will take the time to enjoy life's simplest pleasures.

Let the Truth Be Told

*"It is not your environment, it is you— the quality
of your minds, the integrity of your souls and the
determination of your will that will decide your
future and shape your lives."*
—BENJAMIN E. MAYS, EDUCATOR

Most of us desperately hope to make our mark on the events
of our lives. But how? There seems to be so much unnecessary confusion regarding the truth about success and achievement. What do successful men and women know that so many
do not?

· They know that altitude is determined by attitude; they shoot
  for the stars.
· They know that the road to success is a worthy destination.
· They take chances; they walk to the beat of a different drum-
  mer.
· They come early and stay late. They make the forty-hour
  work week look like child's play.
· They dream big dreams and then work on making those
  dreams come true.
· They know the law of averages. They know that success is
  a statistical event.
· They know that if you don't stand for something you will fall
  for anything.
· They make choices and not excuses.
· They have a strong faith, belief in God, and respect for their
  fellow human beings.
· They know they are responsible, and they respond with abil-
  ity.
· They know their stuff!

I now know the difference between success and failure. I will act
on what I know.

Excuses, Excuses

"You don't make progress by standing on the sidelines, whimpering and complaining. You make progress by implementing ideas."
—SHIRLEY CHISHOLM, FORMER CONGRESSWOMAN

Wouldn't it be great if we could rid ourselves of excuses? We know that an excuse is any reason for inactivity. We've heard and used them all before. For example, many of us have said:

If only I had more money. . . .
If only the circumstances were different. . . .
If only I could have made adversity work for me. . . .
If only I had followed my dreams. . . .
If only I hadn't listened to others. . . .
If only I were the "right" color or right sex or came from the right side of the tracks. . . .
If only I had more schooling. . . .
If only things had gone according to plan. . . .
If only I had had more time. . . .
If only I had married a different mate. . . .
If only I had more influential contacts. . . .
If only I had gotten the "breaks". . . .
If only I had listened. . . .

And if only I would stop making excuses riches would be within my reach.

I am in control of my life. Each day I will eliminate those excuses that stand between me and my good.

Say, Do You Know Where I Can Find a Job?

"Man, if you gotta ask, you'll never know."
—LOUIS ARMSTRONG, MUSICIAN

We were all saddened to learn of the death this week of one of our most hardworking citizens—Someone Else!

Someone Else's passing creates a huge void in our community that will be difficult to fill. Else was with us for many years. The level of his caring and commitment was highly evident. Someone Else did far more than a normal person's share of the work.

Whenever there was a job to do, overtime to pull, or a meeting to attend, one name was on everyone's lips: "Let Someone Else do it." It was common knowledge that Someone Else was the hardest worker in our neighborhood. Whenever there was a need, everyone just assumed Someone Else would volunteer. Someone Else was a wonderful person, often appearing superhuman. In all honesty, everyone expected too much of Someone Else.

Now Someone Else is gone! What will happen to our schools, our churches, our children, our neighborhoods? Someone Else left a marvelous example to follow. But who is going to do the work Someone Else did?

Black America cannot depend on Someone Else anymore to build our communities, develop our institutions, and uplift our race. It is up to *you*!

Today I will take the initiative to help my community move forward.

Affirmative Action

"The future is purchased by the present."
—DAISY LEE BATES, JOURNALIST AND CIVIL RIGHTS
ACTIVIST

An affirmation is a positive thought that you repeat to yourself. Using affirmations allows you to implant quality thoughts into your subconscious so that you can feel and perform better.

Let's assume that you have a splitting headache. Here is your opportunity to combine the power of words with the power of thought. You begin to repeat to yourself, "My head feels wonderful!" or "My head is relaxed and at ease."

As you engage in self-talk, no doubt a little voice in the back of your mind will say, "You know you're lying. Your head feels lousy!" However, if you continue with the positive affirmations, the thought that you are feeling better will take root in your subconscious. You will indeed start to feel better, and an hour later you'll barely remember your headache.

You can use affirmations in a variety of areas. For example, in your relationships: "People always treat me with love and respect. I treat all people with love and respect." For your mental attitude: "Every day in every way I am getting better and better." For your prosperity: "I feel healthy, I feel good, and I feel prosperous."

The possibilities are endless. If you choose to make affirmations a part of your life, you will find them to be a powerful tool.

Today I will engage in positive self-talk that will draw me closer to my goals.

Growing Pains

"You've got to make haste while it's still light of day. My godmother used to say, 'I don't want to rust out, I just want to work out.' If you stand still long enough, people will throw dirt on you."
——BEN VEREEN, ENTERTAINER

What is the key to your unlimited growth and personal development? Perhaps the following tale will provide a clue.

One day a farmer was walking through his pumpkin fields and happened to find a one-gallon glass jug. With nothing better to do, and finding himself in an experimental frame of mind, he poked a small pumpkin through the neck of the jug and left it. A year later, when the time came to harvest the pumpkins, the farmer again came across the glass jug. Oddly enough, the pumpkin had filled it completely and, with no more room to grow, had stopped growing. The farmer broke the glass and held a pumpkin that had assumed the exact size and shape of the jug.

Experts point out that people are like that pumpkin. They poke themselves into jugs beyond which they cannot grow. The difference here is that somebody else doesn't poke them into the jug—*they do it themselves*. Each of us decides how much we are going to grow and what kind of world we are going to live in.

We can only grow as large as the jug we're in—and we are the ones who decide its size and scope. The person who finds his world closing in around him, who finds it dull, routine, and uninteresting, has outgrown his "jug" and should start looking for a larger one.

Today I will break out of my jug. I will utilize my potential.

Who Is That Masked Man?

"America's greatest crime against the black man was not slavery or the lynching, but that he was taught to wear a mask of self-hate and self-doubt."
—MALCOLM X, PAN-AFRICANIST AND HUMAN RIGHTS ACTIVIST

For many years as an intern at Harlem Hospital in the Department of Psychiatry, Dr. Alvin Pouissant studied the problems and challenges of New York's black, urban poor. The results of his findings have been published in many scholarly journals. Dr. Pouissant wrote, "It's important for Black Americans to learn to function independently. We must realize deep within our hearts that 'black is truly beautiful.' It's also important that our children see successful role models; we must undo the negative conditioning that we are not capable of succeeding, that we are not worthy."

Many of Dr. Pouissant's patients who had lost their self-respect and pride due to years of psychic disrepair, developed a positive self-image, self-confidence, and established clear goals for their lives after therapy. They took off their masks of despair. Unfortunately, like many of Dr. Pouissant's patients before therapy, some of us wear a mask of poverty—living a life of lack and want, never finding wealth because we search through eyes of limitation. Some of us wear a mask of chaos and confusion—blind to peace and tranquillity because we see only darkness and doubt. Some of us wear a mask of sickness and pain—we look for hurt and disease and, sooner or later, we find it.

Does this sound familiar? If so, what mask are you wearing? And why are you wearing a mask? You are the star of the show. You may not be the most skilled, most engaging person on earth, but you do have hidden strengths waiting to be unveiled. The moment you remove your mask and expose your unique talents, you will be one step closer to success.

I know who I am. I am unlimited potential.

Love Never Takes a Holiday

"My great hope is to laugh as much as I cry; to get my work done and try to love somebody and have the courage to accept the love in return."
—MAYA ANGELOU, WRITER

Years ago my youngest daughter asked, "Why does Valentine's Day come only once a year?"

For a little girl the excitement of making simple but colorful valentines, adding a little message in a childish scrawl, and giving them to all her friends was something very special. And best of all, my daughter received just as many notes and gifts as she gave.

I tried to explain a bit of the history of Valentine's Day. My wife thoughtfully added, "It doesn't have to come only once a year, it can be anytime you want it to be."

Surprisingly my daughter kept that thought, and even now, years later, she sends us little notes composed during her caring moments, not only on Valentine's Day. My wife and I do the same.

Valentine's Day is special, but a thoughtful note can brighten any day. "Love is sharing a part of yourself with others," says Clara "Mother" Hale. This practice has paid dividends for our family. Perhaps it can do the same for yours. We've found that love never takes a holiday.

Love is a little word, but I will make it grow.

Rest in Peace

"Find the good and praise it."
—ALEX HALEY, WRITER

We all have the potential for finding inner peace. The way to inner peace often lies in our willingness and ability to enter into the lives of others and share their experiences. The following tale drives home this point.

Once a widow's son died in a tragic accident. The woman, overcome with grief, mourned her loss so deeply that no one could provide her with comfort. At last a friend took her to the house of a holy man, where she made a sobbing plea: "Use your powers to bring back my son. Surely you are able to induce the Almighty to lighten my grief." The old man listened before giving the following instructions: "Bring me a mustard seed from a home that has never known sorrow. I will use that to remove the pain from your life."

Immediately the woman set out to search for the mustard seed. "First I will visit the home of a wealthy family," she thought. "Tragedy is less likely to strike them." Soon she approached a beautiful mansion, knocked on the door, and spoke to the woman who greeted her. "I am in search of a home that has never known sorrow. Is this such a place?"

"Never known sorrow!" cried the woman who had answered the door. "You have come to the wrong house." As she sobbed, she began to describe all the tragedies that had touched her life. The widow remained in that home for many days before moving on. When she left to resume her search, she visited a home about a mile away. The experience was the same. Wherever she traveled, from mansion to hut, she was greeted with tales of sadness and sorrow. After months of travel she became so involved with the grief of others that she forgot about her quest for the magic mustard seed, never realizing that it had indeed driven the sorrow from her life.

I will find inner peace by helping others.

Don't Just Stand There!

*"I act as if everything depends upon me and pray
as if everything depends upon God."*
—OPRAH WINFREY, TALK-SHOW HOST

Don't just stand there. Do something! To this often-heard exclamation, the logical response is "What should I do?" Unfortunately nobody can tell you what you should do. Only you know what your goals are. Many people are frustrated because they want to be successful teachers or doctors or lawyers or students. But they don't know how to move their greatest obstacle—themselves. They are *motivated*, but not *mobilized*.

To mobilize, according to Webster's dictionary, means "to put into action or motion." The word, adapted from military terminology, once carried the idea of "marshaling troops for a specific battle." You, too, can marshal your own troops for your particular battles if you remember a very important principle that can change your outlook on life: *What you do is often more important than how much you do!*

Mobilizing yourself involves three key steps: First, decide what you want to achieve most. Second, determine and plan your first step toward getting what you want. And, third, do the first thing that will move you toward what you want. A thoroughbred horse never looks at the other racehorses. It just concentrates on running the fastest race it can. On our track to success we have to fight the tendency to look at others and see how far they've come. The only thing that counts is how we use the potential we possess and that we run our race to the best of our abilities.

I will place my personal power in gear and steer it toward my goal.

Clean Your Plate—
People in China Are Starving

"Positive anything is better than negative nothing."
—LORRAINE HANSBERRY, PLAYWRIGHT AND ACTIVIST

I remember as a child being reminded that I should be grateful for all the good things I had in my life. My mother told me to say grace, say my prayers, and to be thankful for plenty of food, a warm bed, and all the other things that I took for granted. I even recall the times I was told to write a list composed of the items I was grateful for.

Years later I was able to place the "attitude of gratitude" into a whole different perspective. As I discovered more of how our minds work and began to see that we have in our lives what we think about, it registered that in order to continue to enjoy good fortune, I needed to feel fortunate.

It is imperative that we be thankful for what we have in every area of our lives. All great achievers are united by this single principle: *Count your blessings.*

Look around and see the goodness that God has offered. I once read a legend of a man who found the barn where Satan kept his seeds ready to be sown in the human heart, and on finding the seeds of discouragement more numerous than others, he learned that those seeds could be made to grow almost anywhere. When Satan was questioned, he reluctantly admitted that there is one place in which he could never get them to thrive. "And where is that?" asked the man. Satan replied, "In the heart of a grateful man." Be grateful for what you have, not regretful for what you haven't.

Thankfulness leaves no room for discouragement. I will begin to give thanks for the blessings that I already possess.

Waiting to Exhale

"Fires can't be made with dead embers."
—JAMES BALDWIN, WRITER

The lessons of living center around healing. Health is the greatest gift in the world. We do not need to add anything to our lives to be healed. We need only to tune in to the flow— the very flow that the Creator is always whispering in our ear. Health is our natural condition.

There is a legend about a butcher who used the same knife for twenty years without having to sharpen it once. The townspeople were astounded, and one day one of his customers asked him, "How can you do so much cutting and keep the blade sharp?"

"It's very simple," he explained. "I do not try to cut through bone or gristle. Where I feel resistance, I move the knife slightly and make the necessary adjustment. My knife is always speaking to me, and I work in harmony with it." The physical body speaks to us in the same way, and if we are willing to listen to its messages, we can avoid disease.

Instinctively our bodies speak to us through the process of breathing. An infant's first breath is followed by approximately 600 million more before he "breathes his last." In between we "wait with baited breath" and enjoy "breathtaking" scenery. When tired, we "take a breather"; when nervous, we "take a deep breath"; and when out of danger, we "breathe freely." Few people pay much attention to breathing. But doing so can help us regulate our health. Here's a quick experiment to demonstrate the healing effects of breathing. Start breathing quickly, taking shallow, irregular breaths, and close your eyes. What kind of thoughts arise? Since your breathing is shallow when you feel stress, whatever is stressful in your life probably came to mind. The lesson is twofold: First, our breathing influences our mental state; and second, when upset, we should breathe more slowly. A deep breath enlivens our nervous system. To revive yourself, simply stand up with your hands held high and take in all the air you can. Wait a few moments, then exhale. You'll feel more alive, much more positive, and much healthier.

I will stay attuned to my body through my mind.

High Five

"Lack of self-confidence and the fear of failure are opposite sides of the same coin."
—CHARLES JOHNSON, AUTHOR, *THE MIDDLE PASSAGE*

A little boy was overheard talking to himself as he strutted through the backyard, baseball cap in place, toting a ball and bat. He said, "I'm the greatest hitter in the world!" Then he tossed the ball into the air, swung at it, and missed. "Strike one!" Undaunted, he picked up the ball, threw it into the air and said to himself, "I'm the greatest baseball hitter ever," and swung at the ball again. And again he missed. "Strike two!" He paused a moment to examine his bat and ball carefully. Then a third time he threw the ball into the air. "I'm the greatest hitter who ever lived," he said. He swung the bat hard again, missed a third time. After a brief pause he cried out, "Wow! Strike three! What a pitcher! I'm the greatest pitcher in the world!" and proceeded to give himself a number of high fives.

Many times in life we resemble this child. There's something we want—a new job, a new business, or a home. We want it, but we hesitate to reach for it. What stands in our way? A lack of confidence.

When you maintain an air of confidence, obstacles are easily overcome. You believe within your heart that you will accomplish your objectives. Deny the voices that tell you that you can't or that you won't; because *you can and you will!* And when you reach your goal through the trait of self-confidence, give yourself a high five. *You've got what it takes!*

I will always believe in myself.

When Will It Ever End?

"The secret to the fountain of youth is to think youthful thoughts."
—JOSEPHINE BAKER, ACTRESS, DANCER, AND
ENTERTAINER

Creativity is one of the characteristics of Infinite Intelligence. Actuarial tables seem to confirm that high-achievers have an innate need to be more creative. As a group, creative men and women—research scientists, inventors, painters, writers, and philosophers—not only live longer but also remain productive longer than their noncreative counterparts.

For example, A. G. Gaston is still negotiating business deals. He's one hundred years old! At seventy-eight T. M. Alexander is still selling life insurance. At seventy-five Dr. Selma Burke completed the requirements for her Ph.D. In a teaching career that spans more than eighty years, John Morton Finney earned his fourth bachelor's degree at seventy-five. At eighty-two Dorothy Height still voices the cause of black women's rights. Edward Kennedy "Duke" Ellington, one of the most respected figures in the history of jazz, gave one of his finest recitals at New York's Carnegie Hall at the age of seventy-five. Benjamin E. Mays, a man who received fifty-one honorary degrees in his lifetime, gave his most meaningful lectures while in his eighties.

We age not by years but by events and our emotional reactions to them. Faith, courage, interest, and optimism bring us new life and more life. Futility, pessimism, frustration, living in the past, are not only characteristic of "old age," but they contribute to it. Time is always on the side of the achiever.

Age is only a number, not my outlook on life. I will live today by my "inner clock" and worry less about age.

Everything's Coming My Way

"We must conquer our own doubts and fears. It is the greatest mistake to sit and do nothing. Each of us must do what we can."
—JANE BROWNING SMITH, DIRECTOR, INROADS, INC.

Many of us go through life searching for favorable breaks. Perhaps the biggest break you could ever receive is to *decide exactly what it is you want*. You must be certain in uncertain times; definite with the indefinite. Decision is the most important ingredient in the recipe for success.

Some people call it "want to," others call it the "will to win." No matter what you call it, it's the secret that most people overlook. You can have everything going for you—money, contacts, and connections—but if you don't possess the desire to make your life count, success will elude your grasp.

Some people want success so badly, it becomes an all-consuming passion. For example, when asked for his key to achievement, Dr. Benjamin Carson said he "had to become a successful surgeon."

Through symphony and song Quincy Jones wanted desperately to carve his name on the tablet of success. Toward this end he was willing to stake his entire existence on it.

Though barred from law schools because of his race, Thurgood Marshall dreamed of making an impact within the courtrooms of America—and nothing would deter him.

Nothing stops the man or woman who *desires* to achieve. Decide now exactly what you want and the breaks will start coming your way.

Today I will write down exactly what I want.

It's About Time

"I've only just a minute, sixty-seconds it; forced upon me, can't refuse it, didn't seek it, didn't choose it."
—BENJAMIN E. MAYS, EDUCATOR

Dr. Benjamin E. Mays was both an educator and a preacher. His robust and optimistic life could be summed up in his favorite poem, entitled "I've Only Just a Minute." The ideas expressed in the poem are as valid today as when Dr. Mays set them down more than a half-century ago. The poem's stirring power reminds us that life only allows us a little time to do what we want. We must make the most of every moment.

It takes a lot of energy to waste time. Why should we knit or play checkers, for example, when we might spend that "tension-relieving" time reading self-help books for personal development? Each of us can think of a number of activities in our daily lives that are relatively unproductive and unrewarding. Why not replace them with something productive and rewarding?

I don't think watching an hour-long television rerun will ever add to our lives. Therefore, instead of doing something routinely tension-relieving, why not do something goal-achieving? Why not think about how we spend the minutes of our days and see if our habits are allowing precious time to slip away unused? Walter Turnbull, founder of the Harlem Boys Choir, knows the value of time. It took him nearly twenty-five years to establish his boys as the preeminent singing ensemble in the country. "Whenever we waste time," he says, "we should remember that Father Time never makes a round trip."

By correcting our habits and making use of the time we would otherwise have wasted, we will stay young in heart and in mind, no matter how long we have been around.

Eternity can be found in a single minute. I will use each minute wisely.

Which Way Will You Turn?

"Some people succeed because they are destined to, but most people succeed because they are determined to."
—ROSCOE DUNJEE, ENTREPRENEUR AND ACTIVIST

Who among us has not been tempted to exclaim, "I wish I could chuck the whole thing and get away from it all?" Who has never become "fed up" and known an urge to escape? Who has never cried, "I've had about as much as I can take!" Yet would fleeing be the answer? Would not our frustrations still hound us? Would we not take our problems with us?

When tempted to run away, you must call on your resolution, not your doubts and fears. You sharpen your abilities when you encounter something difficult and battle against it with determination and courage. You never get your second wind except in the long race. You never learn to swim in shallow pools. You never learn to play tennis with the net down. You never gain sturdiness if you quit before reaching the top of the first steep hill.

It is persistence that most often separates the achievers from the also-rans. After your arms and back are tired from swinging the ax, it takes that solid lick to split the log. If you quit before the final blow, all your efforts are wasted. Nothing takes the place of persistence. Ultimately the man with determined "push" replaces the man with deferential "pull." Success smiles on those who persist, who refuse to be stopped by rebuff but keep on trying. When you are tempted to run away, call on your inner resources and persist.

Success comes to those who hang on long after others have given up. I will persist in spite of the difficulties.

A Flash of Inspiration

*"The greatest inspiration is often born of
desperation."*
—COMER COTRELL, FOUNDER, PRO-LINE CORPORATION

Just as we are now, each of us has all that we need to succeed.
You and I are thoughts in the mind of God, and God cannot
be defeated. One sage said, "There is no invention—only discovery." The people who succeed are those who adapt, combine, create, and make the best use of what they have been
given to work with. George Washington Carver, for example,
was a God-inspired genius of the highest caliber. When most
of us look at the peanut, we see a tiny seed. But Dr. Carver
saw more than three hundred different uses for the peanut, including washing powder, shaving cream, bleach, paper, ink,
and synthetic rubber. He also discovered 118 uses for the
sweet potato. In short, he accepted what was given, recognized
its uniqueness, and served the world through it. Dr. Carver put
into action the maxim, What you are is God's gift to you; what
you make of yourself is your gift to God.

No matter what our past, our troubles, or our limitations,
there is always a way for us to turn seemingly futile circumstances into splendid success. There is, for example, a powerful story of a woman in New England who lost the use of her
arms and legs but refused to be beaten. She put a paintbrush
in her mouth and began to draw the lovely country scenes she
saw from her porch. Now she sells many of her paintings as
Christmas cards. Her business is successful in more ways than
one.

We are different from all other creatures because of the gift
of imaginative wisdom. Animals see things as they are, but we
see things as they can be. We have been given the divine ability to transform. It is exactly this wisdom that enables us to
transcend circumstances.

**I can change any conditions I find undesirable by using my in-
born creativity.**

Dear Abby

*"Don't ask for anyone's advice unless you are
prepared to use it."*
——SAMMY DAVIS, JR., ENTERTAINER AND PHILANTHROPIST

You are never more vulnerable than at those moments when you need advice. But you also are never more in control: You are the one who decides whom to turn to, how to listen, and how seriously to act on the counsel of others.

A man was on the practice tee when the club golf pro brought another golfer out for a lesson. The pro watched his student swing several times and started making suggestions for improvement, but each time the pupil interrupted with his own version of what was wrong and how to correct it. After a few minutes of this interference the pro began nodding his head in agreement. At the end of the lesson the student paid the pro, congratulated him on his expertise as a teacher, and left in an obviously pleased frame of mind.

The observer was so astonished by the performance that he asked, "Why did you go along with him?"

"Son," the old pro said with a grin as he carefully pocketed his fee, "I learned long ago that it's a waste of time to sell answers to a man who wants to buy echoes." Some people aren't good at taking advice. They can't admit when they need help. They can't deal with conflicting opinions. They only hear what they want to hear or what confirms their own opinion. They listen to the wrong people—or to too many people. And even if they seek advice from those whose wisdom is widely sought, they misinterpret the advice or they don't follow through.

Always remember these four rules concerning advice: *Admit you need it. Consider the source. Go to the right source. And develop a board of advisers.* Don't be afraid to use these keys.

I will be particular regarding whose advice I accept.

One Size Fits All

*"It's a two-way street; too many of us clothe
ourselves in poverty."*
—JULIANNE MALVEAUX, ECONOMIST AND SYNDICATED WRITER

Sometimes, we must admit, we should be doing more with our lives. Too often we follow the crowd instead of pursuing our own goals. We worship the masses instead of our hopes and dreams. Our outlook is analogous to the man who went to a tailor to be fitted for a new suit. When the suit was ready, he stood before a mirror for final alterations. "I think the sleeve is a bit too short for my arm," he told the tailor. "You may have to lengthen it."

"The sleeve is not too short," answered the tailor. "Your arm is too long. Just draw up your arm into the sleeve and it will look fine."

Reluctantly the man did so, but this threw the collar of the jacket out of whack. "Now the sleeve looks all right, but look at the gap between my neck and the jacket!"

"There's nothing wrong with the jacket," the tailor said defensively. "What you need to do is to raise your left shoulder a few inches."

The man again complied, but now the rear of the coat was lifted far above the waist. When he showed the tailor this misalignment, he was instructed, "Lower your head and lean forward, and there will be no problem." Finally the man walked out of the shop, convinced of its proper fit, but he had to walk in a contorted position. As he stepped onto a bus, the man next to him laughed and said, "I know where you purchased that suit."

"How do you know that?"

"Because there's only one tailor who could fit a man as crippled as you!"

The Creator did not intend for any of us to blindly follow the crowd. We will begin to make our mark when we follow our own thoughts.

I will not sell myself short. I will open myself up to new ideas and opportunities.

Fast Food

"All that you accomplish or fail to accomplish in life is a direct result of the images you hold in your mind."
—HORTENSE CANADY, PRESIDENT, DELTA SIGMA THETA SORORITY, INC.

We can never advance any further than the thoughts we allow to occupy our minds. It is important that you feed your mind with nourishing thoughts just as you feed your body with nourishing food. Let me illustrate.

In the heart of a thriving city was a hot-dog vendor who sold fine-quality hot dogs. Business was booming, customers loved his product, and they kept coming back for more. The owner believed in his business and the need for someone to do what he was doing. He was so busy advertising and selling hot dogs that he didn't even have time to read the newspaper or listen to the radio. Consequently he never heard a word about the recession or the need to cut back. As long as he continued to offer his hot dogs, his customers bought them.

Then one day his well-educated son informed him of the economic recession. His son told him that people didn't have money to buy his hot dogs. The old vendor believed this news, so he quit advertising. He began ordering fewer hot dogs. He even removed his roadside signs. And sure enough, people stopped coming to his stand. Customers stopped buying his hot dogs, and he went broke.

Take notice of what you feed your mind. Bad thoughts are what some people call junk food. It has no nutritional value. *Not only are you what you eat, but you are what you think!*

I will place my mind on a mental diet with thoughts of success and prosperity.

Bo Knows

"Don't measure yourself by what you have accomplished, but by what you should have accomplished with your ability."
——BEN CHAVIS, EXECUTIVE DIRECTOR, NAACP

What makes someone great in the eyes of the world? Are our heroes supermen and superwomen who have come from another planet with exceptional powers? Or are they human beings, like ourselves, who have used just a bit more of the potential for greatness that is shared by all? You can always do a little bit more than you think you can. In fact we must become better, or we cease to be alive and to grow. The margin of greatness is quite small.

For example, most professional baseball players bat an average of about .250, which means that they get one hit for every four times at bat. This is viewed as a respectable average, and if a batter is also a good fielder, he can expect to enjoy a secure career in the major leagues. Anyone who hits .300—three hits out of ten at bat—is considered a star. By the end of the season there are perhaps only a dozen players (out of hundreds in the leagues) who have maintained a .300 average, and these hitters are honored as the great ones. They get the big contracts, the acclaim, and the athletic-shoe commercials.

What is the difference between the greats and the also-rans? *One hit in twenty!* A .250 hitter gets five hits out of twenty, and a .300 hitter gets six hits out of twenty. In the world of baseball one hit out of twenty is the margin of greatness! This slim margin of greatness symbolizes the dynamics of greatness in life. When we exercise just a tiny bit more of our potential—a minuscule amount—we become outstanding human beings.

The purpose of my being is not to win acclaim or glory but to be more of what I can be.

Knocking on the Wrong Door

"You're on earth for a purpose. Everyone's goal should be to find that purpose and to walk on the path to your destiny."
—DAMON WAYANS, ACTOR AND COMEDIAN

Opportunities come and go. Sometimes we're insightful enough and lucky enough to seize them. And unfortunately there are moments when we allow our hopes and dreams to go by the boards simply because we failed to open the door once opportunity knocked. Who among us hasn't had missed opportunities? But there is good news. Opportunity will surely knock again.

What is opportunity and when does it knock? It's knocking now if we will only listen. Opportunity is desire. Desire is the force of forces. You may possess anything that you so desire, provided that you know exactly what you want, want it badly enough, confidently expect to attain it, and are willing to pay the price for its attainment. Furthermore, desires not only develop and evolve within you, the individual, but they attract the conditions, circumstances, and people consistent with your desires. In other words, if you know what you want—if you knock on the right door—opportunities will certainly come your way.

You are opportunity, and you must knock on the door leading to your destiny. Begin now to prepare yourself to recognize opportunity and to pursue and seize these magical moments. And who gives you this right ? You give it to yourself. Only you can fulfill your God-given destiny.

I am alive to opportunity. When it comes my way, I will take advantage of it.

Attracting Wealth

"Always strive to be more than that which you are,
if you wish to obtain that which you are not."
—S. B. FULLER, ENTREPRENEUR

Everyone wants to grow and prosper. It's natural to seek joy, love, self-esteem, security, creativity, and meaningful pursuits. How are these qualities realized? Some people think they need to earn a great deal of money first. But I suggest that reversing the process might be more useful. The secret is to create only that which answers your deepest needs.

Most people believe that money will bring them something they don't have, such as power or love. Worries will vanish, they think, as they shuck their burdensome duties and pursue a life of leisure. But they have it backward. Money and material possessions alone won't fill their needs or supply these feelings. They should *first* acquire the quality they think money will furnish. *Then* the quality will draw the money into their lives.

It's important to learn to view money and material goods not as creations to fill a lack but as outcomes of expression and growth. In fact, to work merely for money's sake can be self-destructive. Don't say, "I will spend less time doing things I love so I can spend more hours working for the money I need." Instead ask, "What can I do that will make me feel more alive?" Ask yourself what you think more money will give you that you don't possess now. What needs or desires would money satisfy?

Begin now to meet those needs. You can begin to fill your life with joy and soar toward your potential without material possessions.

I will do my best to separate my wants from my needs.

The Truth About Obstacles

"If there is no struggle, there is no progress."
——FREDERICK DOUGLASS, ABOLITIONIST

An orthopedic surgeon will tell you that a broken bone, if healed properly, is stronger than the original bone.

Did it ever occur to you that without rocks and pebbles in a stream there would be no music of running water? It's the *obstacles* in the path of the water that causes the babbling brook.

If a stream is to be made useful and serviceable, what is the first thing to be done? The hidden power of the water must be released. Immediately an *obstacle* must be put in its path—a dam must be built. The water is then backed up and given depth. Now the strength of its flow generates power. As a result factories can be operated and goods produced. The water now has begun to provide a useful service. But remember, it could never have become useful in this manner without the obstacle in its path.

You and I must form the habit of accepting discouragements and hardships as only great opportunities. Just as there is no physical power on this earth strong enough to hold a moving stream, there is no obstacle strong enough and powerful enough to hold back the stream of your life. If the sand didn't irritate the oyster, there would be no pearl.

I now recognize that strength grows out of struggle.

Promises, Promises

"The richness of the promise has not run out. Keep the faith. Don't get discouraged. Maintain the course."
—WILLIAM A. JONES, FOUNDER, NATIONAL BLACK PASTORS'
CONFERENCE

Have you ever felt that life was all tangled up and you couldn't find the way out? The best response to this situation is to sit beside a lake or stream just as the stars come out. All will be calm and peaceful. Somehow a quietness will come over you, and you will feel capable of tackling life again. No matter where you are in life . . . no matter who you are . . . no matter what you have accomplished . . . no matter when or where or why you may have failed in the past, you must promise yourself always to stay in touch with your divine potential. *Promise yourself to be so strong that nothing disturbs your peace of mind:*

· Talk health, happiness, and prosperity to every person you meet.
· Make all your friends feel that there is a power inside them.
· Be optimistic and look at life's sunnier side.
· Think only of the best, work only for the best, and expect only the best.
· Be just as enthusiastic regarding the success of others as you are about your own.
· Forget the mistakes of the past and press forward to the greater achievements of the future.
· Wear a cheerful countenance at all times and greet every living creature with a smile.
· Give so much time to improvement of yourself that you have no time to criticize others.
· Be too large for worry, too noble for anger, too strong for fear, and too happy to allow the presence of trouble.

Today I will raise my consciousness. I will live up to my divine potential regardless of outer circumstances.

Two Key Ingredients

"I don't know the key to success, but the key to failure is trying to please everybody."
—BILL COSBY, ENTERTAINER AND PHILANTHROPIST

There are two main criteria of success: (1) Do others think you are a success? (2) Do you think so?

These two are related the way a straw is to an ice-cream soda. If you want to enjoy an ice-cream soda fully, it is nice to have both. But if you are to have only one, it is certainly far better to have the ice-cream soda than to have only the straw. For the straw is worthless alone. Similarly it is both worthless and futile to have the whole world thinking that you are a success if you do not think so yourself. The ice cream of success is your own inward knowledge of it. Given that, you do not need the acknowledgment of the outside world.

Trouble arises when we try to fashion our success to the world's expectations even though these are not the expectations drawn up in our own hearts. For whom are we succeeding—for ourselves or for someone else? Success, if it is to be meaningful, must be personal. It springs from the very depths where personality itself arises, and it often takes insightful probing to find out for ourselves what our own ideas of success actually are.

Too often we conform to the world's definition of success without thought or analysis, just as we conform in other areas of life. Only those brave souls who have the courage to think for themselves enjoy any measure of success and freedom.

Success is something that I define. I won't allow anyone to define success for me.

Prime Time

"Lost time is never found again."
—THELONIOUS MONK, JAZZ PIANIST

John H. Johnson, founder and president of Johnson Publishing, once remarked that he regarded every hour of his time to be worth a thousand dollars. "A man who won't keep his appointments," Johnson said, "generally won't keep his word. *Time is money.*"

We tend to waste what we value too lightly. Though it has been said often, every successful person knows that time is a valuable commodity. It can be invested or spent unwisely. Time is your greatest asset. As the ol' folks use to say, "Lost time is never found again. Don't put off until tomorrow what you can do today." It is the one commodity that is completely nonrefundable, indispensable, irretrievable, and irreplaceable. Once it's gone, it's lost forever. But you can change time into any form of riches you so choose. If you want to live a well-balanced, successful life, you should recognize the need for a systematic schedule by which to direct your time toward ends that will ensure success.

- Take time for work, it's the price for success.
- Take time to think, it's the source of power.
- Take time to play, it's the secret of youth.
- Take time to read, it's the foundation of wisdom.
- Take time to make a friend, it's the road to happiness.
- Take time to dream, it's a way to reach the stars.
- Take time to love, it's the highest joy of life.
- Take time to laugh, it's the music of the soul.

Winners value their time. I will take time to do all the things that truly matter in my life.

A Higher Calling

"I'm the son of a minister and I just can't tell dirty jokes. Even if I could, I wouldn't. You can be funny without cursing and doing sex jokes."
——SINBAD, COMEDIAN

In the operating room of a large metropolitan hospital, a young nurse was completing her first day on the job. "You've only removed eleven sponges, Doctor," she said to the surgeon closing an incision after surgery. "We used twelve."

"I removed them all," the doctor declared. "We'll close the incision now."

"No," the nurse objected. "We used twelve sponges."

"I'll take the responsibility," the doctor said grimly. "Now suture!"

"You can't do that!" the nurse blurted out. "Think of the patient."

Just then the doctor smiled, lifted his foot, and showed the nurse the twelfth sponge. "You'll do," he said. He had been testing her integrity—and she had it. This story illustrates a key component of integrity: having the courage of your convictions—sticking to your guns, doing what you believe is right, and not fearing to speak out. Such actions are sorely needed. We need to witness a reemergence of integrity as one of the predominant values in the collective human character.

Those who do have integrity and consistently try to exercise it have discovered something the rest of the world ought to know: *Integrity makes life easier, as well as more joyful and powerful.*

I realize that integrity is a virtue, not a gift.

It Never Fails

*"I knew I had to make it. I had the determination
to go on, and my determination was to be
somebody."*
—JAMES BROWN, THE "GODFATHER OF SOUL"

What is the principle that never fails? By grasping this key you'll add quality and richness to your life, eventually drawing you closer to the goals you seek. The principle I speak of is *persistence*. The power of persistence is characteristic of those who have achieved greatness. It is not brains or talent or resources as it is persistency of effort and constancy of purpose that draw one toward greatness.

There's a simple story that highlights this principle of persistence. One day the devil decided to close up shop in one part of town and reopen in another. A "going out of business" sale was announced. One of his customers who was quite fascinated with the various instruments on display noticed that of all the devil's tools the highest priced was the one called discouragement.

"Why is this one so expensive?" the customer inquired. "Quite simple," replied the devil. "It's my favorite. With the tool of discouragement I can pry into anyone's mind and end all dreams and hopes."

Those achievers who succeed in life are men and women who keep their shoulders to the wheel, who may not believe themselves overly talented but who realize that if they are ever to accomplish anything of value, they must do so by a determined and persistent effort.

Richard Wright, the acclaimed novelist, wrote, "It is no disgrace to begin again. *This thing we call failure is only the process of staying down.*"

Persistence is the measure of how much I believe in myself; and I know that I am capable of success.

Do I Have to Tell You to
Do Everything?

*"I wouldn't ask others to do for me what I wouldn't
do for myself."*
—JEWEL LAFONTANT, CORPORATE EXECUTIVE

When you trust the inherent worthiness of your dreams, visions, and intuitions, you start down the path that leads to happiness and success.

But there are times when we fail to trust our worthiness—when we do as we are told and blindly follow orders. Consequently, we live marginal lives. Ironically, some people have to be dragged kicking and screaming to a better life.

There is a story of a sentry standing day after day at his post with no apparent reason for his being there. One day, a passerby asked him why he was standing guard in that particular spot. "I don't know," the sentry replied, "I'm just following orders." The passerby then went to the captain of the guard and asked him why the sentry was posted in that location. "I don't know," the captain replied. "We're just following orders." This prompted the captain of the guard to ask the king. The king didn't know but his curiosity was piqued. He summoned his wise men and asked *them* the question. The answer came back that one hundred years before, an African prince planted a rosebush and had ordered a sentry placed there to protect it. The rosebush had been dead for eighty years, but the sentry still stood guard. He was waiting to be told to move.

Each of us has a personal path that only we can follow. No one can travel this road but you. No one can force, drag, push, or command you to experience life's journey. You must take the initiative. It is only to the extent that we find the courage to walk our own path that we will be truly effective and at peace with ourselves.

I do not need to be pushed, pulled, or forced to experience my good. I will lead myself to success.

Your Right to Be Rich

"Wealth will never come to those who fail to appreciate it."
—FATHER DIVINE, EVANGELIST AND ENTREPRENEUR

"Wealth is not how much you have," remarked basketball great Cheryl Miller, "but how much you enjoy." Producer Quincy Jones thinks along the same lines. He said, "You're wealthy when your children love you, your critics respect you, and you have peace of mind." And concert pianist Andre Watts took this idea one step further when he said, "Prosperity only comes to those who seek it for others first." In the course of life you may hope to acquire money, but you would be wiser to pursue a more valuable gift instead: *The riches of peace of mind.* The following story illustrates this point.

A businessman had an angel visit him. During their meeting the angel granted him one request. The man requested a copy of next year's stock market quotes in advance. As he studied the future prices on the New York and American stock exchanges, he boasted of his plans and the increased riches that would be his as a result of his "insider" look into the future. He then glanced across the newspaper page and saw his own picture in the obituary column. Obviously, in the light of his certain death money was no longer important.

We are all aware of the many gifts and pleasures that money can buy, but how many of us realize the priceless treasures that money cannot buy? For example, money can buy: A bed, but not sleep. Food, but not an appetite. A house, but not a home. Books, but not brains. Education, but not knowledge. Medicine, but not health. Pleasure, but not happiness. Lust, but not love. A gold watch, but not time; and seemingly "valuable" possessions, but not peace. *Search for peace.*

I will reach for the true blessings in life, those things that matter most.

Who's in Control?

"I've got my own life; I make my own decisions.
I'm in control!"
—JANET JACKSON, SINGER

We were not equipped with minds of our own so that we could abdicate control of our destiny to someone else. It makes no sense to believe that we are in any way designed to be kept under the care and control of another. We were not designed to follow. *We were designed to achieve, to strive, to build.* We must control our lives. To do otherwise is quite literally to waste them.

Ron Leflore, a product of Detroit's inner city, grew up under the worst of conditions. At age fifteen he was tried and convicted for his part in the robbery of a local nightclub. When asked by a judge why his young life was spinning dangerously out of control, Leflore replied, "I guess I got mixed up with the wrong crowd." As the days of his sentence slipped by, he often sat in silence dreaming of a better life beyond the prison gates. The future all-star center fielder for the Detroit Tigers soon realized that he was not powerless and that he was imprisoned because of his attitude toward life. He vowed to take control.

Ron Leflore, the prisoner, knew the true meaning of his dream. For him a wasted existence was to permit his life to be spent under the control of someone else. Yet we, too, each in our own way, are prisoners. We must break through the bars of conformity that we have constructed around ourselves. We must not permit our lives to be spent trudging in circles behind another, who follows another, who follows another, *who might ultimately be following us.* We are equipped with the ability to lead our own lives. The moment we break from the pack to follow our hopes and dreams is the day we assume complete control of our lives.

I choose not to follow where the common path may lead. I will follow my own path instead.

There Goes the Neighborhood

*"The kind of ancestors we have is not as important
as the kind of descendants our ancestors have."*
—PHYLLIS A. WALLACE, FIRST AFRICAN-AMERICAN FEMALE
TO RECEIVE A DOCTORATE IN ECONOMICS FROM YALE

One of the most important aspects of the study of achievement is training the eyes to see properly. Sight is an interesting phenomenon. We see things not as they are but as we are. Our perception is shaped by past experiences, according to our faith and consciousness. In other words, seeing is not believing; believing is seeing. *We can only see in others what lies within ourselves.*

There is a story of a man who comes to the outskirts of town. There he finds a gatekeeper sitting quietly. The traveler tells the gatekeeper that he has just left his old town and that he is thinking of moving here. "What's this city like?" he asks.

"What was it like in the city you just left?" responds the gatekeeper.

"It was a lousy place. The people weren't too friendly."

"Well, that's just what you'll find here," explained the gatekeeper. The traveler moved on. A few hours later another man with a suitcase arrived, seeking a home.

"What's this town like?" the stranger asked.

"What was your old town like?" the gatekeeper shot back.

"Oh, it was a nice place. The people were friendly and caring. I really hated to leave, but I was forced to take a new job."

"Well, that's what you will find here," the gatekeeper continued, and the man happily entered the city.

How we use the function of sight is crucial to our finding and receiving what we want out of life. Success, love, and abundance are not given to a privileged few. Those who enjoy happiness do so because they have learned to see with their inner eye.

I will see the good in others because I will see the good in myself.

It Ain't Over Till It's Over

"I look forward to every new day. I want to keep going and playing music, and doing what I feel is important."
—LIONEL HAMPTON, JAZZ MUSICIAN

By the mid-1950s psychologists had erroneously theorized that man's mental powers reach their peak at age twenty-five and then begin a gradual decline. Such nonsense as "you can't teach an old dog new tricks" still persists despite the fact that current research has shown that our learning ability never declines. Many people needlessly go downhill after retirement. They feel their productive years are completed and their job is done. Consequently they become bored, inactive, mentally and physically atrophied, and often suffer a loss of self-esteem. Some develop a self-image of a useless, worthless, worn-out "hanger-on." As a result their hopes are dashed and their prospects for the future are bleak.

It is not retiring from a job that dims the prospects of these individuals, *it is retiring from life*. It is the feeling of uselessness, of being washed up; the dampening of self-esteem, courage, and self-confidence, which our present attitudes of society help to encourage. People grow old only by deserting their ideals. Years may wrinkle the skin, but to give up interest wrinkles the soul. You are as young as your faith, as old as your doubt; as young as your self-confidence, as old as your fear; as young as your hope, as old as your despair.

Don't despair! In the central place of every heart there is a recording chamber. So long as it receives messages of beauty, hope, cheer, and courage, you are young.

The mind knows not time. As long as I continue to transform my thoughts, I am forever young.

Instant Credit

"My father always told me that 'I was the best.'
That there was no one better than me. Being able
to define myself is something I attribute to my
father and his 'positive arrogance.' "
—CHARLAYNE HUNTER-GAULT, NEWS REPORTER

The ego craves appreciation and receives pleasure from the approval of others. Approval, praise, and love are the great motivators in life. When we're patted on the back, we feel happy and worthwhile. When we're criticized, we feel inadequate and out of balance. Why do we feel good when we are praised? Because praise is an acknowledgment and confirmation of our worth. Praise tells us that we are respected, needed, and appreciated—that we belong.

So often we withhold praise. Sometimes it's because we don't want to appear patronizing or too personal. At other times we simply don't make the effort. We forget that everyone enjoys appreciation, a pat on the back, a word of praise.

So praise others, and don't forget to praise yourself when you deserve it. "The best way to appreciate your friends," said Michael Espy, Secretary of Agriculture, "is to imagine yourself without any." And North Carolina Mutual Insurance founder Charles Clinton Spaulding lived by the maxim: "A slap on the back often pushes out the chest." It is so easy and so pleasurable to participate in someone's life by saying a few constructive words. Sincere praise takes little effort and less time, but the effect is enormous and immediate. The recipients of your praise will hold their heads higher and try a bit harder to confirm your opinion. You will feel a glow from the warmth you have spread.

I will give praise where praise is due.

Have You Immunized Yourself from Success?

"Show me someone content with mediocrity, and I'll show you somebody destined for failure."
—JOHNETTA COLE, PRESIDENT, SPELMAN COLLEGE

Mankind was not created for mediocrity. Our imagination, for example, is most merciful. As a result we cannot imagine those things that we cannot accomplish. We would not be equipped with the ability to imagine future accomplishments and conditions if we were not correspondingly equipped with the ability to turn those ideas into reality.

On the surface, mediocrity may seem comfortable. Those of us who have settled into routine jobs at routine salaries may appear comfortable and content. But beneath the surface we are forced to contend with the rationalizations we accepted and the nonuse of our true abilities. As we consider our potential, the resultant uneasiness is anything but comfortable.

I can are two powerful words that make an even more powerful exclamation—*I can!* For the overwhelming majority of people that sentence can be a true one. People can do what they believe they can do. Perhaps no other quality has the power to lift the poor out of poverty, the hopeless out of despair, the ill out of sickness, the downtrodden out of grief, as belief. For example, Norman Rice could not become Seattle's first African-American mayor unless he believed it first. Cito Gaston, skipper of baseball's Toronto Blue Jays, could not become the first African-American manager to guide his team to a World Series title unless he believed it first. And Clifton Wharton, Jr., the Deputy Secretary of State, could not become the first African American to receive a Ph. D. in economics from the University of Chicago unless he believed it first! The gap between what an individual thinks he can achieve and what is actually possible is very, very small. *But first, he must believe that he can.*

I will examine my life and identify those areas where I can utilize my special talents.

Greatness Takes Time

"The way to be successful is through preparation. It doesn't just happen. You don't wake up one day and discover you're a lawyer any more than you wake up as a pro football player. It takes time."
—ALAN PAGE, MINNESOTA SUPREME COURT JUSTICE

The eagle is a familiar and popular creature within the framework of achievement. Its regal presence, its reputation as the king of birds, its dwelling in high and lofty places, and its freedom, strength, and speed as epitomized in its majestic flight make it a fitting symbol of greatness.

Although classified as fowl, eagles are not as easily produced as chickens or other birds. Eagles are not hatched in a brood. Nor is the reproductive cycle an overnight process. Chickens may be produced in twenty-one days and may be ready for the market in eight or nine weeks. But the eagle is much more deliberate. It takes time to produce an eagle. An eagle's reproductive cycle can last one year. Furthermore their young remain in the nest as long as 130 days before leaving the roost. In comparison the robin and blue jay take flight within a month.

So you see, *greatness takes time.* Babies are born every minute—hundreds of thousands each day. But Howard Thurmans, and Fannie Lou Hamers, and Booker T. Washingtons and Thurgood Marshalls are produced infrequently. It takes time and special effort and care to produce greatness. Our Creator seeks "eagle" men and "eagle" women—leaders who aren't afraid to stand in the face of adversity, men and women who are willing to continue the struggle no matter how uncomfortable or challenging. *Men and women like you!*

I will be patient; greatness takes time.

Your Best Investment

"You survive by using your best investment. By saying no to drugs, no to teenage pregnancies, no to disrespect. You survive by having a 'don't quit' attitude."
—ARTHUR E. THOMAS, PRESIDENT,
CENTRAL STATE UNIVERSITY

Our Creator never confines us to a place where we cannot grow. Wherever our place may be—on the farm, in the office, behind a counter, at a teacher's desk, in the kitchen, or in the operating room—when we fill that place to the best of our abilities, personal growth is inevitable. Three things begin to happen: We do a better job; we expand our talents through vigorous use; and we fit ourselves for larger responsibilities and wider opportunities.

We can give our current position the benefit of our finest effort. We've all heard someone say, "I'm too good for this job. It's too small a position for a person of my talents. There is no opportunity for me to expand." In his contempt this individual refuses to invest his complete capacities in his current position. Inevitably he becomes dissatisfied, restless, and unhappy. He fails at his task; he falls short of the mark; and he cheats himself. A successful and revered businessman says that in his early years his mother gave him a priceless gift—*the gift of service*. "John," she told him, "it is not how much you can get from a job that's important. It is how much you can put into it that counts."

Talent, like muscle, grows through exercise. If we fail to extend ourselves and merely go through the motions while we wait for something more suited to our abilities, we are headed for continual frustration. Begin now to flex your muscles.

I will fill my present position to overflowing.

I've Got a Bone to Pick

"People ask me how I built my business. I tell them
"I didn't have much, but I used everything I had."
—THOMAS BURRELL, FOUNDER,
BURRELL COMMUNICATIONS

A man overheard an elderly gentleman giving some advice to a young boy who was boarding a ship to seek his fortune. "Now, my lad," the old man said, "just remember the *three bones* and you'll get along just fine." The curiosity of the bystander prompted him to ask the old man what he meant by the "three bones."

With a twinkle in his eye the old man replied, "I'm speaking of the wishbone, the jawbone, and the backbone. It's the wishbone that keeps you chasing your dreams. It's the jawbone that helps you ask the questions that are necessary to finding them. And it's the backbone that keeps you at it until you realize them!"

Each of us must use the three bones, and we must *use them now*! To find the happiness that comes through making the most of our abilities, we must persevere in using them and make them responsive to our bidding. Undoubtedly this will give life new meaning, a new outlook. By utilizing these bones we just may be able to light a fire under some tired old bones.

I will become totally enthusiastic about life.

Wonder Bread

*"Death is not the end for someone who
has faith."*
—DESMOND TUTU, SOUTH AFRICAN ACTIVIST
AND ANGLICAN ARCHBISHOP

During an interview with a nationally known magazine, John Morton Finney, a man who earned eleven college degrees in his lifetime, was asked to list the men and women he admired most throughout history. Names such as Hopmer, Cervantes, DuBois, Aristotle, Shakespeare, and the greatest of them all, Jesus Christ, came immediately to mind.

If I were to name my list, I would include individuals like Marcus Garvey, Malcolm X, A. Philip Randolph, Ida B. Wells, Phillis Wheatley, and Martin Luther King. These achievers knew that man lives not by bread alone but by faith.

Bread is vital. But in appraising an individual for greatness, wealth—or bread—is never a criterion. Nobody stops to ask how much wealth people like Frederick Douglas or Harriet Tubman or Sojourner Truth or Mary McLeod Bethune possessed when they died. They achieved historical immortality long after bread ceased to sustain their bodies.

Man must live by faith—faith in himself and faith in others. We must trust the doctor to heal our bodies. We must trust those who drive our school buses. We must trust the banks that manage our money. We must trust the pilot who takes us from one destination to another, thousands of feet above the earth. Though we live by faith in others, more importantly we must live by faith in ourselves—faith to believe that we can develop into useful men and women.

I will seek the real bread of life—faith and understanding.

Rejoice and Be Glad

*"Success is difficult; it's gut-wrenching and
pain-inducing."*
—PARREN MITCHELL, FORMER CONGRESSMAN

*Blessed are you when people revile you and persecute you and
utter all kinds of evil against you falsely on my account. Rejoice and be glad, for your reward is great in heaven (Matt.
5:11–12).*

Be not dismayed if you are criticized—you're in good company. You're in the company of Noah, who was criticized for
building a boat in the middle of the desert. You're in the company of Moses, who was criticized for leading the children of
Israel into the wilderness. You're in the company of Booker T.
Washington, who was criticized for daring to educate southern
blacks, or Roy Wilkins, who risked life and limb to urge
blacks to exercise their right to vote. You're in the company of
Marian Wright Edelman, who is still criticized for condemning
a nation's social policy as it pertains to its children. You're in
the company of Jesse Jackson, who had the audacity to consider himself a presidential candidate, thereby challenging the
political status quo.

So remember, bless those who criticize you; rejoice and be
glad. Though your name may be cast out, keep going. Though
you may be criticized when giving your best, keep going. And
though others may falsely accuse you—*keep going!*

The only power that criticism has is that which I give it. I will
empower criticism no longer!

A One-Track Mind

*"It took me twenty years. But I knew what I
wanted and I knew what I could do."*
—WALTER TURNBULL, FOUNDER, HARLEM BOYS CHOIR

Each of us is born with two minds: a "can do" mind and a
"can't do" mind. An excellent way to get acquainted with
these two types of minds is to look upon the subconscious as
a garden. You are a gardener and you are planting seeds
(thoughts) in your subconscious mind based on your thinking.
As you sow, so shall you reap. That which is possible only becomes possible after you have used your "can do" mind. The
"can do" mind believes in success, abundance, health, and
prosperity. The "can't do" mind, on the other hand, succumbs
to negative thinking, fear, and disbelief. It nurtures feelings of
lack, limitation, ignorance, and discord.

In one respect both achiever and failure alike deploy their
greatest gift—the use of their minds. However, while one uti-
lizes the positive, the other employs the negative. One makes
use of the "can do" mind and reaps all the blessings that it
bears. The other struggles senselessly with the sadder side of
life and all too often adapts to life's shortcomings. Those who
have carved their names onto the tablet of success have a deep
understanding of the workings of these two minds. Long before their goals became apparent, they made a conscious decision to "lose their minds" and rid themselves of all negative
thinking.

The same applies to you. In order to change external conditions and experience all the good this world has to offer, you
must first make a conscious decision to lose your negative
mind.

I will use the key to my success. I will use my "can do" mind.

Cast the First Stone

*"Many people need more hope than help.
Keep hope alive!"*
—JESSE JACKSON, FOUNDER, THE RAINBOW COALITION

When the great library of Alexandria was burned, one book was saved. A poor man bought it for a few coins. It was not well written, but it was unique. Within its binding it contained a thin strip of parchment on which was written the secret of the "touchstone."

The touchstone was a small pebble that could turn any common metal into pure gold. The writing explained that it could be found on the shores of the Black Sea lying among thousands and thousands of other rocks that looked exactly like it. But the secret was this: The real stone would feel warm, while ordinary pebbles are cold. So the man sold his few belongings, bought some simple supplies, camped on the seashore, and began searching among the pebbles.

He knew that if he picked up ordinary stones and dropped them because they were cold, he might pick up the same pebble hundreds of times. So when he felt one that was cold, he threw it into the sea. As his hope faded, he spent days, weeks, months, and years searching for the touchstone. Yet he continued his routine—pick up a pebble, see if it's cold, then throw it into the sea, and so on. But one morning he picked up a pebble that was warm. Inadvertently he still threw it into the sea! He had gotten so used to discarding the stones that when he found the one he wanted, he still threw it away!

Don't give up your hope. It's the magic touchstone. Without hope there is nothing. Keep hope alive. *Don't throw it away!*

I will keep hope alive. My future depends on it.

May I Have the Envelope, Please?

"People always ask, 'How did you succeed?' Simply put, I chose not to fail."
—XERNONA CLAYTON, CORPORATE EXECUTIVE, TURNER BROADCASTING SYSTEM

At some point in life most of us are made keenly aware that we must make choices—choices that determine our destiny. It is as though at birth we are given two sealed envelopes, each containing orders by which our lives are to be governed. One envelope contains a list of the blessings we will enjoy if we recognize the power of our mind, take possession of it, and carefully direct it to the desires of our choice. The other envelope contains the penalties we will pay if we neglect to use this power constructively. We have to decide which envelope to open. Our mind is the only thing we can control. We can either think positively or negatively. *The choice is ours.* The following story drives home this issue of choice.

Before two brothers could ride ponies on their uncle's ranch, their uncle insisted they shovel a pile of manure out of the stall. One brother resisted and grumbled his way through a few half-hearted scoops. The other brother laughed, sang, and attacked the task with abandon.

"Why are you so happy?" the first brother asked.

"Well," the second replied, "with all this manure, there must be a pony in here someplace!"

So it is with our mind. When life throws out its daily problems, we can moan and groan over our fate, or, in the midst of confusion and difficulties, we can tell ourselves, "There must be some good in here someplace!" We have the power to choose our destiny.

To live is to choose, and I choose to live a positive, fulfilled life.

Let Me Break It Down for You

"There is in this world no such force as the force of a man determined to rise. The human soul cannot be permanently chained."
—W. E. B. DUBOIS, EDUCATOR AND SCHOLAR

Have you ever driven your car with the brakes on? I suppose that most of us who have driven for any length of time have had that experience. I can remember times when I have arrived at my destination and reached down to apply the parking break, only to find that it had been on the entire time I had been driving. Yet without realizing it I had moved from point to point with my brakes partly set. The horsepower was there, but the car's vast potential was blocked, bottled up, and restricted.

Traffic signals teach the same lesson. Signs and signals that regulate traffic are necessary for all the obvious reasons. But when you stop because of the red light on your "mental dashboard," what are the real reasons that you hit the brakes? Have you asked, "Am I stopping for realistic reasons, because I hope to avoid some impending danger, or am I stopping because I do not believe myself capable of reaching my objective?"

How do you view yourself? Are you driving with your mental brakes on? If so, release your brakes and avoid all unnecessary stops. You'll reach your goals much sooner.

The light is green and I'm ready to go. I release everything that is holding me back.

Wake Up and Smell the Coffee

"Every movie that I produced I saw in my mind first."
——MARIO VAN PEEBLES, ACTOR AND FILM DIRECTOR

Are there special traits, habits, or qualities common to all successful people? For centuries mankind has been seeking common chords in all achievers, but these traits are not as obvious as one would expect. You need only to read a series of profiles of famous individuals to realize how different each is from the other, how varied are their methods of operation, how different their work habits, how unique their personal lives.

Still, there is one practice that many have in common, especially during their leaner years. They were able to vividly picture themselves having already attained their goals, and they constantly retained that image in their minds. In other words they were aware that as a man thinketh, so is he. There is a significant saying in the Book of Job: "The thing that I have feared has come upon me," and I have seen the truth of this demonstrated many times. On a flight to the Far East, for example, a man was complaining bitterly when the stewardess neglected to serve him coffee. "She passed me by," he reported. "She served everyone around me and left me sitting here. But that always happens to me. I fully expect it."

Sure enough, on the return flight with an entirely new crew the stewardess not only forgot to bring his coffee, she forgot to serve him his meal. Fiery mad, he pressed the call button. "I'm so sorry," she said. "I can't imagine how I overlooked you."

"They do that all the time," the man confessed. Again, Job was right. Your imagination is your magic wand. Use it to visualize success.

I will visualize my positive goals in order to reach them.

Sleeping with the Enemy

*"The triumph song of life would lose its melody
without the minor keys."*
—MARY MCLEOD BETHUNE, EDUCATOR

The Master taught you to "love your enemies." Why? When
we look at our "enemies" as our teachers, they cease to be our
opponents and eventually become our greatest assets.

We are told of an ancient Greek who paid someone a daily
wage to follow him through his affairs and insult him so that,
through learning to remain steadfast in the face of criticism, he
would develop strength of character. Considering his example,
perhaps we should be thankful that our adversaries are doing
us such a valuable service. Throughout her workshops, tennis
great Althea Gibson demonstrates this principle. She urges her
students to select skilled, competitive opponents. Why? Because superior opponents force us to do our best.

And so it is with the inner game of life. We want to grow;
we want to improve our skills in life. If you have mastered
any field of endeavor, you know the value of challenge, adversity, and discipline. The violin virtuoso welcomes with enthusiasm a new and difficult piece of music. He must flex his
musical muscles to master the piece. He knows that through
the practice of overcoming the challenge his proficiency is enhanced. "The same hammer that shatters the glass," Marcus
Garvey explained, "forges the steel."

Looking at adversity and challenge in this manner, we really
can love our enemies. They serve us hard shots until we learn
to return them.

I will embrace my difficulties and grow from them.

When Bad Things Happen to Good People

"If I were to say, 'God, why me?' about the bad things, then I should have said, 'God, why me?' about the good things that happened in my life."
—ARTHUR ASHE, TENNIS GREAT AND AIDS ACTIVIST

During a Sunday service at New York's Abyssinian Baptist Church, Reverend Calvin Butts challenged his congregation to answer the question "How much can God do?" The Bible tells us, among other things, that God can heal us, deliver us from tribulation, lead us, guide us, and inspire us. It tells us that God is a mighty fortress.

But just how much can God do? God can do *almost* anything. That may sound strange to those of us who have been taught that "with God all things are possible." But there are some things that God *cannot* do. Because God is a God of love, he rules by divine principle. In other words, he cannot break divine law. He cannot make exception to the rule. He cannot bring disease or suffering or lack. If he could do all these things, he would not be God at all. *Because God is love.*

Because God is always the loving Father, more ready to give than to receive, we can go to him with full confidence, knowing that he will hear and answer our prayers—not because we seek a special favor, but because, as a child of God, success is our divine heritage.

How much can God do? God can solve our problems, he can heal our bodies and our conditions. He can remove our fears, doubts, and frustrations. He can deliver us from evil. But God cannot do everything. He can only do good! Let us pray for the wisdom to understand our experiences, both good and bad.

Today I will take a few moments to seek spiritual understanding.

Come on In ... the Water's Fine

*"Money doesn't make the man. Some people have
money, and some people are rich."*
—THOMAS A. DORSEY, FATHER OF GOSPEL MUSIC

Take a look at some of the limiting beliefs concerning wealth
in general, and money in particular. Have you, even to a slight
degree, bought into any of them? "It takes money to make
money." "Money is the root of all evil." "People resent the
rich." "The best things in life are free." "It's easier for a camel
to go through the eye of a needle than for a rich man to enter
the kingdom of heaven." It's easy to see how believing even
a few of these myths not only keeps money away from us but
also might make us want to get rid of the money we have.

There is no lack in the universe. Instead the universe is
filled with ideas flowing through time and space, and it's up
to us to take out of this flowing river an abundance of what
we want. Our unlimited abundance is analogous to the mighty
Mississippi River. It is a vast body of water made up of many
other smaller rivers leading into tributaries. These tributaries
assist it in developing its strength and power. There is only
one Mississippi River. So, too, there is also only one universal
law, which, when rightly used, will lead us to peace, joy, and
abundance.

Standing in the flow of the universe and saying that there
isn't enough wealth to go around is like standing in the middle
of the Mississippi River and thinking, "I can't have any more
water. All of my water just passed by." It's as if you have a
blank check. Use it to write yourself a fortune in happiness.

I will hold my bucket under the fountain of prosperity.

The People's Court

"The most effective recourse is the quality of your performance. Your energies should be directed to doing the best possible job you can."
—CLIFTON WHARTON, JR., DEPUTY SECRETARY,
U.S. DEPARTMENT OF STATE

We should judge ourselves by what we feel capable of doing, not by what we have done. Nothing else will motivate you to greatness so much as a belief in your own inherent potential. There is a potency inside of you that will transform your dreams into realities if you tap into it. *You be the judge.*

You should not be afraid to think too highly of yourself. The Creator made you and is not ashamed of the job. He pronounced his work good, and you should respect it. Persistently hold the thought that you are eternally progressing toward something higher and greater. The constant struggle to measure up to such a worthy ideal is the only force in heaven or on earth that can make a life great.

Your self-image depends on your ideal of yourself; the mental picture of the person that you are, the *you that you are meant to be*! It is you who will define your own greatness. No one can stop your date with destiny; no one can cast your fate. You are the judge and the jury. The vision that grips your heart, that longing of your soul to do something significant, that dream of high achievement that occupies your imagination, is not a mere fantasy. It is a prophecy of the great things you will do if you believe in your own potential.

I will never sell myself short; I will never underestimate my own ability.

Headfirst

"If you expect somebody else to guide you, you'll be lost."
—JAMES EARL JONES, ACTOR

One day a traveler in a remote country town, convinced that he was on the wrong road, came to a halt in a village. Calling one of the villagers to the car window, he said, "Friend, I need help. I'm lost."

The villager looked at him for a moment. "Do you know where you are?" he asked.

"Yes," said the traveler. "I saw the name of your town as I entered."

The man nodded his head. "Do you know where you want to be?"

"Yes," the traveler replied, and named his destination. The villager looked away for a moment. "You're not lost," he said, "you just need directions."

Emotionally speaking, many of us are in the same position as that traveler. We know where we are—sometimes disappointed, dissatisfied, and experiencing little peace of mind. And we know where we want to be—at peace, fulfilled, and living life abundantly. Like the traveler, we are not lost—we just need directions.

It doesn't take much to find the high road to success, the path that leads to life's most precious treasures and triumphant possibilities. But to discover those joys and feel zest for the future, you desperately need an agenda for the present. You need directions for today. *You need a purpose.* Listen to the advice Niara Sudarkasa, president of Lincoln University, gave to a group of incoming freshmen: "Your life can't go according to plan if you have no plan." With that the darkness can be pierced.

I will make the most of my life by planning my work and working my plan.

The Thrill of Victory

"Today's global marketplace demands highly skilled, effective managers."
—EARL G. GRAVES, FOUNDER, *BLACK ENTERPRISE*
MAGAZINE

Some people fear competition. The danger of defeat paralyzes them. But head coach Clarence "Big House" Gaines of the Winston-Salem College basketball team knows how to prepare his players. In a career that has spanned forty-seven years, Coach Gaines has won more than eight hundred games—second only to hall-of-famer Adolph Rupp of Kentucky.

"There are only four keys to winning," Coach Gaines contends. "Plan purposefully, prepare prayerfully, proceed positively, and pursue persistently. The price for success in any field requires preparation."

But preparation is worthless without *effectiveness*. Effectiveness means not only getting the job done, but getting it done right. For example, the winner of a two-hour marathon need only be a few seconds ahead of all the other runners to win. In business, sales leaders often make only five more phone calls per day than average, or read a few more journals per month, or get five more good ideas per year. These men and women are highly effective. They not only get the job done, they get it done effectively—and right. Through preparation and enhanced effectiveness, you will be certain to experience the thrill of victory.

Today I will use my preparation to increase my effectiveness.

Pay per View

"We usually see things not as they are but as we are."
—LOUISE BEAVERS, SILENT FILM STAR

What do you think and feel about yourself? When you look in the mirror, do you see the person that you will one day become? Perhaps the following story will help you answer these questions.

There was once an African prince who was born a hunchback. On the prince's thirteenth birthday the king asked him what he would like to receive as a birthday gift. Bent over and looking up, the boy replied, "I would like a statue of myself."

The king was confused. The last thing in the world he wanted for his young son was for him to be mocked. In an effort to change the boy's mind, the king asked, "Surely there must be something else you desire?"

But the prince was steadfast. "No, I want a statue of myself. But I do not want a statue of myself as I appear now. Rather I would like a statue of how I would look if I stood straight! Furthermore, I'd like the figure to be placed outside my window in the garden where I can see it every day."

After the statue was built, the hunchback boy stood before his likeness each morning. Day in and day out he stretched and strained to mimic the six-foot replica. He did this without fail for eight years! On his twenty-first birthday he stood shoulders erect, head straight, staring eyeball to eyeball with the bronze image. What was the prince's secret? As the poet says, "What thou seest, that thou beest."

I will visualize success.

What Color Is Your Parachute?

"What could be more fun than reading, exploring the unknown?"
——MAE C. JEMISON, ASTRONAUT

One sure way to enhance your chances for success is to take in new and additional information. *Earning* more is always preceded by *learning* more. Naturally it is best to stay in school, for school is the best place to learn. But for those who have dropped out or have not completed their formal education the answer is the same. *Learn!*

A priest, a Boy Scout, and a college professor were the only passengers on a small plane. The pilot came back to the cabin and said that the plane was going down, but there were only three parachutes and four people. The pilot then added, "I should have one of the parachutes because I have a wife and three small children." So he took one and jumped.

The college professor said, "I should have one of the parachutes because I am the smartest man in the world and everyone needs me." So he took another parachute and jumped.

The priest turned to the Boy Scout and said forlornly, "You are young and I am old. I have lived a rich life. You take the remaining parachute, and I'll go down with the plane." The Boy Scout smiled back and said, "Relax, Father, that smartest man in the world—the professor—just jumped out with my backpack."

Learn all you can and keep learning, whether you are six or sixty. The minute you stop learning, life will begin to pass you by. Consider the fate of the college professor who jumped out of the plane without a parachute. The only way to succeed in our fast-paced, ever-changing world, is through constant learning.

I will dedicate myself to lifelong learning.

Like Nobody's Business

"If a man is called to be a streetsweeper, he should sweep streets even as Michelangelo painted, or as Beethoven composed music, or as Shakespeare wrote poetry. He should sweep streets so well that all the hosts of heaven and earth will pause to say, here lived a great streetsweeper who did his job well."
—MARTIN LUTHER KING, JR., CIVIL AND HUMAN RIGHTS ACTIVIST

There's a well-worn story of a man who approached two masons who were laying bricks. He paused to ask each, "What are you doing?" The first laborer said, "Can't you see, I'm laying bricks?" He then walked over to the second bricklayer and asked, "What are you doing?" The workman looked off with a faraway mystic expression in his eyes and answered with pride, "I'm building a cathedral. One whose spires will reach heaven itself; a structure that is an important factor in the spiritual life of this community."

Both were physically doing the same thing. But the first laborer was occupied with his present task, and the other was concerned with the ultimate goal. The quest for excellence gives dignity to a person. It gives character to a business. It gives satisfaction to customers. So long as you seek excellence and accept nothing less, your business will succeed *like nobody's business.*

As Dr. King recited in many of his sermons, "If you can't be a tree on the top of a hill, be a shrub in the valley. But be the best little shrub by the side of the hill; be a bush if you can't be a tree. If you can't be the highway, just be a trail. If you can't be a sun, be a star. For it matters not in size that you win or that you fail, but be the best at whatever you are."

I will never do less than my best.

Who Are You Kidding?

*"Status is a bridge from where you are to where
you want to be."*
—GLORIA NAYLOR, WRITER

I love the story of a man who was very insecure. One day he was promoted from major to colonel and was ushered into his new office. He gazed proudly at his new surroundings. Suddenly there was a knock at the door. In walked a corporal.

The colonel said, "Just a minute, Corporal, I have to finish this phone call." He picked up the receiver, pushed a button, and said, "I'm sorry about the interruption, General. Now, where were we? Oh, yes sir, I'll take care of it. Of course I will, sir. I'll check my schedule and see when we can meet for tennis. It's true, we're close friends, and yes, I'll call the President immediately after I'm finished talking with you, General. You're welcome, sir."

The colonel ceremoniously put the phone down, turned to the young man, and asked, "Now, what can I do for you?" The corporal answered, "Well, sir, I just came in to connect your phone."

Far too many people walk through life with a low self-image. They are overly concerned with their weaknesses rather than with their strengths, and they try to conceal them with a false sense of status. The person with a healthy, happy attitude toward his world recognizes his imperfections and strives to find his strengths. Never forget that you have strengths and talents waiting to be developed.

I release any need for false status. I am comfortable with who and what I am. As I develop my strengths, I will uncover my greatest gifts.

Your First Impression

*"You have only one chance to make a first
impression. Make it count."*
—MARKITA ANDREWS, GIRL SCOUT WHO HOLDS RECORD
FOR COOKIE SALES

What constitutes a pleasing personality? The Bible offers a well-known guideline: "And as ye would that men should do to you, do ye also to them." This statement appears in various forms in many religions and philosophies. It is appropriately called the Golden Rule. You and I are forced to coexist in a world inhabited by others. How we approach and treat all members of society—and how society reacts toward us—is partly determined by how well we adhere to this mandate.

A bus driver had a female passenger who was really irritated. She let loose with a string of unrepeatable words. Everybody was ashamed. When the profane passenger got ready to disembark at her bus stop, the driver said, "Madam, you left something behind." She asked him what it was and he said, "A very bad impression."

Your personality is the medium by which you will negotiate your way through life. Your personality will demonstrate, to a large extent, your ability to associate and cooperate with others with a minimum of friction. Your personality is the sum total of your mental, spiritual, and physical traits and habits and distinguishes you from all others.

Never underestimate the power of a smile, a firm handshake, or a warm greeting. These are the tools that fashion long-lasting, positive relationships.

I know that others will respond to me in the manner in which I respond to them. I will be sure to cast a good impression.

You Did That on Purpose

*"We must all find our true purpose; like
Michelangelo or Mozart or Leonardo da Vinci. Each
of us must develop a mission in life."*
—MICHAEL JACKSON, ENTERTAINER

Occasionally we can see a strange sight at sea. The wind, the tide, and the surface ice will all move in one direction, but sailing majestically against these forces will be an iceberg. The reason is not hard to find. We see only a small part of the iceberg. Deep down in the water is the base, controlled by more powerful, deeper currents.

Strength of character is the powerful current that keeps us going in the right direction. Each of us has a unique purpose. People only begin to fulfill their creative potential when they have a high degree of alignment in their lives—that is, when their pursuits and goals are in line with their own purpose. *The most fundamental definition of personal power is having the capacity to realize your purpose.* Personal vision is the key to unlocking its power. Vision is the picture of the future that you wish to create. Vision is the vehicle for bringing purpose into the realm of acts and commitments.

More people should realize that each of us needs a settled purpose in life—an aiming point. Then by doing our very best every day, we will reach this point on which we have set our compass. Those of us who do remarkable things in our lives have a clear vision stemming from a deep and pervasive sense of purpose.

I will align my purpose with my goals.

Love—the Great Equalizer

"There is more pleasure in loving than in being loved."
—JEANNE MOUTOUSSAMY-ASHE, PHOTOGRAPHER AND
WIDOW OF FORMER TENNIS GREAT

The real secret of success is love. We must love ourselves enough to know that we are worthy to succeed. You can gauge how well you are succeeding in this game called life by the number of loving relationships you have. Without this recognition of love, the idea of success rings hollow. True love comes to us every moment of each day disguised in many forms, from every possible angle. It is up to us to accept this love into our hearts. There is nothing more important than love. It is humanity's greatest experience.

Love is the one emotion that determines for each of us the space we will occupy in the hearts of our fellow men. It is the solid foundation upon which all of humanity is based. You are love. In other words, you are not only your brother's keeper, *you are your brother's brother.*

A man came up to two boys fighting in the park. He took one aside and began to spank him for his inappropriate behavior. An observing bystander came up to the man and asked indignantly why he didn't do anything to the other boy. The man responded that the child he was disciplining was his son, and he loved him dearly. He loved him enough to teach him lessons for the future.

Real love is selfless and free from fear. It pours itself out upon the object of its affection, without demanding any return, for love cannot be demanded, it must be given.

I will express my love for others.

Learn How to Say "I Can!"

"I know I'm going to make it in spite of my handicap. I will not be a prisoner of the chair. I know what I can do."
—TEDDY PENDERGRASS, SINGER AND SPOKESMAN FOR THE PHYSICALLY CHALLENGED

"I CAN!" wrote the historian Charles Wesley, who dared to tell the world that the black man had a history of note. "I CAN!" whispered Olympian Wyomia Tyus, who became the first person to capture gold medals in the one-hundred-meter race in two consecutive Olympic games. "I CAN!" thought Jewel Plummer Cobb, who was destined to make a name for herself in science and education. "I CAN!" shouted Jack Johnson, who dreamed of being the first black man to wear the belt of "world's heavyweight champion."

No one has ever received, gained, or accomplished anything in life without saying the two powerful words "I CAN!" The statement "I CAN" is not future promise, but an affirmation of what we choose to create now. This principle spells the difference between the person who is the master of his fate and one who sees himself as a victim of uncontrollable forces.

As I learn more about success and achievement, it often occurs to me that you and I are living far beneath our power as persons, and our possibilities as inhabitants of this great planet. Not enough of us say "I CAN." We can be at least ten times more powerful, at least ten times more bountiful and wonderful, at least ten times happier and freer and stronger than we are. We can be ten times more active, more alive, more spiritual, more faithful, more Godlike than we are. Studies have revealed that we use less than 10 percent of our mental capacity. And likewise, we use less than 10 percent of our creative capacity. The only way to gain this unlimited happiness and potential is to learn how to say "I CAN!"

I believe in the two simple words "I can!"

Go Ahead and Work It

"Let's get busy!"
—ARSENIO HALL, TALK-SHOW HOST

"The magic word" is a word that will perform wonders for anyone regardless of age or calling. For any man, woman, or child, the magic word brings new meaning and usefulness to life. This four-letter word carries with it clarity, self-respect, and satisfaction.

The magic word is *work*! To live life to its fullest translates into work. Years ago the people of a very successful civilization thought they had all the answers to success. The king called the wisest people in the kingdom together and said, "I want you to write down all the reasons why we are successful. Place them in writing so future generations will be able to read them and duplicate our successes." They worked frantically for nearly two years and came back with the answer. It consisted of twelve volumes.

The ruler glanced at it and said, "This is great, but it's too long." He then challenged them to simplify their findings. Worn down and beaten, six months later they came back with their findings confined to one sentence. If all future generations understood this one sentence, they would be in a position to conquer anything. The sentence simply read: "There's no such thing as a free lunch!"

Work gives our life meaning. Work raises our self-image. Work is victory. So get busy and work with all your might.

I will find my way in the world through my work.

Greener Pastures

*"We were poor but we did not learn that poverty
was a way of life. We learned that if you went to
church, worked hard, saved your money and got an
education, you could make it."*
—TONY BROWN, JOURNALIST AND TALK-SHOW HOST

Hope seems to spring eternal that opportunities are greater
elsewhere. Many of us spend time thinking about greener pastures when we haven't properly appraised our own. While we
are looking at what others are doing and wishing we were in
their pasture, other people are wishing they were in ours.
Studies have shown that there are more opportunities hidden in
our current line of work than most of us could exploit in a
lifetime. We need only search for them thoroughly enough and
long enough to find them. It's like the story of the African
farmer who sold his land and spent the rest of his life searching for diamonds the world over, only to have the richest diamond mine in the world discovered on the very farm he had
sold.

There is no such thing as a job that cannot, with time and
thought, lead to greatness. But unless we spend time, study,
and effort to become outstanding at what we are now doing,
why in the world should we think we could become great at
something else?

Learn everything possible about the endeavor you are attempting to master. Look long and carefully at the pasture you
now occupy. Chances are it's loaded with opportunities that
someone else is going to exploit; and if the grass is truly
greener on the other side of the fence, it's because someone
else took care of it. Today is big with blessings.

I will take advantage of the opportunities in my own field.

Knock on Wood

"Chances are ..."
—JOHNNY MATHIS, SINGER

By the close of the 1950s, most hotel beds in every room were placed against the same side of the wall. Thanks to an ancient superstition and custom, patrons are able to "get up on the right side of the bed." Many people believed then, and some still do, that the gods and forces of good lived within the right side of the body, while all the forces of evil dwelt within the left side. Superstition and luck get named or blamed for life's many surprises, good or bad. But is it luck that's really in charge?

Personal goals, rooted in our major purpose for living, affect our happiness much more than any run of luck. Life is led more by our expectations than luck. Though very real, luck is not what most people think. *Luck is no commodity*—you cannot run out of it like flour or bread. *Luck is not magic*—no lucky charm attracts it. Stars don't emanate it, so there are no "lucky" ones. *Luck is not transferable*—you can't catch it standing near achievers. *Luck is not chance*—were this a pure-chance world, the odds of you succeeding at anything would be fifty-fifty at best. Half the time you would succeed, the other half you'd fail.

Fortunately this doesn't happen. We get to our place of work more than half the times that we start out. We don't choke on our food half the times we eat. Mostly we succeed at whatever we do. Be thankful it's not a fifty-fifty world. *Luck is something you make happen for yourself.* That's your edge.

I will make my own luck.

Absolutely, Positively Has to Be There Overnight

"If you want wine—think wine!"
—BARBARA KING, PASTOR,
HILLSIDE INTERNATIONAL TRUTH CENTER

We attract to us what we think. If we think and see goodness and prosperity, they shall come to us. In the words of the Master, "As ye sow, so shall ye reap. Cast your bread upon the water and it shall return to you."

Two men were walking to a neighboring town when both fell into a raging river. One man panicked and feared the worst. He feverishly attempted to buck the torrents in a struggle to make his way back to shore. In his resistance the river overcame him and he drowned. The other man decided not to fight the flow. His mind was consumed with thoughts of safety. As a result he relaxed, lay back to the best of his ability, and allowed the river to carry him. Eventually the river deposited the second man onto a calm shore, where he found himself in the town toward which he had been walking.

Every thought is a prayer. Each thought is like an order that we place with God, who is prepared to give us all that we ask for in the form of our thoughts. The more we dwell on any thought, the more likely we are to see that thought manifested in our experience. We can make this principle work for us by focusing on the thoughts that we would like to see turn into events and experiences. We are constantly attracting to us people and conditions that mirror exactly our patterns of thought. Once the laws are clear to us, we can see that "random" or "accidental" events are actually the result of a very intelligently designed system of justified relationships.

So decide upon what you want. Send it up in thought. And before you know it, your desires will absolutely, positively be on their way back to you—the dreamer!

I will make my own destiny.

Push Your Ego Aside

"Never blow your own horn."
—MILES DAVIS, JAZZ GREAT

Suppose the story of Adam and Eve and the Garden of Eden is not allegorical at all, but the truth. Suppose that you and I are like Adam and Eve, our prototypes, brought into existence out of the earth. I find it ironic that our Creator chose to mold us, not from rare precious gems but from dirt. In fact, *dust*! In other words, no one is more important than anyone else.

Dust is cheap. Though people buy dirt, no one buys dust. Although there are many types and grades of dirt, make no mistake about it, there is only one type of dust. *Dust!* You can't catch it; you can't can it; you can't sell it; you can't organize it; and it won't stay in one place. Dust is ubiquitous and totally useless. All it does is wait for the next wind to blow, so it can latch on to someone else. Imagine, we all come from this same dirty stuff—*dust*.

I find it funny that so many people take pride in their dust. They put fancy letters after their dust thinking this will change what they are. For example, their business cards proclaim that they are Dust, "Ph.D.," or Dust, "MBA," or "Dr." Dust, or "President" Dust, or "Reverend" Dust. But the bottom line is they are still just dust.

One day, as fate will have it, we will all see our Maker. And guess where we're going? Back to *DUST*! You will be a better person when you push your ego aside.

I will push my ego aside and see myself as I really am.

What Do You Need?

"I'm not into the money thing. You can only sleep in one bed at a time. You can only eat one meal at a time, or be in one car at a time. So I don't have to have millions of dollars to be happy. All I need are clothes on my back, a decent meal, and a little loving when I feel like it. That's the bottom line."
—RAY CHARLES, SINGER

How do you get others to pull with you instead of against you? How do you get them into your corner, cheering you on, urging you on to victory? Like all great truths the answer is surprisingly simple: *To the degree you give others what they want, they will give you what you want.* It seems incredibly simple. Perhaps it is, if you really understand it. But few do.

For example, the employer must give praise and recognition *first*, then the employee will put forth the extra effort. The parent and teacher must express confidence in the child *first*, then the child will produce better grades. That's the way the law works. You first give others what they want; then they will give you what you want. *But wants and needs are totally separate.* Wants are sometimes frivolous and unnecessary. Needs, however, are the deeper currents of one's existence. They're much more meaningful. For example:

· People want sympathy, but they need empathy.
· People want riches, but they need fulfillment.
· People want power, but they need support and cooperation.
· People want prestige, but they need respect.
· People want adoration; but they need love.

What do others need? Look within yourself for a clue.

What I need, others need. And what others need, I will give.

I'm a Bud Man

"From the day you're born until the day you ride in a hearse, there's nothing so bad that it couldn't be worse."
—SMOKEY ROBINSON, SINGER AND SONGWRITER

At every moment you can make either of two cases for the condition of your life. You can point to evidence that it's a thicket of thorns or a bed of roses.

When you buy roses, have you noticed that the stem is always covered with thorns? When the thorns are removed, the flower wilts more quickly. That's why the thorns are usually left on. When you are presented with a rose, do you say, "Why are you giving me this stem with thorns on it?" No, you focus on the positive—you admire the beauty of the rose. The same choice exists at every moment in life.

Think of the young boy who brought home his report card heavy with poor grades. His mother asked, "What have you to say about this?" The boy replied, "One thing is for sure, you know I'm not cheating!"

Focus on the positive. Look at your surroundings and notice all there is to appreciate. Start by developing a gratitude attitude. Give thanks for the things you have and don't worry about the things that you don't have. Notice the things you take for granted—a place to rest, comfort, and shelter. These necessities that we take for granted are important to our well-being.

Notice how much better you feel when you focus on the positive. At any given time there are two attorneys in your mind, one gathering evidence for "life is awful" and the other defending "life is great." The jury is in. Court is adjourned. *Life is worth living!*

I will focus on the positive aspects of my life.

Jumping to Conclusions

"Worry is interest paid on trouble before it is due."
—MIRIAM MAKEBA, FOLKSINGER

I recently heard about a man who worried about getting to work on time. Each day he followed the same routine. His alarm went off at 6:30 A. M. He rose briskly, shaved, showered, gulped down his breakfast, brushed his teeth, grabbed his briefcase, got into his car, drove to the nearby ferry, parked his car, rode the ferry across to the downtown business district, ran to his office, marched to the elevator, rode to the seventeenth floor, and arrived at his desk no later than 8:00. He followed this same routine for nearly ten years.

One morning his alarm failed to go off and he slept fifteen minutes late. When he awoke, he was panic-stricken. He rushed through his shower, nicked himself when he shaved, skipped his breakfast, snatched his briefcase, leaped into his car, sped to the ferry landing, jumped out of his car, and looked for the ferry. He saw it out in the water a few feet from the dock. He ran down the dock at full speed until he reached the edge of the pier, then lunged out over the water, and landed miraculously on the deck of the ferry with a loud thud. The captain rushed down to make sure he was all right and said, "Man, that was a tremendous leap. But if you would have just waited another minute, we would have reached the dock and you could have walked on."

Most time spent worrying is wasted. If you spend time worrying, you will accomplish little. A time management expert asserts that the majority of fears are unnecessary. Of the 8 percent of the worries that are real and legitimate, 90 percent revolve around things we cannot influence. So why worry? Learn to spend your time in more productive ways.

I can't change the past, and I won't worry about the future.

You Must Be Dreaming

"In one hand I have an idea, in the other, I have an obstacle. Which one grabs your attention?"
—HENRY PARKS, ENTREPRENEUR

There is no dream in life that is beyond your ability to accomplish. The Creator would not plant a seed in your mind if He did not plan to give you the means to nurture and cultivate it into a beautiful flower. Once we know that God is working with us and not against us, we can cherish our dreams as divinely inspired visions of our new life. Then all we need to do is hold firmly to our dream, especially during the moments of doubt and challenge. The key to transforming your life is to keep your mind and heart on your dream. As Amway supersalesman George Halsey once remarked, "Obstacles are what you see when you take your eyes off your goal."

Your dream is a sprouting creation that needs desire and support to develop to full maturity. Then it returns the care by nourishing the dreamer as well as those who promote it. Every great achievement begins as a dream. A vision of success is a seminal idea that must be cultivated and strengthened by the individual who believes in his or her dream to stand by it in moments of difficulty.

Are you willing to stand by your dream in times of opposition? Are you willing to say yes to yourself and your idea when others stand against you? If you have answered yes to these questions, then you are certain to succeed. For your dream is none other than God's dream for you.

Today I will say yes to my dreams, changing my life in the process.

The Millionaires' Club

"It is far better to be free to govern, or misgovern yourself, than to be governed by anybody else."
—KWAME NKRUMAH, FORMER PRESIDENT OF GHANA

In this fast-paced, chaotic world it is easy for the average person to feel insignificant. After all, there are more than five billion people on earth all wondering what the future holds for them and the rest of mankind. Yet it is individual thought that collectively shapes and determines the course of human history. Men and women neither more nor less skilled than you and I have made large contributions to help the world become a better place to live.

There are no open doors to the temple of success. Everyone who enters must forge his or her own way. "But how?" you ask. By assuming personal responsibility. It is our responsibility to carve out a meaningful life. You have the power to subdue the earth. You have dominion. This is the crux of our personal responsibility.

The greater your lot, the greater your responsibility. The man in the biblical story who was given five talents was fully responsible for those five talents. If you acknowledge the talents given to you by the Creator—your mind, your health, your freedom of choice, to mention a few—then you must also know that you are eventually answerable for these talents.

What would you do if you had a million dollars? Well, you do have one million dollars' worth of potential, talents, and capabilities. Be sure to take the responsibility to develop these gifts.

Today I will take the responsibility to develop my talents.

Strong as an Ox

*"What you ought to do, you should do; and what
you should do, you ought to do!"*
—OPRAH WINFREY, TALK-SHOW HOST

Centuries ago in Africa a great drought plagued the land. The wheat fields were completely dry. Without adequate water there would be famine.

A young farmer sat on a riverbank. He had just returned from the village shrine, where he had prayed for rain for hours. As he sat on a ledge overlooking the winding river, the stories told to him by his grandfather began to overtake him. In his grandfather's day hundreds of thousands of people perished because of famine. Faced with similar prospects for his generation, he thought of ways to avert a catastrophe. What could he do?

With the flash of inspiration he had a vision. He would develop a treadmill that was propelled by an ox. When the animal walked, it moved in a circle, scooping buckets of water from the river and dumping them in a trough in the wheat fields. Since that time, there hasn't been a famine because of a lack of rain. Day after day, in a most mundane task, an ox would turn the treadmill that would supply water to drought-stricken crops.

If we're not careful at various points in our lives we can resemble an animal on a treadmill—not one that raises water from a river but one that is weary and frustrated. How can we get off? By utilizing the same keys used by the African farmer: motivation, a burning desire, and the ability to think. Otherwise you might need to be as strong as an ox.

Today I will examine those areas that keep me stuck in place.

Pick the Tough Ones

*"Go after the tough ones. You've got to be willing
to stick your nose in places people may not want
you to be. You have to have great curiosity."*
—ED BRADLEY, *60 MINUTES* COHOST

Do some serious daydreaming and set your sights high. A professor of psychology gave a test to his class with three categories of questions. He instructed the students to answer questions from any section on the test. The first category was the hardest and consequently was worth fifty points. The second, which was not as difficult, was worth forty points. The third, the easiest, was worth ten points.

When the papers were returned, the students who had chosen the hardest questions, the fifty-pointers, were given A's, even if they'd gotten the answers wrong. The students who had chosen the forty-pointers received B's. Those who had attempted to answer the ten-point questions—the easiest ones—were given C's. The students didn't understand the test results, so they asked the professor how he had graded the exam. The professor leaned back, smiled, and explained, "I wasn't testing your knowledge, I was testing your aim."

When manufacturers first produced golf balls, they made the covers smooth. Then they discovered that a ball would travel farther if it was made rough. Soon sporting-goods companies began producing golf balls with dimpled covers. So it is with life. It takes some rough spots in your life to make you go your farthest. It takes the same amount of effort to fail as it does to succeed. So avoid the path of least resistance and pick the tough ones.

I will choose the hard road in order to better myself.

Fatal Attraction

"The only way to catch a cold is to chase one."
—HELEN CARRY, MINISTER, CHRIST UNIVERSAL TEMPLE

Are you guilty of asking for something that you really don't want? Some people are. Have you ever seen someone come to work with a sniffle? You comment on the sniffle only to have the person respond, "Well, it just started this morning, but my colds don't get too bad until the third day, and then I can barely get out of bed." That person is asking for what he really doesn't want.

Think of the person who goes to work with a slight headache. Somebody comments on it, and the person responds, "Well, it's slight right now, but it always is in the morning. It's not until about three o'clock in the afternoon that it begins to kill me!" This person is asking for what he doesn't want.

Have you ever looked at your watch late at night as you lay down and said to yourself, "Boy, I bet I'm gonna be tired and feel lousy in the morning"? If you have, then you've been guilty of asking for what you didn't want. It's a shame that we use our imagination in such a negative way when we could use it in a more constructive, positive manner. I am reminded of King Solomon's request to his counselor to tell him "something that will make me happy when I am sad and make me somber when I feel too happy." A few days later his aide gave the king a ring with these words inscribed on it: "This, too, shall pass."

Why not try another approach? Talk to yourself in a positive fashion, and you'll discover that it's nice to ask for—and even nicer to get—the things you want.

I will speak only of those things that I truly desire.

You Can Get There from Here

"The main reason I wanted to be successful was to get out of the ghetto. My parents helped direct my path."
—FLORENCE GRIFFITH-JOYNER, OLYMPIC CHAMPION

Where will you be when you get where you're going? In other words, where will your dreams take you? What are your ambitions and goals? Perhaps you're like the hopelessly lost salesman who stopped at a general store in an old country town and asked for directions home. The store owner winked at his friends and very convincingly replied, "You can't get there from here." Is that the way you feel about your goals and dreams? Do you say to yourself, "I can't get there from here?" If you do, you're probably right. Here are three keys that will help you reach your dreams.

First, don't be afraid to dream. Decide what you want. Research has shown that dreaming while you're asleep is critical to your emotional stability. Dreaming while you're awake is just as important if you expect to reach your potential. Second, identify the obstacle that stands between you and your goals and develop a plan to overcome it. Third, don't be afraid to fail. Everyone encounters failure. It's how you deal with setbacks and disappointments that separates productive, fulfilled individuals from the also-rans.

"Success," says supersalesman and hair-care tycoon Comer Cottrell, "is the ability to hitch your wagon to a star *while keeping your feet on the ground.*" Happy is the person who dreams big dreams and is willing to take the steps to make them come true. Don't be afraid to start climbing.

From where I stand, I can go anywhere in life.

The Good Ol' Days Are Here and Now

"My kid's idea of a hard life is to live in a house with only one phone."
—GEORGE FOREMAN, FORMER HEAVYWEIGHT CHAMP

These are the best of times. As a matter of fact today is the best of days. Today is the best time to be alive. Not yesterday. Not tomorrow. But right now. This is *the* good ol' day. Every generation has experienced its share of problems. Unfortunately some people emphasize the negative and forget the positive. For example, one hundred years ago life expectancy was less than forty years; but today we are expected to live past seventy. Just a few years ago polio was the scourge of every school-age child. Now, at the close of the twentieth century, there are less than one hundred cases of polio reported throughout the country.

A century ago men wore six-shooters, sanitation was primitive, childbirth was hazardous, and women were not allowed to hold public office. Today there are more minorities and women in college than ever before. More children of color are becoming doctors, lawyers, teachers, and other professionals. As a matter of fact 1991 witnessed more black students receiving doctorate degrees than any previous year and more women holding public office.

On par, we are living longer, eating better, and enjoying life more than our predecessors ever dreamed. Although the jury is still out, the 1990s may be tabbed as the greatest decade of the century. You and I are living in a great era. These are the good ol' days. Make the most of them, since they're the only ones that really matter.

Today I will rejoice in today.

A Change Is Coming

"There's a freshness and uniqueness about dance because it constantly changes. Variety is the spice of life."
—JUDITH JAMISON, DIRECTOR, ALVIN AILEY DANCE THEATER

Two caterpillars were crawling across the grass when a butterfly flew over them. As they looked up, one nudged the other and said, "You couldn't get me up in one of those things for a million dollars."

You've heard it said that we should never change a proven success formula. Generally speaking, the majority would agree with that statement. If it ain't broke, don't fix it. But sometimes there is a time and a place for change.

Imagine what it would be like if the owner of an aquarium never changed the water in the tank. It wouldn't be long before the fish died. Changing the water and keeping it circulating allow the fish to thrive in their habitat. It is much the same with us. Without change we would stagnate. Although many of us resist it fiercely, change forces us to grow and evolve, to become more flexible, resilient, and confident. Our task is to transcend any fear of the unknown and encourage ourselves to change what needs to be different in order for our lives to flow freely and creatively.

An African proverb tells a story of a teacher who gave her student a silk scarf snarled in many knots. The student's assignment was to untie the knots, a chore he struggled with until he realized that, in order to succeed, he had to untie the last knot first. To change our lives for the better, we must untangle our most immediate challenge—or our last knot of difficulty—so our scarf will be permitted to flutter gently in the breeze.

From this day forward I will welcome change. I will embrace a break from the routine.

Rush Hour

"Don't worry, be happy."
—BOBBY MCFERRIN, SINGER

A story is told about a group of U.S. citizens who were making their way through a remote island. They had employed a group of locals at the seaport and had informed them that they were pressed for time. The first day they moved quickly through the countryside. The second day they continued their relentless pace. The third morning, when they were frantically preparing for another day of rapid travel, they found the natives squatting under the trees refusing to move. When the bewildered and helpless travelers asked them why they were not ready to start, they simply said, "We shall rest today to let our souls catch up with our bodies."

Our failure to take time to live actually prevents us from deriving the best from life. For workaholics there's no end. Life consists of the endless routine of sitting at the desk, or being on duty at the station, or getting up every morning at five-thirty to catch a six-thirty express train to the city. For the workaholic days turn into months that turn into years of the same old thing—the long commute, the conference calls, the mail we must answer.

We should remember that we do not live to work. We work to live. Mankind assuredly was never meant to beat out his life in hurry and tumult. My grandmother was right. I can still hear her voice: "Take your time, baby." Good, hard work is one of humanity's greatest gifts. But perhaps we can enjoy greater peace of mind if we strive less, or at least reduce the tension of our effort. What good is it to succeed if we cannot enjoy life in the process?

Today I will take a "mental health break" to rest, replenish, and revive my soul.

The Light Is On and Somebody's Home

"I believe in miracles. I'm living proof anybody can come back from the dead."
—JOHN LUCAS, NBA COACH AND A RECOVERING ADDICT

"I don't want to treat this man," the doctor thought. Though he would not say it aloud, his heart wasn't in it. Besides being broke, the man was dirty and unkempt. The doctor wondered when his patient had bathed last. Nonetheless he was compassionate and treated his patient's cuts and bruises. The old fellow thanked him and left the office.

Nearly a month later the same man returned. This time he looked much better. He was neatly attired and clean from head to toe. The fellow approached the physician, extended his hand, and said, "I want to thank you for saving my life."

"What do you mean?" the doctor responded.

"When I walked through your door last month," the man explained, "I was near the end. Everything had fallen apart. After wandering the streets I decided that I could not go on any longer. I made my way to the nearest bridge, where I intended to jump and end my life. As I approached the top of the bridge, I saw your office lights and decided to give life one more chance. You were kind and helpful even though I had no money and I was such a mess. Doctor, you made the difference in my living or dying. Since you treated me, things have started to go my way, and now I feel that I truly want to live. And I will, thanks to you."

Just like this doctor, each of us has the power to light many lives. And likewise others have brightened and blessed our lives in so many ways. None of us knows the strength and the power of our lights. These lights shine brightest when they brighten the paths of others.

I will be a point of light and light the paths of others.

You Get Out What You Put In

*"My mother told me I was capable of doing
anything. 'Be ambitious,' she said.
'Jump at de sun.' "*
—ZORA NEALE HURSTON, WRITER

We yearn to be needed, wanted, and loved. We want to be important. We need appreciation, satisfaction, recognition, acceptance, and fulfillment. Remember, to the degree you give others what they need, they will give you what you need.

This calls to mind the man in a desolate mountain region who was a laborer six days a week and a preacher on the seventh. He served a small rural congregation tucked far into the hills. The only monetary compensation he received came from the morning offering. One Sunday his six-year-old daughter attended the service with him. Just inside the door of his house of worship sat a table, and on it rested a collection basket. As they entered, the little girl saw her father place a half-dollar in the wicker basket before any of the congregation arrived.

When the service ended and the last member departed, the preacher and his daughter began to leave. As they reached the door, both peered expectantly into the collection plate and found that the only offering was the half-dollar he had donated. After a short silence the innocent little girl said, "You know, Daddy, if you had put more in, you'd have gotten more out." You now have the key to success that will unlock many doors that would otherwise be closed. Follow the advice of this young child: *You can only succeed and achieve to the extend that you give and share of yourself.*

If you feed others, you will never go hungry.

You'd Better Eat Your Wheaties

"There are no shades trees on the road to success."
—LEONTINE KELLY, FIRST AFRICAN-AMERICAN FEMALE
BISHOP, METHODIST EPISCOPAL CHURCH

In all of life's endeavors your own efforts will help you the most. Loose wires give out no musical notes, but when their ends are fastened, the piano, the harp, or the violin is born. Free steam drives no machine, but harnessed and combined with the piston and turbine, it makes useful machinery. An unhampered river drives no dynamos, but dam it up and you can generate sufficient power to light a city. So our lives must be disciplined if we are to be of any real service in the world. There are many well-intentioned people who will tell you not to worry about the future—all you have to do is place your faith in God. So you should, but with the complete understanding that the Creator helps those who help themselves.

Determination and discipline are the opposite of "chance." When we practice determination and discipline, we take our destiny into our own hands. The determined person refuses to surrender to the random winds of circumstance. If we rest our fate in the hands of fortune, we shall sometimes succeed and sometimes fail, but we will always be weak. In taking charge of our fate, we will succeed most of the time and fail some of the time, but we will always be strong. We will have no regrets about our life, for we know that we gave it all we had to give.

Be determined, be disciplined, be strong. Seize opportunities. Remember that you will never be faced with a challenge you cannot overcome.

Today I will gather the strength to become more determined and disciplined in order to reach my goals.

Your Most Faithful and Humble Servant

"We realize that our future lies chiefly in our own hands. We know that neither institution nor friends can make a race stand unless it has strength in its own foundation. In order to succeed it must practice the virtues of self-reliance, self-respect, industry, perseverance, and economy."

—PAUL ROBESON, WRITER, SINGER, ACTOR, AND SCHOLAR.

We increase in value whatever we praise. The entire universe responds to praise. Animal trainers pet and reward their charges with treats for acts of obedience. Children glow with joy and gladness when they are praised by parents and loved ones. Even the plant world grows fuller and healthier for those who praise and nurture it. We can praise our own ability and in turn expand and increase our potential as we speak words of encouragement. Whatever we increase in potential increases in value. The unfailing law of increase is, Whatever is praised and blessed multiplies.

The Creator gave you dominion over the earth. Count your blessings and they, too, will increase. Everything is your servant. If you are working for someone else and you desire a better job or more pay, start by blessing and being thankful for the job you have. Bless your current line of work; be thankful for every opportunity it gives you to acquire greater skill and the ability to serve others. Bless the money you earn, no matter how little it may be. Be thankful for the opportunity to serve faithfully, no matter how small the immediate reward. Give your best, give it cheerfully, gladly, thankfully, and you will be amazed how quickly your increase will come.

I will praise life and stand poised to enjoy my good.

I've Learned My Lesson

"Life is a short walk. There's so little time to give and so much to achieve."
—JOHN OLIVER KILLENS, WRITER AND PLAYWRIGHT

Each year thousands of people are nominated for membership into the Horatio Alger Association. Wealth cannot purchase a place among the honored ones, nor can power or influence. The one key to receiving the prestigious award is poverty. All recipients must show that at some point in their lives they were poor and that, on their own merit, they became successful, despite all setbacks. In 1990 Robert J. Brown was inducted into the society. As the great-grandson of slaves, Brown had no difficulty proving his poverty-stricken past. And today, as a businessman and noted philanthropist, his success is apparent to everyone.

Bob and his brother were raised in North Carolina by their grandparents. He remembers that their leaky old house seemed to be in constant need of repair and they never had enough to eat. "We didn't have a lot of material things," he recalls, "but we did have a great deal of love and affection." No matter how tough their circumstances, his grandmother was always willing to share with others in need. Her generosity taught him one of life's most important lessons.

One summer day when Bob was a young child, a tattered elderly man trudged up the steps of their house. He walked up to Bob's grandmother and said, "Miss Nellie, I'm hungry. I haven't eaten in days. Can you spare a bite?" She invited him in to share what little they had. After he left, Bob asked his grandmother, "Grandma, why do you continuously feed all these people when we don't have a thing?"

She said, "Son, if I never teach you anything else, I want to leave you with this: Life is all about serving and giving. There's nothing else in life greater than that." Life will pay handsomely if you learn this lesson well.

I will assure my greatness by becoming the greatest server.

Smarty Pants

"A person isn't educated unless he has learned how little he already knows."
—THOMAS A. FLEMING,
NATIONAL TEACHER OF THE YEAR, 1992

The president of one of the largest rubber companies in the country was recently making a speech. After he finished, the chairman opened the meeting for questions. A young man in the front row said, "Would it be too personal if I asked you how you got to be the president of this corporation?"

"Not at all," was the president's reply. "I was working in a filling station and not making much progress. One day I read that if a person wanted to get ahead, he must know all there is to know about his particular product.

"So, during one of my vacations, I went back to the home office and watched them make rubber tires. I watched them put in the nylon cords, took notes, and asked a million questions about the process. And I didn't stop there. During another vacation I traveled to Africa to watch workers plant rubber trees and extract the crude rubber used in our tire facilities.

"Now when I talk about my product, I don't say, 'This is what I'm told,' or 'This is what I read,' or 'This is what I think.' No, I say, *'This is what I know.'*"

He then continued. "There is no force in the world that has a greater impact than the statement of a knowledgeable person fortified by confidence and experience. An individual who knows, and *knows that he knows*, can speak with authority that has no comparison. The world makes way for the man or woman who knows what he or she is doing."

Today I will begin a disciplined program of reading, study, and meditation.

Word Perfect

"Words embolden. Words help us with future conquests. Words enlarge our spirit."
—CARL ROWAN, SYNDICATED COLUMNIST

Words unify and words break. Words heal and words destroy. Words bless us and words curse us. For example, the words I just heard will linger throughout the day. Words shape our lives. Those who have earned the world's respect and admiration for their outstanding accomplishments are always quick to point out how words of encouragement and inspiration helped them throughout their career.

We do not live in a vacuum, nor can we harvest the better fruits of life without help and encouragement from others. As members of society, our growth depends to a large degree on how well we handle our relationships with those who cross our paths every day. Without friendship and assistance the successes we enjoy will be few. Friendships are best cultivated through kind words.

Why is it, then, that so many of us go out of our way to offend others with criticism that so often comes back to haunt us? Why do we allow our big mouths to dig ruts in our path so deep that our march forward comes to a halt? If you lose your temper, you'd be better off not to try to find it again. If your tongue has been busy accumulating enemies for you—enemies who can impede your progress—now is a good time to watch what you say as well as how you say it. "Blunt and harsh words," says former Oakland *Tribune* publisher Robert Maynard, "often have the sharpest edge." Form the habit of offering encouragement and inspiration and you will lift up your life in the process.

I am always compensated for the words I speak.

I Have a Dream

*"There's nothing mysterious about success. It's the
ability to stay mentally locked in."*
—MONTEL WILLIAMS, TALK-SHOW HOST

Success is creating a state of mind that allows you to obtain the desires of your heart. Success resembles human survival. Both depend on future vision, seeing ourselves in specific situations as healthy, thriving, and full of positive expectations.

As a college student in Houston, Texas, Dr. Barbara King, pastor of Hillside Truth Center in Atlanta, Georgia, overcame a life-threatening bout with tuberculosis. When she was cleared to resume her studies, after spending four years in a sanitarium, Dr. King discovered that her classmates had either graduated or dropped out while she was convalescing. Now faced with doctor bills as well as tuition, she worked hard as a maid on campus to get through school. After finally completing her coursework, she was asked how she managed to endure. What powers did she possess that others lacked? How did she manage to stay focused? She gave a clue in a speech before a group of college hopefuls.

"I never thought of quitting," she said. "*I kept my eye on the prize.* I had faith. There's enough faith in the world to accomplish anything, but you must claim this faith for yourself. *Claim it!* Don't let anybody tell you that you can't be what you want to be. *Claim it and be it!* Believe in yourself. Believe that you have something to give to the universe."

Focusing your energies in a single direction can work wonders. If you want something badly enough, long enough, and consistently enough, don't be surprised if you get it.

I will focus my mind on my goals.

Why Don't We Ever Talk?

"The divorce rate would be lower if, instead of marrying for better or worse, people would marry for good."
—RUBY DEE, ACTRESS

Experts claim that one of the most serious problems facing a marriage, and one of the prime causes for its failure, is the inability or reluctance on the part of husbands and wives to communicate. For example, a sign on the wall of a marriage counselor reads, WHEN A WOMAN MARRIES, SHE GIVES UP THE ATTENTION OF SEVERAL MEN FOR THE INATTENTION OF ONE. Or as comedian Eddie Murphy says in one of his routines, "What frightens most men about marriage is not another mouth to feed—but another one to listen to." It seems the longer two people live together, the more they tend to drift apart and take each other for granted.

Over the years married life has the tendency to resemble the experience of driving a new car—at first it's exciting, but with time, well, it's just a car. People are not machines, and this kind of attitude toward a wife or a husband spells doom for the marriage. A couple with such an attitude might put on the appearance of a happy marriage, but it is only a facade. If there is anyone on earth you can talk to, it should be the person with whom you have agreed to spend your remaining days.

Try this recipe guaranteed to cook up a happy marriage:

1 cup: *speaking*	1 cup: *conversing*
2 cups: *concentration*	3 cups: *listening*
5 spoons: *understanding*	2 spoons: *sharing*
2 quarts: *communication*	4 quarts: *caring*

Take speaking and concentration and mix thoroughly with caring. Blend it with communication, sharing, and understanding. Add listening. Sprinkle abundantly with laughter. Bake in sunshine. Serve generous helpings daily.

I will not take my mate for granted.

A Real Basket Case

"Opportunity does not send letters of introduction."
—NAOMI SIMS, MODEL AND ENTREPRENEUR

Your future is bound in your present. Today's thoughts and actions will define your tomorrows. If you hold hopes of a better future, then you must change your thoughts today.

Today is yesterday's tomorrow. How do you like today's experiences? Are they as good as you thought they would be yesterday? Actually there is no such thing as tomorrow because today is always here. If you waste today, you'll waste tomorrow.

As a rite of initiation, a tribal youth was given a basket and told to pick the finest ears of corn in a given row. The only requirement was that she was to choose as she went along—she could not retrace her steps. She admired the fine quality of corn before her. However, as she felt one ear after another, she left them on the stalks, always thinking that better ears lay ahead. Suddenly, to her dismay, she came to the end of the row and had gathered none of them. Without realizing, her opportunities went fleeing before her.

When you put off your good until a "more opportune time" or until tomorrow—just like this young girl—you are placing your treasures beyond your reach. Do not act as if you had a thousand years to live. Move now toward that which you desire most. I admit, it's proper to plan ahead, but remember, all successful planning must be founded upon an appreciation of present opportunities.

I will take advantage of my opportunities now!

Rise and Shine

"It's no disgrace to start over or to begin anew."
—BEBE MOORE CAMPBELL, JOURNALIST AND WRITER

Dinner was over. The host of the party and his guests assembled in the library. They chatted idly before the conversation turned serious. They talked of personal setbacks and obstacles to success, and of the great need for courage and faith in overcoming such experiences.

"I have a philosophy that has evolved over the years," the host admitted. "It has helped me through every disappointment. My grandmother shared this advice with me before she died." At his guests' urging he offered his grandmother's words, sharing his secret of calm and serenity, of rising above every distressing circumstance, of going on with courage and hope.

"What looks like the end of the road," he said, "is only a turn in the road, the beginning of a new and more profitable experience. *You are never beaten unless you give up.* I have lived by this philosophy, and it has kept me happy." The dinner host was Ralph Bunche, statesman, diplomat, and secretary-general of the United Nations. Among Dr. Bunche's guests that evening was a newspaper editor who felt that Dr. Bunche's words would help others, so he suggested he write an article about his philosophy.

Ralph Bunche complied with the editor's wishes. His article appeared and created something of a sensation. Countless men and women, impressed by Bunche's valiant way of life, adopted his outlook and attempted to live by his principles.

My greatest glory is not in never falling but in rising every time.

Lead, Follow, or Get Out of the Way

"A good leader takes a little more than his share of the blame, a little less than his share of the credit."
—SAMUEL L. GRAVELY, FIRST AFRICAN-AMERICAN ADMIRAL
IN THE U.S. NAVY

Best-selling author Myles Munroe writes, "The world is filled with followers, supervisors, and managers but very few leaders." Leaders are ordinary people who accept or are placed under extraordinary circumstances that bring forth their latent potential, producing qualities that inspire the confidence and trust of others. The following tale is a good example of effective leadership.

One day a proud lion was determined to make all the animals in the jungle realize that he was king. He was so confident that he bypassed the smaller animals and headed straight to the bear. "Who is the king of the jungle?" the lion growled. "Why, you are," the bear replied.

Next he approached the tiger. "Who is the king of the jungle?" The tiger confessed, "Everyone knows that you are."

Then the lion addressed the elephant. "Who's the king of the jungle?" The elephant immediately grabbed the lion, shook him, whirled him around, and slammed him into a tree. The lion—beaten, bruised, and battered—struggled to his feet. He looked at the elephant through blackened eyes and said, "Look, just because you don't know the answer is no reason to be sore about it!" The lion was anything but a leader.

"A boss may create fear," explains Jewell Jackson McCabe, founder of 100 Black Women, *"but a leader creates confidence."*

Leaders have confidence in themselves and create confidence in others. Like leaders before you, you, too, can develop these qualities.

Today I will develop the confidence and enthusiasm that breed leadership.

The Largest Room

"One way to make the world better is by improving yourself."
—WILLIE WILLIAMS, LOS ANGELES POLICE CHIEF

What's the largest room in the world? Regardless of what others say, it's the "room for improvement." There's always room for you and me to improve the quality of our lives. I like the tale of the wise professor who was so learned that he could teach whatever he chose—biology, history, or astronomy. One day he decided to motivate a young student by planning a canoe trip in the wilderness. He hoped to show him how meaningful education can be.

Early one morning they boarded a canoe. As they drifted downriver, a leaf fell into the stream, prompting the professor to ask, "Now, tell me, young man, do you understand the leaf?" The boy answered no. The wise old man said, "If you do not learn biology, you will miss out on one of life's potential joys."

As the canoe rounded a bend, rocks that hovered above the water's edge revealed markings of Indians from days past. The professor said, "See those markings? Do you know which Indian tribe made them?" The boy said, "I don't know." "If you don't learn history," said the professor with increased impatience, "you'll miss out on much of life's enjoyment."

Shortly after, darkness fell, and stars began to appear. Looking up, the old man asked, "What star is that?" Once again the boy shrugged his shoulders and said, "I don't know." "My son," the professor said, "if you don't understand biology or history or astronomy, you'll miss out on life."

Suddenly they heard a loud roar and realized the canoe had hit a rock and was about to capsize. As they prepared for the worst, the student asked, "Professor, do you know how to swim?" The old man shook his head. As the boy dove into the river and swam to safety, he yelled back, *"Then you're missing out on life!"* Life will pay off on our terms if we constantly engage in self-improvement.

I will concentrate on learning what I need to learn.

Busy Bodies

"When your dreams turn to dust, vacuum."
—DESMOND TUTU, SOUTH AFRICAN ACTIVIST AND ANGLICAN
ARCHBISHOP

We've all heard the saying, "Use it or lose it." The familiar proverb embodies one of the most important principles of human nature: To become proficient in any field, you must practice. However, we tend to think of this maxim in terms of our bodies. For example, if I place your right arm in a cast for three months, it will atrophy to almost nothing by the time the cast is removed. Only months of regular exercise will restore it to normalcy. As we grow older and our lives become more sedentary, we cease to put regular strain on our muscles. As a result, our bodies become soft and fragile.

We lose our physical conditioning through failure to use our muscles, and as a consequence we are easy prey for sickness and disease. Regular and systematic use of our bodies prevents such deterioration. "If some people didn't lift their eyebrows," jokes Lee Haney, Mr. Olympia, "they would never get any exercise." Becoming a "busy body" has its advantages.

So, too, with the more intangible parts of our natures. We must use our courage, or it deserts us; we must use our determination, or it leaves us; we must exercise our power of decision, or we soon find that we have none. To achieve a standard of excellence, to accomplish anything extraordinary, we must be disciplined and willing to devote long hours to the task at hand. It means using both our physical and our mental muscles in order to reach our objective. Each of us best fulfills our destiny when we operate full blast, when we are fully extended.

I will exercise both my physical and my mental muscles.

Nothing to Write Home About

"The freedom of slaves is measured by the length of their chains."
—JOSEPHINE BAKER, ACTRESS, DANCER,
AND ENTERTAINER

Life is, for the most part, the way we see it. So whenever we encounter challenges or injustices, we may want to adjust our focus or perspective. Your perception of reality will change the ever-changing shape of your reality. *In other words, change your seeing to change your scene.* The following letter was sent by a college student to her parents with the hope that they would receive bad news in the "right perspective:"

"Dear Mom and Dad, I'm sorry it has taken me so long to write, but my stationery was destroyed the day the demonstrators burned down the dormitory. I'm out of the hospital now, and the doctors said my eyesight should be back to normal—sooner or later. That wonderful boy, Bill, who saved me from the fire, kindly offered to share his cozy, little apartment with me until the dorm is rebuilt. He comes from a good family, so you shouldn't be too surprised to learn we're going to get married. In fact, Mom and Dad, you always wanted to have grandchildren, so you should be real happy to learn you're going to be grandparents—*next month*!

"Mom and Dad, please disregard the above practice in English composition. There was no fire, I haven't been in the hospital, I'm not pregnant, and I don't even have a boyfriend. But I did get a D in chemistry and a F in French, and I wanted to make sure you received this news in the proper perspective. Love, Mary."

If your picture of life is out of focus or off center, start by adjusting your perspective.

Today I will view circumstances in the right perspective.

Happy Hour?

"Before I ride with a drunk, I'll drive myself."
—STEVIE WONDER, SINGER AND ENTERTAINER

Two brothers sat at a cluttered kitchen table. The house reeked of stale alcohol. Flies hovered over piles of dirty dishes. Dad was drunk on the couch. One child was perched in front of the television while the other was immersed in his schoolwork. One father—two boys. One situation—an alcoholic father, an absent mother. Both boys lived out the same hell on earth with daily verbal and physical abuse and neglect.

One brother ran with a fast crowd who helped him find an escape. Like his father, he found it in drugs and alcohol. This second-generation alcoholic lived from bottle to bottle, barely finding odd jobs, earning just enough money to continue his habit. The second brother buried himself in his schoolwork. A teacher praised his efforts, and consequently he excelled. He worked hard and won a scholarship to an Ivy League school. He went on to become a well-respected lawyer. One day a newspaper chose to write a profile on their local hero. The reporter asked the young man, "Is it true your father was an alcoholic?"

"It's true. I had an alcoholic father—that's why I am where I am today. I decided early on I wasn't going to waste my life the way he did."

Meanwhile the first brother continued on his path of destruction. Eventually his employer gave him the choice of losing his job or entering a rehabilitation clinic. He chose the latter. The counselor in the rehab program listened as he described his childhood: "I had an alcoholic father—that's why I'm where I am today." Same home. Same father. But different outcomes. Thank goodness we can control the outcomes of our lives.

Only I am in control of my life. I will take full responsibility for my circumstances.

Great Expectations

"We have the ability to shape, change, accept or reject anything we want. Open our minds to positive thought and faith, and prosperity can become a reality for each of us."
—JOHNNIE COLEMON, PASTOR,
CHRIST UNIVERSAL TRUTH CENTER

We impose meaning on day-to-day events, and what we say to ourselves about them leads us toward either success or failure. World-class tennis star Zina Garrison was the seventh seeded player in the 1990 Virginia Slims tournament. But she was eliminated by an unseeded player in the first round.

Why? She told a *New York Times* reporter, "My mind wasn't there at all. . . . I had no motivation, no pickup. And when you're playing so bad, you just don't know how to get out of it, or if you can."

What crushed her spirit? What made her think so negatively? A silly superstition. She went on to say, "I'm superstitious, and it seems like I have one good, one bad year, and every even-numbered year is usually a bad one."

Do you think a hand on high deliberately alternates Garrison's good and bad years? Of course not. Like many of us, she's the victim of her own self-defeating thinking. Superstitions are merely poor mental habits given an external cause. Anyone can fall prey to such misconceptions—even a professional athlete who receives careful coaching.

Every situation is always fresh and new. Yesterday's failure means nothing about today's possibilities—unless you make up wild superstitions about it. You can make the most of every opportunity. Create positive expectations, and you'll have positive results.

It's better to expect too much of yourself than too little.

Tools of the Trade

"Start where you are with what you have, knowing that what you have is plenty enough."
—BOOKER T. WASHINGTON, EDUCATOR

Whitney Young, founder of the National Urban League, gave a group of civic leaders a clue as to why equal opportunity is so important: "If you give us the tools," he said, "we will finish the job." Young's words are worth remembering. How many times have you labored at an unsuccessful activity only to find out that having a particular tool could have saved you a great deal of time, energy, and frustration?

This is because we think of tools as tangible instruments. However, to make the most of success, we must use the word *tool* in a much broader sense. We've heard the expression "climbing the ladder of success" so often that its significance is lost in its simplicity. A ladder is nothing but a tool—just an instrument to help facilitate work. Likewise a job is a tool to be used in arriving at our goals in life.

A ladder is designed for vertical but not horizontal use. It is to be used for an upward climb. Also, a ladder cannot be climbed except by using one rung at a time. Just as people do not stumble into success but rather grow into it, a ladder offers only a progressive means of movement. We use each rung as a foundation to reach greater heights. If we try to skip a rung, disaster is imminent.

Perhaps the most important similarity between one's vocation and a ladder is that it requires effort to climb in either case. Not all are willing to make the sacrifice to reach the top of the ladder, but those who climb high enough will escape the congestion at the bottom.

Dreams are the tools of the successful. I will dream big dreams.

Are You Trying to Hustle Me?

*"One-tenth of the folks run the world. One-tenth
watch them run it, and the other 80 percent don't
know what the hell's going on."*
—JAKE SIMMONS, JR., OIL INDUSTRIALIST

Charles Clinton Spaulding, supersalesman and founder of
North Carolina Mutual Insurance Company, was asked what it
took to get to the top. "The same thing it takes to succeed in
any undertaking," he replied. "Hard work and determination.
But, most important, you've got to hustle!"

Those who make things happen share this quality. They all
hustled. No matter how intelligent or able you may be, if you
don't have a sense of urgency or the initiative to exploit your
potential and put forth the effort to realize your goals, you will
fall short of your mark. You've got to hustle! The world is full
of highly competent men and women who honestly intend to
accomplish grand dreams but fall prey to indifference and idleness. Their accomplishments seldom match those of less-
talented people who are blessed with drive, ambition, and
energy. There's no substitute for hustle!

What is hustle?

· Hustle is doing something that everyone else is certain cannot
  be done.
· Hustle is getting the sale because you got there first or hung
  on after others gave up.
· Hustle is burning the midnight oil; it's blood, sweat, and tears.
· Hustle is missing lunch.
· Hustle is getting the customer to say "yes" after he or she said
  "no."
· Hustle is believing in yourself when no one else does.
· Hustle is winning and encouraging others to win.
· Hustle is heaven if you're a hustler, and hell if you're not.

Hustle is the only way you will reach dreams.

**Today I will wear out the shoe leather and hustle toward my ob-
jectives.**

Who Is Your Scapegoat?

"Each of us must earn our own existence. And how does anyone earn anything? Through perseverance, hard work, and desire."
—THURGOOD MARSHALL, SUPREME COURT JUSTICE

The Old Testament book of Leviticus describes the sacred custom of using a scapegoat once a year to atone for the sins, mistakes, and failures of the Israelite nation. In a solemn ceremony Aaron, the high priest, would lead a goat to the outskirts of the camp. There he would place his hands on the goat's head and confess over it all the sins of the Israelite people. Through this symbolic act the goat took on the sins. It was then allowed to escape and wander in the wilderness, presumably to die.

The term *scapegoat* is still with us today, but it is not used in reference to a sacred ceremony. Now people use it to describe what or who they choose to blame for their problems or mistakes. Some people make scapegoats of their parents; others blame their woes on the government, the economy, their school, their company, or their boss.

Instead of working on what is going on *inside* them, they try to blame what is going on *around* them. It's always easier and more convenient to assume that the answer or the blame lies elsewhere. But life is a *do-it-yourself* proposition. "We increase our ability and stability," says rhythm-and-blues great Curtis Mayfield, "when we increase our sense of accountability and responsibility." You must accept personal responsibility for the quality of your performance. You are responsible for your reaction to the circumstances in your life.

I am responsible for me. I point no fingers, give no excuses, and offer no scapegoats.

A Credit to the Race

"I had heard all kinds of rumors about MIT. They used to say that even the janitors at MIT had master's degrees. At first I wasn't going, but then I couldn't run away from a challenge. I had to compete with the best."
—RONALD MCNAIR, *CHALLENGER* ASTRONAUT

One of the best interpretations of success I have ever discovered is a training film that recounts the running of a marathon in a small town in Brown County, Somewhere, USA. More than one hundred runners are entered in the race, but the focus is only on three. The first is a young woman whose goal is to better her time by at least a few seconds. She knows that many of the marathoners can beat her best time—3 hours and 58 minutes, slow by running standard—but that doesn't concern her.

Next we meet a young man who looks hopeful but not completely confident. His idea of success is simply finishing the marathon, something he has failed to do in several attempts. He isn't interested in running a 3:50 or even a 4:50. For him success will be crossing the finish line.

The third runner is another young hopeful who has decided to "go for broke." He's not sure he can win, but he is intrigued by reaching down inside to see how good he really is.

The gun sounds, and all three runners break from the starting point with dozens of other entrants. Soon they spread out along the highways of Brown County and settle in to run at their own pace. Who wins the race? Not any of these runners. A stranger, new to the area, grabs the honors. But does that mean that all the others lost? It depends on how you look at it. Externally there can be only one winner. But internally everyone can win. The finish line that really matters is not the one drawn by race directors but the particular goal set in the mind of each participant. As in life, no one needs to be a loser. The real prize is not first place, but competing in the race itself.

By doing my best I'll win the race of my life.

Know When to Say When

"Enough is enough!"
—FANNIE LOU HAMER, CIVIL RIGHTS ACTIVIST

I recently read the story of a little boy who went with his mother to the toy department of a store. A big sign read, CHILDREN ARE NOT ALLOWED TO PLAY WITH THE TOYS. Ignoring the sign, the little boy climbed on a hobbyhorse and began to rock back and forth.

His mother said, "Come on, darling, you must get down, you cannot play with the toys." He pushed her away and held on to the neck of the horse, even though his mother scolded and tugged at him. Finally a clerk approached and said, "Sorry, but the sign says, 'No children allowed on toys.' " The boy ignored him and the clerk, in turn, called the assistant manager, who grabbed the boy's arm and repeated, "Sonny, you're not allowed to play with the toys!" The boy pushed him away, too.

Soon a manager came over and in a pleasant tone of voice said, "Sonny, if everybody began to play with these toys, they would soon be broken and we could not sell them." The little boy hung on tighter. Finally a tough, burly old man, who had been watching the entire scene, approached the frustrated motivators and said, "Let me talk to him." He went over and whispered something in the boys' ear. Immediately the child jumped off the horse and said, "Okay, Mama, let's go home." Surprised, the mother asked, "What did that man say to you?" The youngster replied, "He told me, 'You get off the horse or I'll spank you!' "

As you chase your dream, it's wise to remember, some things just aren't worth the risk, such as your health and well-being. It is always smart to constantly assess your position.

I know when to say yes and when to say no.

You Make Me Laugh

"Try to make the world laugh—it already has enough to cry about."
—RICHARD PRYOR, COMEDIAN AND ACTOR

Stand-up comic and performer Damon Wayans has called life, with all of its tragedies and twists, a human comedy. There's a lot in life that seems unfair, but seeing the absurdity, finding something to laugh at, makes it easier to endure and certainly a bit more fun. It may also combat illness.

For example, I read a story about a cancer patient who was anticipating a bone-marrow transplant. One day, while lying in his room, he overheard his doctor tell his wife in jest, "You know, what your husband really needs is a brain transplant." Though terribly ill, the patient laughed at the joke, reminding himself that not everything was completely grim. He continued to laugh throughout his hospital stay. Interestingly enough, this man left the hospital in half the time predicted, forcing his roommate to think, "Perhaps if I laughed more, I'd be on my feet sooner."

When you laugh, all kinds of wonderful things happen to benefit your body and mind. Endorphins are released in your brain, which give you a natural "high," and your respiratory system gets the kind of workout that it may get from jogging. Furthermore, laughter relieves pain. You can only laugh when you are relaxed, and the more relaxed you are, the less pain you feel.

On a late-night talk show before his death Sammy Davis, Jr., asked his host, "Do you know what's the difference between heaven and earth? On earth, the most frequently asked question is, Where's the bathroom? And the most frequently asked question in heaven is, Why did I take life so seriously?" Laughter is the pulse of life.

This is the day that I will laugh at myself.

Different Strokes for Different Folks

"Not everyone likes chocolate ice cream."
—NIPSEY RUSSELL, COMEDIAN

For years the best coaches have used the same technique to build successful teams: They accept the fact that different players possess varying but equally important skills. Some players are fast runners, while others can kick or hit a ball great distances. The trick is to put each player into a position that emphasizes his strengths and minimizes his weaknesses. The following fable demonstrates the power of this skill.

Once upon a time the animals of the forest decided to develop a school. They developed a curriculum of running, climbing, swimming, and flying. All of the animals took all of the courses. As you might guess, the duck was excellent in swimming, in fact better than the instructor. But he only made passing grades in flying and was poor in running. Since he was slow in running, he had to drop swimming and stay after school to practice his sprints. This caused his webbed feet to blister. As a result he became only average in swimming.

The rabbit started at the top of his class in running, but developed a nervous twitch in his leg muscles because of so much makeup work in swimming. The squirrel was excellent in climbing, but encountered constant frustration in flying class because his teacher made him take off from the ground instead of the treetops. He developed a charley horse from overexertion and consequently lagged in climbing and running. The eagle was disciplined for being a nonconformist because he beat all the others to the top of the tree in climbing but insisted on using his own way of getting there.

The moral of the story is obvious: You must identify your greatest strength as well as the strengths of those around you.

I understand that different does not mean inferior.

All You Have to Do Is Ask

"Life has more questions than answers."
—GEORGE HALSEY, ENTREPRENEUR

Several years ago George Halsey, a highly successful Amway distributor, taught me the value of setting clear, specific financial goals. Over lunch in an exquisite North Carolina restaurant Halsey shared a story with me about an elderly millionaire and a young man who desired to be rich.

"Do you want to be rich?" the millionaire asked. "I most certainly do," the young man answered.

"Then write down the amount of money you want and how much time you'll devote to acquiring it." The young man furrowed his brow. "Do you think money will fall from trees just because I write a figure down on paper?" he questioned.

"Yes, I do," said the millionaire. "Every millionaire I've met told me he became rich only after he set an amount and a date by which to acquire his wealth. If you don't know where you're going, chances are you won't get there.

"Most unsuccessful people aren't aware that life gives exactly what you ask. So you must ask for exactly what you want. If your request is vague, what you'll get will be just as muddled. If you ask for the minimum, you'll receive the minimum.

"Do you doubt me? Just ask someone how much money he wants to earn next year. If this person is on the road to success and doesn't mind confiding in you, he'll answer immediately. But nine out of ten are incapable of answering this question.

"Theirs," the millionaire said, "is the common mistake. Your mind desires to know just what you expect from it. *If you do not ask for anything specific, that's just what you will receive.*"

Right here and now I know exactly what I want.

Open for Business

"The haves and have nots can often be traced to the 'did's and didn't dos.'"
—WILLIAM RASPBERRY, SYNDICATED COLUMNIST

In the final analysis each of us is in business for ourself. That is, each of us is the president of his or her own corporation. As you assume this office, you alone are responsible for your firm's success or failure. A parable illustrates this notion well.

A businessman on a crowded city street dropped a dollar into the cup of a man selling pencils and hurriedly stepped aboard a train bound for his office. However, on second thought, he backed off the train, walked over to the beggar, and took several pencils from the cup. Apologetically he explained that in his haste he had neglected to pick up his pencils and hoped the man wouldn't be upset. "After all," he said, "you're a businessman just like myself. You have merchandise to sell and it's fairly priced." Then he caught the next train.

At a civic function a few months later a neatly dressed salesman stepped up to the same businessman and introduced himself. "You probably don't remember me and I don't know your name, but I'll never forget you. You are the man who gave me back my self-respect. I was a beggar selling pencils until you came along and told me I was a businessman—that I was responsible for my future. And for that I thank you."

A wise man once said, "Many people have gone further than they thought they could because someone else thought they could." The most you can do for anyone is to reveal his own wealth to him.

Everything that I do prospers. I'm in business to stay in business.

Awaken the Giant Within

*"Living in Hollywood can give you a false sense of
reality. I try to stay in touch with my inner
feelings—that's what's really going on."*
—WILL SMITH, ACTOR AND COMEDIAN

A number of years ago a poor farmer discovered oil in his
backyard. Though he was once poverty-stricken, the discovery
of oil made him quite wealthy. One of the first things he purchased with his newfound wealth was a new car—a Mercedes-
Benz. He wanted everyone in town to notice his car. So, when
driving through town, he turned to the left and right to speak
to everyone in sight. As a matter of fact, he often turned completely around to speak to folks behind him. Yet he never had
an accident while driving. Why not? The reason is simple.
Directly in front of that shiny new car were two horses pul-
ling it.

Local mechanics said there was nothing wrong with the
car's engine. The old man had simply never learned how to in-
sert the key and turn on the ignition. Underneath the hood of
that luxury car were hundreds of horses—highly engineered
horsepower ready, willing and raring to go—but the confused
farmer was only using the horses on the *outside*.

Closer to home, many people make the mistake of searching
in their external world to find horsepower—or the answers to
their problems—when they should look inside—within themselves. You will not find success or happiness in your external
world. You will always find them within. "How great we all
could be," singer and songwriter Valerie Simpson told a group
of children, "if we would only search within and release our
hidden power. Turn inward and find your true greatness."

I go forth in life with the realization that the kingdom lies
within.

Don't Get Too Comfortable

*"We must define ourselves by the best that is in us,
not the worst that has been done to us."*
—EDWARD LEWIS, PUBLISHER, *ESSENCE* MAGAZINE

As you pursue your goals, attempting new and various methods of reaching your objectives, you will experience uncomfortable moments. Count on it; that's part of the process. Anything new, different, or untried lies outside the comfort zone—in the land of the uncomfortable.

As you approach the edges of your comfort zone, you begin to experience a host of negative emotions: fear, guilt, unworthiness, depression, and possibly anger. These are feelings that usually accompany people who say, "I'm uncomfortable." For many the explanation "I'm uncomfortable" is sufficient reason not to venture out. It's little wonder, then, that these people seldom reach their dreams. They choose comfort over goals.

The subtle ways in which the comfort zone keeps you from your dreams are remarkable. The comfort zone reacts with "Don't do it!" messages long before we begin to take action. When we even think about doing something new and different, the comfort zone kicks in. Since birth we have been programmed to do whatever it takes to avoid fear, guilt, unworthiness, and hurt. Therefore we think about something else—something more comfortable.

To reach your goal—to live out your dream—you must choose, moment by moment, to take steps in the direction of your dream no matter how uncomfortable you may feel. Reaching one's goal is not a matter of comfort—it's a matter of achievement.

The best way out is always through.

Just the Facts, Ma'am

*"The only thing you can learn from studying
poverty is how to be poor."*
—ROBERT WOODSON, DIRECTOR, NATIONAL CENTER FOR
NEIGHBORHOOD ENTERPRISE

One of the most common reasons people have for not pursuing their dreams is the state of the economy. To these types the economy or the timing or the circumstance is never quite right for success. These individuals never stop to realize that the economy is not something "out there;" it is something "in here."

No matter where the economy is (or is headed), those who study economic facts and figures have the perfect reason for not chasing their goals. For example, the same people who study poverty or crime can prove, unequivocally, that you cannot walk three blocks in New York City without being badgered by the poor, nor breathe for three minutes in Los Angeles without succumbing to smog.

Successful people don't depend on fortunate circumstances. For example, S. B. Fuller, an uneducated man born to sharecropper parents, experienced the type of poverty that is thankfully rare today. His father left home when he was quite young, and his mother died when he was in his teens. Twenty years later he arrived in Depression-laden Chicago with nothing more than a briefcase full of ambition and a capacity for hard work to match. Before his death he would build a business empire worth more than $10 million.

Even if times are so tough that *only one percent* of the population is fulfilling their dreams, with a U.S. population of 275 million, the fact remains that more than 2.75 million people are reaching their goals. *Certainly you can be one of them!*

I know the facts. I can be, have, or do whatever I wish. I can live a more prosperous life.

Meeting of the Minds

"Your mind is what makes everything else work."
—KAREEM ABDUL-JABBAR, FORMER NBA GREAT

It has been said that "the rational mind is a wonderful servant, but a terrible master." We must control the mind instead of giving it free rein to run wild. If we do not control the mind, it will team up with the mouth and the tongue, and together they can lead us into trouble.

A man was troubled with dizzy spells. He went from one doctor to another, but none could diagnose the problem. He began to lose weight, and he stopped sleeping at night. His health began to deteriorate. He soon lost hope that he would ever recover, so he decided to prepare for the worst. He made out his will, bought a cemetery plot, and even made arrangements with the local undertaker for what he was convinced was his imminent demise. He even decided to buy a new suit of clothes to be buried in. He picked out shoes, socks, coat, pants, and asked for a size 15 shirt. The store clerk said, "But, sir, you need a sixteen-and-a-half shirt, not a fifteen." The man insisted he wore a size 15. Finally, in exasperation, the clerk said, "But if you wear a size fifteen you'll get dizzy spells."

We can stay out of trouble by using our minds. I am not speaking of the emotions but of wisdom of the soul. Alonzo Herndon, an ex-slave who was worth millions when he died, spoke discreetly about the mind. "Sometimes it's best," he said, "if a person spends a moment or two thinking. It's one of the toughest things an individual can ever do. *The mind is one of our most prized assets.*" Our rational mind—when under control—will never steer us wrong. The mind is real. It cannot be misled, because it does not confuse facts with wisdom.

I will keep my rational mind under control.

Dial 911

"After my daily therapy the pain in my legs feels good. It gives me hope that one day I'll be able to walk."

—DARRYL STINGLEY, ACTIVIST FOR THE PHYSICALLY CHALLENGED

If you could have one wish, what would it be? High on the list would be, "Just give me a life without pain." However, upon a closer look you may want to think twice. The following story, which ran in a local newspaper nearly thirty years ago, demonstrates the challenges associated with a life totally free of pain.

Little Barbara Smith, born in Dayton, Ohio, almost never cried. She didn't cry when she fell down; she didn't cry when she bumped her head; she didn't even cry when she burned her hand or cut her finger. She cried only when she was hungry or angry. Doctors soon discovered that she had a defect within her central nervous system for which there is no known cure.

The child could not feel pain. Medical experts told her mother that she must constantly watch her baby in the event that Barbara might break a bone and continue to play on it before it could be properly set, or cut herself without knowing it. Spanking her to make her wary of life's inadvertent dangers would do the little girl no good because she couldn't feel the spanking. Life without pain was perpetually dangerous.

A life without pain is apparently not the Creator's intention. We will always experience the bumps and bruises of life. Only the abnormal never hurt. Success by its very nature demands a period of overcoming, a process by which we become strong in broken places. So as you continue to chase your dream and you find yourself battered and bruised along the way, don't quit. Moments like these will pass. Just mentally dial 911 and replenish your soul.

I acknowledge that pain is natural, and I will overcome it.

Too Legit to Quit

"I've always believed no matter how many shots I miss, I'm going to make the next one."
—ISIAH THOMAS, BASKETBALL GREAT

Every adversity, every failure, and every unpleasant experience carries with it the seed of an equivalent benefit that may prove a blessing in disguise. Failure and defeat are the common language that Nature uses to speak to us and bring us under a spirit of humility so that we may acquire wisdom and understanding.

A wise man once said that it would be impossible to live with a person who had never failed or been defeated in any of his endeavors. This same man also discovered that people achieve success in almost exact proportion to the extent to which they meet and master adversity and defeat. And he made another important discovery—that the truly great achievements were attained by men and women past the age of fifty. He expressed the opinion that the most productive years were between sixty and seventy.

You, too, can ride the success beam by learning to discover and build on the seed of an equivalent benefit in each of your setbacks. Since defeat in some form inevitably overtakes each of us at one time or another, it's obvious that the Creator intends you to gain strength, understanding, and wisdom through struggle. Adversity and defeat cause you to develop your wits and go forward.

It is often difficult for us to recognize the equivalent benefit in our adversities while we are still suffering from the wounds. But time, the greatest of all healers, will disclose the benefits to those who sincerely search for and believe they will find them.

Great achievement is born out of perseverance.

Parental Discretion Advised

"Children could keep on the straight and narrow path if they could get information from someone who's been over the route."
—MARIAN WRIGHT EDELMAN, FOUNDER,
CHILDREN'S DEFENSE FUND

When the proud mother and father hold their seven-pound bundle of joy in their arms, it's difficult to imagine that someday that little package will be a six-foot, two-hundred-pounder or a five-foot beauty who will make major contributions to the world. Positive parents, however, have the capacity to "see the future," to use their imaginations, to visualize that child growing up to be a loving, creative, successful adult.

Just as the renowned sculptor Selma Burke sees her masterpieces in granite and stone long before she strikes the first blow, so must parents confidently project an image of the fine young man or woman who will emerge from that tiny "block" of humanity. It is the responsibility of the parent to nurture that impressionable child through successive stages into positive adulthood.

Of course, the nurturing process is not easy. A well-baked cake consists of many ingredients blended in the correct format for the proper length of time. To raise children who will be winners in tomorrow's world, parents must use many essential ingredients—love, tenderness, discretion, and other qualities all wrapped in an abundance of care and commitment for the children's eventual well-being. We can't take for granted that our children will feel as good about themselves as we want them to, but we can set the stage for success by giving their egos a nudge here and a kiss there. Raising positive children is no small task by any stretch of the imagination, but it can be fun, exciting, and tremendously rewarding.

Today I will let my child know that he or she can succeed.

The Last Shall Be First

*"I'm not a self-made man. I cannot forget those
who have sacrificed for me to get where I am
today."*
—JESSIE HILL, CEO, ATLANTA LIFE INSURANCE

Often we see plaques on the walls in people's homes that read, GOD FIRST, FAMILY SECOND, WORK THIRD. That's wrong. It's wrong as a credo because they are *all* first. We are spiritual beings living in a spiritual universe. That spirituality permeates our family, our work, and our entire life. Our choice is to recognize it and work with it, or deny it and have it work against us.

In work, in finance, in health, in many areas of our lives, we use terms that we all immediately recognize. But when we get to spirituality, we frequently disagree over terminology. The following story will help define the term *spirituality*.

Several years ago there was an extremely wealthy old woman living in one of the most expensive suites of a four-star New York hotel. The cost was anything but modest, and she began to feel guilty about spending all that money on herself. One day, as she exited the hotel, she saw a disheveled beggar stumbling down the street. Feeling somewhat remorseful, she walked up to him and placed a hundred-dollar bill in his hand. As she walked away she said, "Godspeed."

The next day as she was coming out of the hotel a neatly dressed, cleanly shaven man walked up to her, placed ten hundred-dollar bills in her hand and said, "Godspeed paid 10 to 1!" This only goes to show that one person's spirituality is another's racehorse. Spirituality involves more than the mind or intellect; it involves the soul. When we do something spiritual, we do it from the soul. We do it for ourselves.

You have a spiritual side. Find it and pour your soul into it.

School Days

"Remember, luck is opportunity meeting up with preparation, so you must prepare yourself to be lucky."
—GREGORY HINES, ACTOR AND DANCER

Life is a persistent teacher. It will repeat a lesson over and over until it is learned. How does life know whether or not we have learned a lesson? Until we have changed our behavior. Until then, even if we intellectually "know" something, we haven't really learned it. School remains in session. The good news is that we eventually learn all we need to know.

For some, however, eventually is not soon enough. If you can learn something that will make your life happier, healthier, and more productive, *why not learn it now*? That brings happiness, health, and productivity to you sooner—and it avoids a lot of painful lessons along the way.

Others aren't content with learning only what they need to know. Getting by is not enough. They want more; they're eager learners. But what if we're curious about things that seemingly can't be answered? When faced with this quandary we need to refer to the words of Johnetta Cole, president of Spelman College: "Society curses ignorance whether among the rich or poor. *To be educated is the greatest gift in life.*" Marva Collins, founder of Chicago's Westside Prep, agrees: *"The world itself is a university,"* she said to a reporter. "Children learn from every facet of life. *Whomever evades learning misses out on life.*" When we continue to learn, we learn how to succeed.

You're not in school for only a few years, you're in school for the rest of your life.

Who's Laughing Now?

"Nothing is easy to the unwilling."
—NIKKI GIOVANNI, POET AND WRITER

If we are to survive and live triumphantly, then we had better learn to live with the naysayers—those who would doubt our abilities and make light of our efforts.

A boy watched an artist paint a picture of a muddy river. He laughed at the artist because he had painted so much mud. The artist told him, "You see mud in the picture but I see beautiful colors and contrasts, beautiful harmonies." His painting eventually sold for thousands of dollars.

Cynics and doubters will always be among us. When you dare to step out of the crowd, people will always laugh. But if you know you're right and believe in your abilities, then the smirks of others will turn to smiles of approval.

When Richard Allen proclaimed that he would develop a church where African Americans could worship without hindrance, his fellow clergy laughed. When Dr. Louis T. Wright, a Harvard-trained physician from southern Georgia, invented the neck brace, the medical community laughed. When James Van Der Zee sold his possessions to travel the country photographing the exploits of African Americans, people laughed. In 1973, when Lelia Foley announced to family and friends that she was going to run for public office in tiny Taft, Oklahoma, and become the first black female mayor in the country, her opponent laughed. When William Monroe Trotter demanded "full equal rights for the Negro," America laughed. When Doris Spears sought to become the first black female deputy sheriff in the United States, her fellow officers laughed. And when Emmett Ashford spent his entire life in musty, country towns because he dared to become major league baseball's first African-American umpire, organized sports laughed.

Don't allow the laughter of critics and naysayers to deter you.

Today I will stand and turn a deaf ear to the doubting Thomases. I know what I have to do.

I've Got to Hand It to You

"The difference between luck and ability is time."
—REGINALD LEWIS, ENTREPRENEUR

Are you disenchanted with the hand that life has dealt you? Then change those circumstances to some more favorable. *Your destiny lies within your hands.*

Perhaps a parable will help you see my point. High on a hilltop overlooking the beautiful countryside of East Africa lived an old man whose wisdom was sought by many. Legend has it that he could answer any question anyone might ask of him. Two young boys believed they could fool the old sage, so they caught a small bird and headed for his home.

One of the boys held the little bird in his hand and asked the old man if the bird was dead or alive. Without hesitation the old man said, "Son, if I say to you that the bird is alive, you will close your hands and crush it to death. If I say the bird is dead, you will open your hands and let it fly away. You see, my son, in your hands *you hold the power of life and death*."

When applied to your life, this parable has a much deeper message. Within your hands lie the seeds of failure—or the potential for greatness. You are capable of achieving your heart's desire, and the qualities that are necessary for such accomplishment lie within you at this very moment. Believe that you have been placed on earth for a purpose, and as you fulfill your purpose, you are shaping your own life, your own destiny. Make sure your future is in capable hands.

You can always find a helping hand at the end of your sleeve.

Heavy Metal

"Can't nothin' make your life work if you ain't the architect."
—TERRY MCMILLAN, AUTHOR AND LECTURER

One day a poor, disheveled old man rummaged through a junkyard searching for a piece of scrap iron that he had planned to use as a paperweight. After finding such a piece, he approached the owner of the junkyard with several coins in his hand.

"How much is it?" he asked.

"Let me see," the owner replied, placing the rusty metal strip on a scale. "Well, it's nearly a pound," he said. "I guess that'll be ten cents."

As his impoverished visitor was leaving the yard with his paperweight, the owner walked beside him. "Sir, isn't it funny—that small piece of metal that you just purchased is worth only pennies," said the owner. "But just think, if you heated it and treated it and molded it into cast iron—the type that could be used on tractors that cultivate crops or battleships that defend our nation—why, that piece of metal would then be worth eighty cents a pound—*eight times as much!*

"As a matter of fact," he added, "if that same piece of metal were made into a pair of scissors, its value would increase to ten dollars a pound. Furthermore, if this little strip of iron was molded into fine watch components, the price would skyrocket to five hundred dollars a pound.

"But most importantly," he said, "if you took this rusty strip of metal and created surgical instruments, the type of instruments that guide the hands of the world's most skilled surgeons, why, sir, your paperweight would indeed be priceless." And then the owner paused and said, "Isn't it incredible to think that some of us lie in the junkyard of life? Each of us desperately needs to find ways in which we can be molded and shaped into something more useful. If we find a way, our success is guaranteed."

I refuse to place limits on what I can do. I am priceless.

Home Alone

"The most lonely place in the world is the human heart when love is absent."
—SADIE ALEXANDER, FIRST AFRICAN-AMERICAN FEMALE TO
RECEIVE A PH.D. IN ECONOMICS

My mother called a few places home during her long life—and she had many thoughts to share about her last home, a nursing facility. "I live in a nursing home," she once told a visitor. "Many of my friends live here too. Some really get around, and others are quite ill. Regardless, they have lived long, useful lives.

"Those of us who are mentally alert are still fond of old friendships. Though we may not be quite as mentally alert now, we have pleasant remembrances. We have people residing in our home who have come from all walks of life. There are mothers, fathers, housewives, doctors, lawyers, teachers, secretaries, nurses, and writers—just about any occupation that you could imagine.

"Those of us who can remember the way our friends were when they were healthy can still love and respect them for the person we know they once were. We can still appreciate the good conversation, the friendly visits, and their warm greetings. People who need people are the luckiest people in the world.

"We all must remember that none of us can totally control the future, and that each of us grows older from the day of birth to the day of death. No matter where life may find us, we should all be grateful for whatever home we may call home." Mary Elizabeth Kimbro has made her transition. But before she left, she encouraged those around her, serving as an inspiration to many.

How thoughtless and foolish we are when we forget for even a moment how much our elders have given and are continuing to give to the lives of those they touch.

Today I will thank my aunts, uncles, grandparents, and elders for serving as an inspiration.

You Can't Be Serious!

"The secret of success is to start from scratch and keep on scratching."
—DENNIS GREEN, NFL HEAD COACH

Are you willing to work hard in order to succeed? To go all out? Are you willing to sacrifice certain pleasures because your time and energy must be devoted to your goal? If so, then you possess the key to success. Few extraordinary things ever get accomplished without commitment.

Total commitment is not just hard work, *it is total involvement*. For example, building a brick wall is back-breaking work. There are some people who build brick walls all their lives. And when they die, they leave behind miles of walls, mute testimonials to how hard they labored. But there are others who build walls, who place one brick on top of another, but they do so with a vision—a goal—in mind. They visualize the end result—success.

Yet many people fear all-out commitment—to a person, a job, or a goal. The mental consciousness of "the grass is greener" is a major roadblock to commitment. It implies that you have the option of quitting when things get tough. But commitment is based on the belief that "this is it." People who are always looking "over there" for something better will never make it "over here."

You will never move beyond the surface of a task into the heart of an opportunity if you run from one goal to another. Digging deep, or becoming serious about that which you desire, is the process that reveals the gems. It is often the last key on the ring that opens the door.

Today I will step back and take a hard look at the things I am committed to.

High Tech

*"Ours is a high-tech society. We must constantly be
in the business of raising consciousness."*
—WILLIE B. BARROW, PASTOR, OPERATION PUSH

An editorial in a regional newspaper reported a story about a man in California who built an ingenious machine in his garage. Using spare parts, he produced a machine that contained just about every high-tech device known to the computer world. On the builder's command this huge contraption with its thousands of parts—gears, motors, and switches—would begin its complex operations.

From a control panel on the back of the machine, the operator watched with satisfaction as lights blinked and dials turned as an indication that all was going well. Technicians rated the contraption a marvel of technology. However, there was just one minor flaw. *The machine was not designed to do anything!* It was developed by an absentminded gadgeteer who got carried away with the wonders of the machine age.

We are like this marvelous contraption: not programmed to do anything. But as soon as we develop direction and a plan of action, we begin to realize our full potential. In this high-tech, high-consciousness world, we direct through our thought process the control panel of the greatest machine ever devised—*our mind*!

You are designed for accomplishment, engineered for success, and endowed with the seeds of greatness.

When Close Is Not Enough

"The way I approached my entire racing career is to do it right."
—WILLY T. RIBBS, RACE-CAR DRIVER

Many people are satisfied doing only as much as they need to get by. They're not striving for 100 percent performance.

Of course no one is perfect, and mistakes will be made in every human endeavor. But accepting less than your best can have dire consequences. Efficiency and performance experts believe that we should strive for 100 percent performance or zero defects. At least one study has revealed what life would be like if things were done right only 99.9 percent of the time. You might be shocked. We'd have to accept:

- One hour of unsafe drinking water every month
- Two unsafe plane landings per day at the nation's busiest airport
- Sixteen thousand pieces of mail lost by the U.S. Postal Service every hour
- Twenty thousand incorrect drug prescriptions per year
- Five hundred incorrect surgical operations each week
- Fifty newborn babies dropped at birth by doctors every day
- Twenty-two thousand checks deducted from the wrong bank account each hour
- Thirty-two thousand missed heartbeats per person per year

The truly great achiever never stops trying to improve. He or she shoots for zero defects. "The difference between success and failure," says Greg Baranco, Black America's top car salesman, "is attention to detail. Business teaches us that accomplishments are achieved in areas that also-rans thought were not important and winners did." A commitment to excellence is the shortest distance to success.

It is foolish to think you can do anything perfectly; it is a mistake not to try.

Mo' Money

"It's true, money won't buy happiness, but it will make a helluva down payment."
——REDD FOXX, COMEDIAN

"What would you do if you won a million dollars?" insurance tycoon A. G. Gaston asked me. "It's a question you'd better be able to answer."

Rich is a word that is rich in meaning. It means magnificent, sumptuous, having an abundant supply, fertile, extremely productive, containing choice ingredients, pleasantly full and mellow, warm and strong in color, and amusing. Most of these synonyms don't necessarily have anything to do with money, and yet how often do we think of "being rich" as simply having a lot of money?

The popular misconception is that *riches* refers to things that are scarce, things that only a few people have. Not so. Many of the most magnificent, sumptuous, and pleasantly full experiences in life are readily available for little or no cost. We all have riches. Some of us have them in money, but most have riches in talent, ideas, creativity, loving, caring, wisdom, and beauty. "It is not by a man's purse," said S. B. Fuller, "but by his character, that he is rich or poor."

The secret is to use the riches that you possess and the ones you can obtain to enjoy personal fulfillment.

There are people who have money and people who are rich. Being the latter is much more desirable.

Standing Room Only

"I did what I had to do!"
——HATTIE MCDANIEL, FILM STAR

What are we going to do when we achieve our current goals? Latch on to another dream of course. What do mountain climbers do when they reach the top of a mountain? Find another mountain. So often, people firmly established at the height of success look back on their time of struggle as the happiest years of their life. In other words, winning is fun— that's the purpose of the game—but so is playing.

An old man enjoyed a fall day as he sat on a park bench. He seemed almost unaware of a little boy playing in the leaves nearby. The infant—less than a year old—was trying desperately to stand on his own as his mother watched. The child would look at the old man, try to stand, only to discover that his method wasn't working. After a few seconds he would tumble over in the leaves with a surprised look on his face. The old man smiled.

The scene played again and again, with a few tears and determination added. While his mother was busy chatting with a neighbor, others watched and wondered, "Why doesn't that old man help him? Why doesn't he make it easier for the little boy?"

Then came a brief whisper from his elderly companion, "You can make it, son." And make it he did. The young child planted his sturdy little legs, finally took his hands off the ground, and with a wobbly effort he stood. He was delighted with himself. The old man reached out a gnarled hand to hold the dimpled one stretching forward.

A wise man said, "Sometimes he helps best who only stays nearby and lets growth occur."

Stay focused on your goal and enjoy the journey.

Little Bitsy Things

"Hell, it's not just slavery; it's being harassed by the police and the racial slurs. It's a whole bunch of little things."
—JOHN SINGLETON, MOVIE PRODUCER AND DIRECTOR

A giant sequoia lies rotting on the western slopes of the Rocky Mountains. It was a growing sapling when the Master walked the shores of the Galilee. It was reaching full maturity when Columbus sailed the ocean blue, and it looked down from lofty heights during the Civil War. The giant redwood withstood the ravages of fires, floods, storms, and droughts. It seemed destined to live many more centuries.

Then, a few years ago, a tiny beetle started to burrow into its bark and lay the eggs that would produce other beetles. The few insects multiplied into hundreds, then thousands, and finally into millions. They attacked the bark, then worked deeper and deeper into the trunk, and finally ate the very heart and core of that mighty tree. Then one day, after withstanding the elements for centuries, the rains came, the winds blew, lightning flashed, and the giant sequoia fell. Not because of the elements and not because of its age. It fell because of the weakening effect of those tiny beetles—*those little bitsy things.*

Racism is analogous to this process. To be African American implies that for centuries we have felt the brunt of discrimination and injustice. Perhaps as we seek employment or housing or an education for our children, or even as we browse through certain stores, we are treated like common criminals. It's nothing earth-shattering—*just those little bitsy things.*

Black America, stand tall! Stand rooted in the truth that we were kings and queens in Africa longer than we were slaves in America. Don't allow someone else's negative attitude and poor self-image to steal our dreams.

Today I won't get mad or even. I'll keep my head up and get better!

Your Cup Runneth Over

"Success is when your cup runneth over and your saucer too!"
—NATHANIEL BRONNER, SR., ENTREPRENEUR

Imagine yourself standing before an abundant waterfall. What would limit you from taking your wealth of water from that waterfall? The size of your container, right? If you had a cup, you'd have a cup's worth of water. If you had a gallon jug, you'd have a gallon's worth of water. If you had a barrel, you'd have a barrel of water. If you had a tanker truck, you could supply water, or in this case, "wealth," to all your friends and family.

What if the same were true of all the attributes of wealth? What if your ability to experience peace of mind, health, happiness, abundance, prosperity, love, and opportunity were limited only by your ability to receive? What if each of these qualities were available to you in infinite supply and the only thing limiting you was the size of your container?

Yet most of us don't think that way. We believe that if we have a cup, only a cup's worth of water ever dribbles over the waterfall. This is an illusion—a highly convincing illusion, but an illusion just the same. If we wanted to expand our ability to experience peace of mind, health, happiness, abundance, prosperity, love, and opportunity, we must expand the size of our mind *first*.

You create your container by seeing yourself already in possession of what you want. You enlarge the container by stating, positively and affirmingly, "I am healthy," "I am prosperous," "I am happy." As the container is enlarged, you will inherit the wealth of life.

Today I will dig my well before I'm thirsty. I will affirm what I want.

May the Force Be with You

*"Don't be afraid of what you want. This is your
time. The barriers are down."*
—MORGAN FREEMAN, ACADEMY AWARD-WINNING ACTOR

What is the ultimate power source that can lead you to success? This question is best answered by asking a series of questions. What force . . .

- Travels faster than the speed of light?
- Penetrates all known barriers, whether concrete or steel?
- Transcends time—both past and future—enabling anyone to turn the clock backward or forward into infinity?
- Supplies each of us with an unlimited source of creativity? Splashes oils on canvas to create a masterpiece; blends notes and melodies into a masterful musical composition; conceives dreams in the minds of men and women, raising them out of poverty into new hopes and vistas?
- Sharpens the focus of human attention to needlelike precision until the basketball goes through the hoop or until the student receives his or her diploma?
- Programs data into the subconscious, which calculates breakthrough solutions to what were once impossible deadlocks and unsolvable problems?

What is this force? What is this incredible power? This power that ignites the creative fire is called *imagination*. Imagination is the audio and visual channel that the Creator uses to communicate his dreams to your subconscious. When you are tuned in, you are alive and well. Observe your surroundings and you'll see countless illustrations of powerful achievements racked up by individuals just like you. And how is it done? Through the ultimate power source—your imagination.

Let your imagination roam free—it will ignite your future!

And the Walls Come Tumbling Down

"For years, people have looked at Beamon's record as unattainable. I don't accept that. I believe the Lord has given me a talent. I know the record is inside me and I will attain it."
—CARL LEWIS, OLYMPIC CHAMPION

I am continually amazed at the abilities of athletes who run faster, jump higher, and execute feats of physical skill with greater precision every year. Every day we read about a young athlete who cracks a barrier, who hurdles another wall.

Arguably the toughest athletic barrier was the four-minute mile. Experts in track and field believed for years that a human being could not run a mile in less than four minutes. Runners had been trying to achieve this goal since the days of the ancient Greeks. In fact folklore has it that the Greeks had lions chase their runners, thinking that the lions would make them run faster. But nothing worked. Running a mile in less than four minutes was impossible.

Then one man proved the experts wrong. In 1954 a young medical student named Roger Bannister ran the mile in less than four minutes. The year after Roger Bannister leaped past the barrier, thirty-seven other runners broke the four-minute mile; and the year after that, more than three hundred runners toppled the feat. Today high school athletes scale this wall without thinking twice.

Isn't it amazing how when one person breaks a barrier, others quickly follow suit? The only limits that we have are those we place upon ourselves. Once we clearly understand that most "barriers" are mental limitations, our chances of improving our performances are dramatically improved.

When you realize something can be done, you can bet you will do it.

Stretch Marks

"A problem not worth praying about is not worth worrying about."
—AZIE TAYLOR MORTON, FIRST AFRICAN-AMERICAN
TREASURER OF THE UNITED STATES

According to most medical experts, the things that creates stress are called *stressors*. There are two types of stressors: *internal* and *external*. An external stressor can be a phone call at 10:00 P.M. from a collection agency demanding a payment.

Internal stressors arise from circumstances that you create. Picture a situation where someone calls you and says he needs to meet you to discuss something quite urgent. By the time you meet with him, you imagine every conceivable thing that could be wrong. At the conclusion of your meeting, you find that all of those terrible possibilities were much worse than the actual problem. Your imagination became your enemy because you fed it negative thoughts, and it responded in a like manner. You can be your own worst enemy when it comes to stress. You can create internal stressors in your life.

Stress can also work the other way—especially when you underestimate the severity of a problem. For example, suppose you're transferred into a new department on your job. For some reason you're expecting things to be easy. But your new assignment takes more work than you anticipated, and along with it comes more pressure and aggravation.

This is also true of the way you talk about your circumstances. Sometimes your talk can be so negative that you create additional stress. In other words, you "stretch your stress." If you were just to deal with your problem openly and positively, you'd solve it. But if you continually talk about it in a negative manner, you'll stretch your stress and make your situation worse. *Wake up! Don't stress yourself out.*

Don't stretch your problems out of proportion.

Extra, Extra—Read All About It

"Sometimes it takes years for a person to become an overnight success."
—PRINCE, SINGER, SONGWRITER, AND PRODUCER

Housed within the *Washington Post* building, which towers like a beacon above one of the busiest corners in Washington, D.C., a newspaperman sat at his desk. Just being in his office again, hearing the busy clack of the typewriters, feeling a part of the pulsating life of a great newspaper was sheer bliss. Carl Rowan was home. He was a civilian again after completing a successful tour of duty as a naval officer. He was writing again, and he was happy.

In the Pacific, through all those lonely months, Rowan had dreamed of returning home and of the blessings and comforts of life in the States. A person gets to know what he misses when he is away from it. Nowhere in the world were people surrounded by so many opportunities and advantages. That is how he felt, returning home.

He took out a sheet of paper and penned his thoughts. If there were ever a time to remind people of their many blessings, this was it. He wrote: "The ingredients of success are quite simple. You are not obligated to succeed. You are only obligated to do your best." I guess this says it all.

My success is built on the ability to do better than good.

The Economy Within You

"Don't be afraid to go out on a limb. That's where the fruit is."
—JANIE MINES, FIRST AFRICAN-AMERICAN GRADUATE FROM
U.S. NAVAL ACADEMY

"It is a gloomy moment in the history of our country. Not in the lifetime of most men has there been so much grave and deep apprehension: never has the future seemed so incalculable as at this time. The domestic economic situation is in chaos. . . . The political cauldron seethes and bubbles with uncertainty. . . . It is a solemn moment. Of our troubles, no man can see the end." Those words were not written about the 1991–92 recession, nor about the 1980–81 or 1974–75 declines. They were published in *Harper's Weekly* in October 1857.

The real cause of the Panic of 1857 was *fear*. It was fear of the devaluing of the American dollar, fear caused by the failure of a few large corporations, fear of declining stock values, and fear of worker unrest. Today we call it lack of consumer confidence, but it is the same thing—*fear*. Fear has caused every panic, depression, and recession that has occurred in this country since 1857.

When economic historians write the final chapter on the recession of 1992, they will no doubt conclude that it was made worse by a serious erosion of consumer confidence—*fear*. Such negative influences feed upon themselves and engender even more negativism. Achievers know that negative attitudes can cause individuals to lose their material wealth and much more—their true riches in life. "Keep your fears to yourself," warns Eddie Robinson, Grambling University football coach. *"But share your courage with others."*

Those who have studied and learned the art of motivation can lay the foundation for increased earnings and the acquisition of wealth, just as many did in past financial crises. Your financial state of affairs depends more on the *economy in you* than on any external force.

I will not succumb to fear.

Be Sure to Take Your Vitamins

"The mind is the standard of the man."
—PAUL LAURENCE DUNBAR, WRITER AND POET

We're aware of the process by which the body obtains vitamins through food and water to maintain sound health. To eliminate a vitamin deficiency, you choose food for your diet that contains the necessary vitamins. Through Nature's cyclical miracles the body absorbs vitamins and distributes nutrients to vital organs. Vitamin A, for example, protects skin and hair; the B complex develops stamina; vitamin C wards off disease; vitamin D builds strong bones; and vitamin K enhances eyesight. These vitamins act within and on the body, keeping us healthy and fit, and able to *act*.

But have you heard of vitamin I? Vitamin I develops *inspiration*. To correct a vitamin I deficiency you can purposely select beneficial external influences to help you achieve the motivation you are seeking. Vitamin I can be absorbed from numerous sources, a few of which are: *And Still I Rise,* by Maya Angelou; *A Raisin in the Sun,* by Lorraine Hansberry; *Up from Slavery,* by Booker T. Washington; *Succeeding Against the Odds,* by John Johnson; *Live Your Dreams,* by Les Brown; *Green Power,* by Arthur G. Gaston; and the Bible.

Whereas natural vitamins must be taken on a regular basis for a fit body, vitamin I must be absorbed daily for a healthy and productive mind. Therefore be sure to take your daily supply of vitamin I.

Feed your mind with nourishing thoughts, just as you feed your body with nourishing food.

Eat and Be Merry

"You've got to be hungry!"
—LES BROWN, MOTIVATIONAL SPEAKER AND
TALK-SHOW HOST

How much do you hope to accomplish today? Will work require a significant part of your time? Your family another? Then there's the vacation to plan, the book you've been meaning to read, and the friend you wanted to visit. According to at least one study, 80 percent of Americans fall prey to procrastination.

Procrastination is the grave in which opportunity is buried; it is the art of keeping up with yesterday. Marsha Warfield, a comedienne who has constantly battled with her waistline, quips about the fine art of delaying diets. "One thing you can be sure of—there will be more people going on a diet tomorrow than those on a diet today." Many of us are guilty of putting off tasks until we can accomplish them all at once. At the same time, most of us are too busy ever to afford the luxury of large blocks of time to devote to these tasks. Even when such periods appear to be available, something almost always leads us astray.

So what's the answer? The answer can be found in a riddle: "How do you eat an elephant? One bite at a time." Just as no one can swallow an elephant whole, no one can be expected to tackle a major project at one sitting. Breaking large tasks into thirty-minute sections allows time for the routine, the urgent, and the long-term jobs each of us face. Breaking the project into small sessions makes even the most unpleasant of tasks tolerable and eventually allows us to consume the entire elephant. So dig in, and be sure to clean your plate.

Today I will break my large tasks down into manageable pieces.

Amen

*"If Black America is to ever get on its feet, it must
first get down on its knees."*
—RALPH D. ABERNATHY, FORMER EXECUTIVE DIRECTOR,
SOUTHERN CHRISTIAN LEADERSHIP CONFERENCE

Do you know the surest and quickest way of obtaining your
specific desire? *It's prayer!*

But what is prayer? Prayer is *desire*—not vain repetitions or
religious chants but communication with infinite intelligence.
Our Creator's only requirement of prayer is to expand our consciousness on what we want. Furthermore, prayer is not only
worship, it also unites us with our spirit. "Whatsoever things
you ask for, when ye pray, believe that ye shall receive them,
and ye shall have them." There's only one catch—you must
ask intelligently.

A story is told of two monks who strolled in the garden of
the monastery each afternoon. One day they decided they
would enjoy listening to music during their walks. Each
agreed that they would ask the bishop for permission. The next
day as they came out for their walk, one of the monks was
wearing headphones and carrying a cassette player while the
other looked in amazement.

"Didn't you ask if you could listen to music?" the wired
monk asked.

"I asked permission and was refused," replied his colleague.

"How did you ask?" queried the first.

"I approached the bishop and said, 'Father, when I'm walking and meditating in the garden, is it okay if I listen to music?' and he said, 'Absolutely not!' "

"Well," said the other, "you were refused because of the
way you asked the question. I approached the bishop and said,
'Master, when I am listening to music in the garden, is it all
right if I meditate?' and he said, 'Certainly.' " Prayer is talking
something over with God rather than trying to talk God out of
something.

When the outlook is bad, try the "uplook."

Bourgeoisie

*"Light skin, dark skin. High yellow, jet black.
What's the big deal? Why can't we accept each
other for what we are?"*
—JAMES FARMER, CIVIL RIGHTS PIONEER

In order to accept the fact that we are less than perfect, each of us needs to examine our own biases. Spike Lee's *School Daze* aptly describes the mental conditioning that we African Americans have experienced. His movie chronicles college life through the eyes of an impressionable freshman at a fictitious black institution. In the process Lee surfaces many of the taboos and cultural biases that have been a part of our psyche. Just like any other group, we tend to measure people by their looks, their speech, where they come from, and yes, even the color of their skin. We are just as guilty of making snap judgments or scorning those we do not view as our intellectual or social equals.

This thinking will keep us in bondage. Individuals should only be judged by their character and the gifts they share. We need to listen to the message and not judge the messenger.

A man once had a flat tire outside the gates of a mental hospital. As he removed the lugs from the flat tire to switch them with the spare, they slipped off the curb and fell through the grille of the sewer drain. After he realized there was no way to retrieve them, he began to swear in frustration. Just then an inmate who had been standing near the gate said, "Why don't you remove a lug from each of the three other wheels and put them on the spare?"

"My goodness," said the man, "what a brilliant idea! What in hell is someone as smart as you doing in there?"

"Well, I may be crazy," the inmate replied, "but I'm not stupid!"

Dr. King wrote, "The highest form of maturity is self-evaluation. Never judge others until you've examined yourself first." Each of us must examine our own biases.

As I release old biases, I begin to see the divinity and worth of each individual.

Read My Lips

"Many people don't actually lie; they merely present the truth in such a way that nobody recognizes it."
—ELEANOR HOLMES NORTON, LAWYER AND LEGAL
PROFESSOR

Have you ever wondered how and why certain individuals, corporations, institutions, or organizations became successful and why some who achieved outstanding success subsequently failed? The answer is integrity—or lack of it.

Integrity is the cornerstone in building and maintaining success. The achievement of true integrity and well-rounded character is in itself success. Perhaps the best definition of ethics or integrity was given by Thurgood Marshall, former Supreme Court Justice, who said: "The good thing about telling the truth is that you don't have to remember what you said." The following tale is an excellent example:

A salesman in an expensive restaurant paid his check, turned to the stranger at the next table, and said, "Would you like to buy an airline?" The stranger said he wasn't interested.

"I didn't think so," the salesman said. "I just wanted to be able to say that business was discussed at this meal when I submit my expense account."

There are many reasons why honesty, ethics, and integrity would significantly contribute to your well-being. In a broad sense, they would give added purpose to your life and would focus attention on the many practical benefits of having a regard for the needs of others. Even the most gifted persons fail in their trade or profession if they do not develop inviolable moral standards of integrity.

The truth is one thing for which there are no known substitutes. The quality of truth will be the focal point of my life.

Lean on Me

*"It's when we forget ourselves that we accomplish
tasks that are most likely to be remembered."*
—BESSIE COLEMAN, FIRST AFRICAN-AMERICAN FEMALE
AVIATOR

Ask any achiever the secret of his or her success and you are
likely to hear an answer along these lines: "Well, I was fortunate. I worked hard, didn't make too many mistakes, and happened to be in the right place at the right time."

This is probably true. But the deeper truth, however, is that
in most cases these modest people made their own breaks.
They became indispensable to their employers or enterprises
and snatched opportunities. Management, clients, and customers alike trust, rely, and lean on these hardworking types in
moments of chaos. These movers and shakers take the initiative, assume leadership roles, and can often be found volun-
teering for difficult or unpopular assignments. Indispensable
men and women have the enthusiasm to inspire, and the self-
discipline to stick to a job until it's complete. Unlike the
example below:

A man who had been called for jury duty asked to be excused. "On what grounds?" asked the judge.

"We're very busy at the office, sir, and I ought to be there."

"So, you're one of those individuals who thinks he's indispensable. You think the firm can't do without you, is that it?"

"No, sir—far from that. I know very well it can, but I don't
want them to find out."

"Excused," said the judge.

The best way for you to develop the security that lasts a
lifetime is to become outstanding at one particular line of
work.

The outstanding man or woman will always be in demand.

The Sunny Side of the Street

"I don't understand it. People are always saying that I've got an attitude."
—WHOOPI GOLDBERG, ACTRESS AND COMEDIENNE

There are many facets to the subject of attitude. One of them involves optimism. Talk-show host Montel Williams says, "We all hope for the best, but an optimist expects to get it." Debbie Turner, a former Miss America, continues to inspire our youth through the power of optimism. "Keep your face to the sunshine," she instructs, "and you'll never see the shadows."

The optimist takes action—the pessimist takes a seat. An optimist takes a look at a glass of water half-filled and says it's half full. The pessimist looks at the same glass and says it's half empty. But most importantly, the optimist keeps a smile on his or her face and gives thanks for all things. For example, a minister had a habit in his opening prayer of thanking God for the weather. On a particular cold, snowy Sunday morning, a few members ventured to church wondering how their pastor could possibly refer to the weather with a sense of gratitude. To their surprise he said in his prayer, "Dear Lord, we thank Thee that you send us so few Sundays like these."

Civil rights activist Fannie Lou Hamer drives the point home. Living in a home with few material possessions, she was taught to have a positive outlook. When asked how she managed to survive in such meager surroundings, she responded, "Things don't turn up in this world until somebody turns them up. Circumstances are less dreadful than they seem." Each of us could benefit by utilizing her words.

I will maintain a sense of optimism.

A Few Good Men

"Our job is to put the man back into manhood."
—NATHANIEL GOLDSTON, PRESIDENT, 100 BLACK MEN

If I could offer a single prescription for the survival of America, and particularly of Black America, it would be to restore the family. And if you asked me how to do it, my answer would be to save the boys.

So much of what has gone wrong in America, including the frightening growth of the poverty-stricken, crime-ridden, and despairing black underclass, can be traced to the disintegration of the family structure. Everybody knows it, but too many have been reluctant to talk straight about it. We know that children need intact families that include fathers, but we fear to say it lest we appear to be blaming hard-pressed single mothers for the very problems they are struggling to overcome.

There is nothing wrong with being a black female single parent. Our Creator is a single parent. But there is something wrong with the fact that a black woman is so much more likely to experience this situation. And there is something wrong with glorifying this problem instead of rising up to change it. Millions of children do not know, and will never know, what it means to have a father. Nor do they know anyone who has a father or is a father.

If we are to survive, then our families must be restored. And if our families are to be reconstructed, then our young males must step forward. We cannot rescue our families unless we make up our minds to save our boys. What our community needs, what America needs, is a *few good men*!

I've heard the call and I will answer the bell. I will give my time to be a father or mother to one black male.

Simon Says

"Success always leaves footprints."
—BOOKER T. WASHINGTON, EDUCATOR

Leadership is the skill that is most in demand in today's workplace. "The role of the leader," says Herman Cain, president of Godfather's Pizza, "is to turn weaknesses into strengths, defeat into triumph, and obstacles into stepping stones." But Joe Clark, former high school principal, puts leadership into perspective. "Don't ever follow any leader," he says, "until you know whom he or she is following." All organizations, from the smallest to the largest, require capable leaders. But they also need followers who recognize dynamic leaders.

There's a story about a young woman who wanted to go to college. But her heart sank when she read the question on the college application that asked, "Are you a leader?" Being both honest and conscientious, she wrote "no" and returned the application, expecting to be rejected.

To her surprise, she received this reply from the college: "Dear Applicant: A study of the application forms reveals that this year our college will have 1,452 new leaders. We are accepting you because we feel it is imperative that they have at least one follower!"

The first step toward leadership is to follow the examples of worthy leaders.

Surround yourself with the image of yourself.

Reverse Discrimination

"It ain't nothing to find no starting place in the world. You just start from where you find yourself."
—AUGUST WILSON, PLAYWRIGHT

Here are a few questions to consider. In what direction are you headed? If you follow this course, where will you be in five or ten years? What have you done up to this point in your life? Is there anything in your past that you would change? If you could turn back the hands of time and live your life in reverse, what would you do differently?

I thought about the last question and decided on some changes I would make. If I had my life to live again, I would love more. I would share my love with all those I meet. I would spend more time with my children exploring those things that interest them. I would not be inhibited to express my love openly. And when I am unable to give or express my love, I would offer myself in service.

I would also be more considerate of family and friends. I would pay more attention to people. I'd try to keep close to them and express warmth and affection. I'd try more often to send a greeting of good wishes or a note of cheer. I'd be more careful to answer every personal letter promptly, to keep the channels of communication open, and to keep friendships expanding. I'd take the initiative to make more contacts, especially with those acquaintances I value highly.

If I could live my life again, I would travel lighter. I would start barefoot in the spring and play into the fall. I would go to more parties; I would ride the merry-go-rounds. I'd stop to smell the roses.

There is little I can do about the grains of sand that have already passed through the hourglass. But I can live my remaining years as if I had a second chance—as if I could turn back the hands of time.

None of us can catch up with yesterday, but we can walk side by side with today.

News You Can Use

"Like you, I'm still a work in progress. And the next step beyond failure could be your biggest success."
—DEBBIE ALLEN, SINGER, DANCER, AND TV PRODUCER

Tennis great Althea Gibson remarked, "You must first be a believer before you can be an achiever." In other words, believing is everything. Believing you "can't" keeps you blind to the possibility of discovering how you can. A parable illustrates this point:

A man who was unsuccessful in business visited a palm reader purported to have supernatural powers. She gave him a "magic box" and told him if he wrote down on a piece of paper what he wanted to achieve and deposited the paper in the box, his goal would come to pass. He followed her instructions and shortly thereafter formed a partnership to start a new business. It was immensely successful. A year later he went back to the palm reader to thank her for the magic box. She revealed, "There's no magic in the box. *The magic is in believing!*"

The word that could determine your success in life has only three letters—*can*. Can is one of the most powerful words in the English language. Ironically the addition of the letter *t* to the word spells the difference between success and failure. Throughout history achievements have been made in spite of the word *can't*. One hundred years ago who would ever have thought that a black man would lead the most powerful army in the world? *Colin Powell!* Or that a black woman would travel into space? *Dr. Mae Jemison!* Or that a black man would orchestrate the successful presidential campaign of a white southern governor? *Ron Brown!*

Turn a deaf ear to any news of limitation. Turn instead to the positive, to what's possible. This will be news that you can certainly use.

Believe in yourself even when no one else does.

Will You Be Patient?

"It takes twenty-one years to be twenty-one."
——REGGIE JACKSON, BASEBALL HALL-OF-FAMER

An African fable tells of a young boy who traveled many miles to the school of a great and famous warrior. Impressed that the lad had come so far, the master agreed to meet with him.

"What can I do for you?" asked the warrior.

"I wish to be your student and become the finest swordsman in the land," the boy replied. "How long must I study?"

"Ten years at least," replied the master.

"Ten years is a long time," said the boy, somewhat astounded. "What if I were to practice unrelentingly day and night with all my effort?"

"Thirty years," answered his idol.

"How is it that when I say I will work harder, you tell me that it will take longer?" the student asked, quite confused.

"The answer is clear," said the master. "When there is one eye fixed on your destination, there is only one eye left with which to find the way."

Success is a process that requires both our eyes and all our patience. Furthermore, it requires that we let go of our expectations of how the process will work and engage in our task at hand.

Today I will review my goals and exercise patience.

The Light of My Life

*"It's better to look where you are going than to
see where you have been."*
—FLORENCE GRIFFITH-JOYNER, OLYMPIC CHAMPION

Light is one of the most enjoyable, practical, and accessible gifts we have. Light is an idea that has permeated every religion, spiritual practice, and philosophy known to man. In the Bible God saw that the light was good, and he separated the light from the darkness—*"Let there be light."* While imprisoned, Malcolm X read vociferously by pale beams of *moonlight.* Harriet Tubman risked life and limb and led many slaves to freedom on the underground railroad by *candlelight.* Many nights Benjamin Banneker stood motionless, mesmerized by the *starlight* as he dared to chart the constellations. Spirit-filled as she is, Johnnie Colemon *lights the souls* of others with her message of truth and hope. "Off camera I am really shy," confesses singer and dancer Stephanie Mills. "But when the *spotlight* comes on, I become a totally different person." Each day Marva Collins challenges our youth to dream, aspire, and turn on *the light to their imagination.* The multitalented Wynton and Branford Marsalis *light up our lives* with their soulful melodies of jazz. And as an inspired seminary student at North Carolina A & T University, Jesse Jackson *saw the light* and became our voice for reason and justice.

The first thing to remember about light is just that—all we have to do is to be conscious of it. You must simply acknowledge its presence. You must move toward the light. Each moment we make a choice between light and darkness, between good and evil, faith and despair, positive and negative. Why not focus on the positive? Why not turn on the light that already exists?

Today I will spend a few moments in the light of my imagination.

It's Your Choice

*"Stand on your own two black feet and fight like
hell for your place in the world."*
—AMY-JACQUE GARVEY, BLACK NATIONALIST

One of the greatest powers that you possess is the power of
choice. But in order to benefit from this unique gift, you must
choose carefully. Pay close attention to the following tale.

In ancient times there lived a king whose methods of justice
were both loved and feared by his subjects. The king built a
huge court for himself and his people. At the front, he placed
two doors. When the accused was brought before him, the
king gave the person a choice of which door to open. If the accused man chose the right door, a lovely maiden stepped forth
to take his hand in marriage. But if the culprit chose poorly,
he faced a huge and ferocious tiger that would devour him.

As fate would have it, this king had a beautiful daughter
who fell in love with a handsome but poor young man. And
according to legal custom, any common man who dared to lift
his eyes to the princess would face the king in court. Unfortunately her poor suitor was jailed and informed that the next
day he would stand trial and choose his fate. The princess was
heartbroken. She found herself torn between love and jealousy.
She didn't want to see her lover killed before her eyes, yet she
also didn't want to see him in the arms of another.

That evening she dreamed she saw her lover step forth and
open a door. And just at that moment she awoke. Which did
he choose? As the story goes, you must decide. At some point
in your life the choice of the lady or the tiger will surface.
Your outcome will depend totally on your mental state and the
amount of love in your heart.

Choice, not chance, determines my destiny.

Jet Fuel

*"It's not a question of can you succeed; a better
question is will you succeed."*
—GEORGE JOHNSON, ENTREPRENEUR

Our Creator is on the lookout for people he can trust, men and
women worthy to be endowed with the keys to success. Success is prevalent in this world. But you must be tested before
you can wear this prestigious label.

Several years ago the Lockheed L-1011 TriStar airplane was
introduced. To ensure its safety, the firm that developed it began eighteen months of rigorous testing costing in excess of
$1.5 billion. To test the strength of the jetliner, Lockheed ex-
posed the plane to the roughest treatment possible.

Hydraulic jacks, electronic sensors, and a computer put the
airplane through its paces for more than 36,000 simulated
flights. The jetliner underwent five lifetimes of simulated
flight—amounting to more than one hundred years of airline
service—without one single malfunction.

Test pilots flew the plane into icy clouds. They wanted to
check the operation of the anti-ice system and see how the aircraft would respond to ice accretion. Finally, after hundreds of
tests, the aircraft was given the seal of approval. That plane
has been through it! I wouldn't mind flying on it, and I guess
you wouldn't either.

Life is sometimes like that plane, and the testing no less
easy. But when you've been tested and found worthy, you will
be ready for bigger goals and dreams.

The successful are tested within the furnace of adversity.

Enough Is Enough

"It embarrasses me to think of all those years I was buying silk suits and alligator shoes that were hurting my feet; cars that I just parked, and the dust would just build up on 'em."
—GEORGE FOREMAN, FORMER HEAVYWEIGHT CHAMP

Whenever we start talking about needs and wants—and all we really need are food, shelter, and clothing—some people get scared. Images of homeless people dance in their heads. Surely wealth includes a few creature comforts.

Yes, a certain degree of creature comfort seems to belong to any definition of wealth. But how much is enough, and how much is too much? That depends on what we want. As a tool for obtaining and supporting the things we really want, prosperity is fine. When we begin to accumulate belongings to keep up with the Joneses, we might be inviting disaster. When we worship that "strange god" of materialism, we leave the course of our heart's desire.

Thirty years ago an African diplomat visiting the United States for the first time deplaned and walked directly into a large, modern airport terminal. He stood for a while looking around the enormous airport—so different from his native land, he might have been on another planet. He saw a vast assortment of food, drink, magazines, and newspapers. He sat on padded, upholstered furniture. The restrooms were clean and had hot and cold running water. The airport was carpeted, well lit, and air-conditioned.

Even so, he saw passengers rushing by, hurrying to their flights, seemingly not appreciating any of it. "They live in paradise," he observed. "I wonder if they'll ever know."

Knowing the difference between needs and wants is prosperity.

Get Your *But* Out of the Way!

*"Believe in yourself and your abilities. There are
lots of other folks who'll tell you, 'It can't be
done.' "*
—JASMINE GUY, TELEVISION AND FILM STAR

Unfortunately too many people cannot specify what holds
them back. All too frequently they feel there's "something"—
whether it's called hard luck or the "system"—that binds them
to lives of misery and poverty. Some even boast of what great
heights they could reach if only they could sever the cords that
bind them. Surely they could change their lives for the better
if they could remove the shackles—real or imagined—that
chain them to limited lives.

On many occasions I've counseled men and women in a variety of occupations and I've heard all kinds of stories. Very
often people have said to me, "Dr. Kimbro, I want to do this
. . . but." Or, "Dr. Kimbro, I would like to have that . . . but."
Or, "Dr. Kimbro, I could become this . . . but."

One day I got my fill of all these excuses and reasons for
inactivity, and I blurted out, "You know, you could be what
you want to be, do what you want to do, and have what you
want to have, if you would just get your *but* out of the way!"

For the most part we know what we want out of life. Not
only do we know what we want, we know how to get it. Most
of us have concluded that we have the time, the energy, the
skill, and the opportunity. And the only thing standing in the
way of us enjoying whatever we desire is our big excuse. If
you want to achieve more, declare your reasons unacceptable,
your excuses inexcusable—and then get your *but* out of the
way!

**Get rid of the word *but*. It's the difference between success and
failure.**

This Is the Life

"You've got to give to get. And if you don't plan on givin', then you better not plan on gettin'."
—JOE CLARK, FORMER HIGH SCHOOL PRINCIPAL

A man who works five days a week, buys a little food and some liquor for the weekend, and relaxes half drunk in his easy chair, proclaims to his family, "This is the life."

A youth who forsakes his schooling so that he may work full-time to buy a fancy car and experience life in the fast lane declares to his buddies, "This is the life."

A young woman who views life from the outside in, who compromises her principles and lives in a world of loose money and fast-talking men, flashes her bejeweled hands and designer clothes in front of her girlfriends' eyes, and claims, "This is the life."

The middle-class couple who move into their split-level, ranch-style home and spend all their time chasing cheap thrills and momentary highs, from infidelity to drugs, proclaim over cocktails, "This is the life."

I sincerely wonder if "this is the life" of which the Master spoke. Can life be lived—*really lived*—apart from some task, some duty, some great purpose that strengthens the soul and glorifies the Creator? Is a person really living when he or she has no purpose in life other than eating, drinking, wearing the latest clothing, and being seen with the "right" people?

A wise man said, "We live in deeds, not years; in thoughts, not breaths; in feelings, not in figures on a dial." Character cannot be purchased, bargained for, or inherited. It must be homegrown.

It's never too late to start living a new life.

Body Language

"It takes more than just a good-looking body.
You've got to have the heart and soul to go with it."
—LEE HANEY, MR. OLYMPIA

Psychologists agree that most poverty-stricken people maintain a poverty consciousness. They think in terms of poverty, they fear poverty, they talk poverty, and prophetically they receive poverty in abundance. However, each of us has been given the power to affect the odds in our favor.

For example, a number of years ago a haggard-looking, beaten old man entered the parlor of a fortune-teller. Without a formal introduction the tattered stranger explained to the prophet that a mutual friend recommended he pay her a visit with the ultimate hope of turning his life around. He went on to say he had decided to end his life if he failed to get help.

From all outward appearances the stranger was a failure. He had the dull stare of defeat in his eyes and the drooping shoulders of a man worn down by life. Yet someone had recognized some degree of worth in him to send him to this woman. She pondered what to do for him.

A full-length mirror, which was concealed by drapes, stood in the rear of her parlor. The downhearted visitor was asked to stand in front of the curtain while he was introduced to someone who might be able to help him regain his self-confidence. After building up to a dramatic climax the woman pulled the drapes apart. The dejected old man stared at himself in the mirror. He gazed at his own image, stunned and speechless. After a lengthy scrutiny he realized the answer to his problem. With sincere thanks, he hugged the fortune-teller and went his way.

I can only rise and achieve to the level of my self-concept.

Hallelujah! Free at Last

"This colored people going to be a people."
—SOJOURNER TRUTH, ABOLITIONIST AND PREACHER

"It" never happened to Richard Allen, a preacher from Philadelphia. Nor did "it" happen to Phillis Wheatley, America's first black poet, though she cried many nights for it. And "it" certainly didn't happen to Denmark Vesey, Toussaint L'Ouverture, Crispus Attucks, or Nat Turner—heroic men who gave their lives in the hope that one day they would see "it."

But "it" did happen to Booker T. Washington, a nine-year-old slave on a Virginia plantation. It was a time to rejoice. "It" did happen to Frederick Douglass, a former slave and a grown man in his late forties. He called it the major event in his life. In her autumn years "it" happened to Sojourner Truth, who immediately wrote a letter to President Lincoln expressing the need to allow women's suffrage. "It" happened to John Russwurm, Black America's first college graduate and an abolitionist who migrated to Liberia. When this scholar received the news in West Africa, he immediately sank to his knees and cried, "Thank you, Father." "It" happened to my great-grandfather, a butler from North Carolina. And "it" also happened to Martin Delany, Henry Highland Garnet, Mary Elizabeth Bowser, and Rebecca T. Cole, men and women of distinction and valor. What is "it?"

"It" is freedom. The freedom to be, to have, to do, to hope, to work, to choose, to soar, to dream whatever you wish. Ours may not be a perfect society, but it is the freest nation on earth. This is the environment in which each of us finds ourself. We all stand on broad shoulders—men and women who have gone before us. We owe it to them and to ourselves not to take this freedom for granted.

I will treat freedom with the respect to which it is entitled.

Health Care

"I did it through persistence, dedication and hard work. You've got to find something you can apply your heart and soul to. People will say, 'No way' ... but as long as you're persistent and determined, no one can stop you."
—MATTY RICH, FILMMAKER

Mike Wilson was told he was dying of an incurable disease that he couldn't even pronounce. Consequently he threw in the towel and started acting as if his life was over. He quit his job, ruled out marriage, drank heavily, and turned into a hermit. He was waiting to die, but he might as well have been dead already. Mike's life was empty, even though he wasn't dead—as a matter of fact *he wasn't even dying*.

Nearly five years after the initial diagnosis, another checkup revealed that Mike didn't have the terminal disease. Given this second chance, he has since married and bought a home. Today he feels great.

Nothing had changed except Mike's *attitude*. When he thought he was dying, he set a course for self-destruction. But when he learned he wasn't a victim of a rare illness, he set a course for living and fulfillment. The tragedy is that happiness and success were always within his reach. Mike simply stopped looking for them.

You possess these qualities too. Don't allow your epitaph to read, BORN 1950, DIED 1990, BURIED 2020. *Whatever happens, be sure to live life to its fullest every day!*

Life is God's gift to me; I will cherish every precious moment.

The Difference Between Handicapped and Disabled

"Disabilities can sometimes be definitions. You can think of yourself in terms of what you can't do and never realize the possibilities of what you can do."
—BONNIE ST. JOHN, ATHLETE AND SCHOLAR

For an accomplished world-class skier, winning three Olympic medals is pretty good. For Bonnie St. John it's astounding. Most Olympic skiers first hit the slopes at the age of five and secure the financial backing necessary to support the training it takes to become a winner. Not only did Bonnie have a late start—when a friend took her on a ski trip at age fifteen—but she also didn't have a dime of support to polish her skills.

If testing the limits of the ski slopes seems like the ultimate challenge, it's actually been only one phase of her life. While training for the Olympics, Bonnie transferred to Harvard University, where she maintained a straight-A average. For her classroom excellence she was rewarded with a Rhodes Scholarship, during which she completed the coursework for a Ph.D. in economics.

Bill Demby's accomplishments are no less heroic. A decorated Vietnam veteran, the charismatic Demby is one of the nation's most sought-after motivational speakers. Since 1989 his face has been seen by millions on a television commercial depicting his basketball skills. A onetime high school phenomenon, Demby gave up the hard court for the business world. Through ads and special appearances he now represents Du Pont Chemicals, one of the top firms in the nation.

I could stop the story at this point, but I'm just getting started—and so are Bonnie and Bill. You see, *both are disabled*. Bonnie was nearly six when her right leg was amputated. Bill lost both of his legs to a Viet Cong rocket inside the steamy jungles of Vietnam. Both continue to surge forward, never stopping to count the cost. They choose to focus *on what they have*, determined to use it to the fullest.

Disabled is a physical challenge; handicapped is a state of mind. Remove your mental crutches.

You Can Say That Again

"Some things are better left not said."
—BERNARD SHAW, NEWS ANCHOR

Several years ago a scientist working with two nomadic tribes noticed that not one of the natives stuttered. Being a scientist, he wondered if this was a coincidence or if it was characteristic of this particular tribe. His interest and curiosity led him to study other tribes throughout this land. He didn't find a single native who stuttered, so he studied their numerous languages and discovered why they didn't. They didn't have a word, or even a synonym, for the word *stutter*.

Obviously if there isn't a word for "stutter," it would be impossible for anyone to stutter. Scholars tell us that words paint pictures in our minds. For example, if you read or hear the words *fail*, *can't* or *poverty*, your mind completes the pictures that have been painted by the word. But if you don't have a word for stutter, the mind cannot visualize or paint a picture of a stutter. The result: no stuttering.

I'm convinced you can enhance your self-esteem and change your life by altering your vocabulary. Take the word *poor* and remove it from your vocabulary. Write, feel, and dream the word *prosperity* in its place. Scratch the word *hate*. Don't see it, think it, or say it. Instead write the word *love*. Obviously the list of words to be removed and added is endless—as will be the benefits that follow.

I will watch what I say and how I say it.

Accounts Receivable

"We make a living by what we get, but we make a life by what we give."
—BARBARA HARRIS, FIRST AFRICAN-AMERICAN FEMALE PROTESTANT EPISCOPAL BISHOP

Many people encounter troubles because they demand that life be handed to them on a silver platter.

Do you feel that the world owes you a living, that life should fulfill your desires and needs? The truth of the matter is that all you could ever need has already been provided for you. There is no reason for anyone to sit back and complain that the world has deprived him of his due. As long as we acknowledge the one source behind the universe and realize that within it rests the possibility of all good things, then we understand that everything has already been given to us.

Life owes you nothing, but you are eternally in debt to life. Only you can withhold yourself from life. You are only able to receive to the extent that you are able to give. And what do you have to give? For starters you are alive, an expression of the one source. You can in turn give life to others. By your beliefs, words, and actions you can lift the lives and spirits of those you meet. There is no limit to the number of hearts you can touch. Life has been given to you. Now it's up to you to do something with your life. Experience your good by giving a part of yourself away.

The world owes me nothing; I am in debt to life.

Don't Look a Gift Horse in the Mouth

"You have to keep your mind on what is truly most important—your work."

—SUZANNE DE PASSE, PRESIDENT, GORDY/DE PASSE PRODUCTIONS

Maintaining the right outlook on life can be a bridge over troubled water. The story of an old man who had many possessions explains this idea. This man had a beloved son, a prized horse, and many valuable gifts. But one day his horse broke out of the corral and ran away. In one catastrophic moment he lost one of his most cherished gifts.

Upon hearing of his grievous loss, neighbors offered their sympathy. "Your horse is gone—what bad luck," they said. Each attempted to console him. But he answered, "How do you know it's bad luck?" Sure enough a few days later the horse returned home and brought twelve beautiful wild stallions with it. When the townspeople heard the good news, they congratulated the man, saying, "What good luck, thirteen horses!" And the wise old man replied, "How do you know it's good luck?"

They remembered his words the next day when his son, his only child, was thrown from one of the wild stallions, breaking his leg in the process and leaving him with a permanent limp. When his neighbors got the news, they said, "Your son, a cripple—what bad luck." But again, he countered, "How do you know it's bad luck?"

One year later a warlord came to town, taking every able-bodied young man off to battle. The war was lost, and all the warriors were killed. The only young man left in the village was the old man's crippled son, for he had not been drafted due to his handicap.

What's the meaning of this message? Regardless how circumstances appear on the outside, life goes on.

Regardless of outside conditions or circumstances I will stay fixed on my goal and expect the best.

Please Forgive Me

"People with clenched fists cannot shake hands."
—RALPH BUNCHE, FORMER SECRETARY-GENERAL,
UNITED NATONS

The decision to forgive yourself or someone else is a vote to live in the present moment.

"I'll never forgive him for that!" "How can I forgive myself?"—Are these familiar expressions? If we refuse to forgive others, then we are really saying, "Instead of taking action to improve matters, I prefer to live in the past and blame someone else." When we won't forgive ourselves, we are actually choosing to stay on a guilt trip that only leads to mental anguish.

Some people don't understand this idea of forgiveness. They believe that forgiveness is a one-way street. If they have been hurt or wronged, they believe it is the duty of the other party to offer forgiveness. Usually these individuals withhold their forgiveness until someone apologizes. But anytime we withhold forgiveness, *we* suffer! Half the time the "guilty" person doesn't even know he hurt us and continues to breeze happily through life while we put ourselves through unnecessary torture.

When we choose to forgive, a marvelous principle comes into play. As we change, others change. As we become open and receptive, others respond to us in kind. Somehow the moment we say, "I forgive you," we release others and we are released in the process.

I now release all those who have hurt or offended me. I forgive them completely.

Don't Believe the Hype

"Being successful is not black power. Success means having a place in the sun."
—HERMAN J. RUSSELL, ENTREPRENEUR

Television and other seductive media program us to believe that success includes the following: wealth, vast material possessions, instant name recognition, and a carefree life. Unfortunately this is a mythical standard of success. We need only look at the preoccupation with material wealth to realize that we are in real danger. We cannot buy success, wear it, drive it, live in it, or travel to it. Success is rooted in the inner life, the being and living of life—not the outer trappings.

Three executives were sitting around trying to nail down a definition of the word *success*. One of them said, "Success is being invited to the White House for a talk with the President." Another executive said, "Success is being invited to the White House for a meeting with the President, and when the phone interrupts the conversation, the President doesn't answer it."

The third executive chimed in. "You guys are way off base. Success is being invited to the White House for a meeting with the President, and when the phone rings, he answers, listens for a moment, and then says, 'Here, it's for you!' "

What good are fame and fortune if we miss the really valuable things in life such as love, family, friends, and health, to name only a few? As one well-to-do invalid was heard to say, "There is nothing special about using a gold bedpan. I'd trade all my wealth for two more healthy years of life." Success is a worthy goal to pursue, but let us be concerned, first and foremost, with peace of mind.

Success is knowing that one other human being has breathed easier because you lived.

Roll, Jordan, Roll

*"There's no free lunch. Don't feel entitled to
anything you don't sweat and struggle for."*
—MARIAN WRIGHT EDELMAN, FOUNDER, CHILDREN'S DEFENSE FUND

The people with the strongest self-esteem are those who have learned to stand on their own two feet. They are willing to pass up the fun-for-the-moment and select a course that pays off in the long run. All of us yearn to be free, and our greatest opportunity for freedom is through self-reliance. The eminent historian Dr. Carter G. Woodson expressed it best:

> When you determine what a man shall think, you do not have to concern yourself about what he will do. If you make a man feel inferior, you do not have to compel him to accept an inferior status, for he will seek it himself. If you make a man think he is justly an outcast, you do not have to order him to the back door; he will go there without being told. And, if there is no back door, his very nature will demand one.

At the same time those who maintain a positive self-image tend to be genuinely helpful to others. In fact the two tendencies blend so well that it is hard to tell which produces the other. For example, there are two seas in the Mideast. The Sea of Galilee takes in fresh water, uses it to support much-needed marine life, and then empties it in the Jordan River. The Jordan River in turn spreads this marine life throughout the desert, turning it into a fertile plain. While the Sea of Galilee bustles with life, the Dead Sea is exactly that—a *dead sea*. Its water is so full of salt that it cannot sustain life. Why? It takes in water from the Jordan River and hangs on to it. It has no outlet.

What a perfect picture of the differences in people! Those who "get all they can" tend to become self-centered and afraid that someone will steal from them. But those who give freely of themselves usually end up having more than they can give away.

Don't give until it hurts, but give until it feels good.

The Day Your Life Turned Around

"Most of us measure our success by what others haven't done."
—TINA TURNER, SINGER

Decide, once and for all, that you will be the best you can be in whatever you set out to do. George Johnson, founder of Johnson Products and one of Black America's wealthiest individuals, once offered these comments to a local business group:

"Be the best that you can be. Have faith in yourself. Be a person of worth and know it. Believe in yourself. Hold in your consciousness a vision of the life you desire. Move through each day with a vision of yourself as strong, yet loving—flexible, yet in charge. Act as though failing was impossible. Within you are limitless possibilities waiting for birth. Go ahead, give life to them."

Choose to see yourself, as well as mankind, as the creative expression of a loving God. The Book of Genesis says the Creator, the sovereign of the universe, breathed into our nostrils and gave us life. In other words each of us contains a part of the divine. Only when we are committed to excellence can we begin to measure up to all that we were created to be. Only when we see mankind as the product of a Supreme Being can we explain those thousands of daily strivings that urge us to live up to the best within us.

If you want the kind of happiness and deep personal satisfaction out of life that no one can destroy, search until you find what you do best. Consider who you are. You were born for greatness.

Make a strong commitment to reach your full potential.

It's Hammer Time!

"I don't care how many times you hear the word no. You ain't gonna give up. Either live North or die!"

—HARRIET TUBMAN, CONDUCTOR,
UNDERGROUND RAILROAD

The idea of taking one day at a time may seem very narrow. However, never underestimate the cumulative effect of the days that we live. Take, for example, a single penny. If you see a penny lying on the sidewalk, you hardly feel it's worth the effort to bend over and pick it up. But suppose you began to double that penny each day for a month. At the end of a week you would have only sixty-four pennies. That's not very impressive—but at the end of a month you would have 536,870,912 pennies; or $5,368,709.12—*more than five million dollars*!

One moment may not seem important in one day, but as we begin to multiply those moments, it's astounding how many we would have in a month. My little calculator doesn't have the capacity to tell me how many moments we have in a year, and it is utterly beyond my imagination to think about how many moments could be accrued in a lifetime.

Watch a stonecutter bang away at the stone with his hammer and wedge. He might hit the stone a hundred times with no apparent effect, but on the hundred and first blow, the stone cracks. The point is, the hundred and first lick did not crack the stone itself; it was the cumulative effect of the hundred blows *before* that brought the results.

That is the way our moments and days work. Sometimes it seems we're making little progress; sometimes it seems all of our efforts are useless, but we keep trying; we struggle without giving up. Then one day the victory we have sought belongs to us. *It was not that final effort—it was all the effort that went before.*

Like the stonecutter, I will hammer my way through to success.

A Soldier's Story

"Don't be upset if your dreams don't come true. It could be the best thing that ever happened to you."
—SHARI BELAFONTE, ACTRESS

An old man who had been beaten and robbed on an old country road was rescued by three soldiers. In an effort to show his appreciation he granted each soldier one wish. "Before you decide," he counseled, "be very cautious. You'll only get one wish."

The first soldier, who was poor, requested riches. By the time he got the words out of his mouth a trunkful of treasures appeared at his feet. The soldier thanked the old man and headed for home with his newfound wealth. As the old man closed his eyes, he saw that the soldier would have many friends and the best that money could buy. But he could also see that one day the soldier's riches would run out, leaving him both penniless and without friends.

The second soldier was very ugly. He desired good looks. As soon as he made his wish, the soldier felt his face change—he had indeed become handsome. He, too, thanked the old man and left for home to show everyone his new face. As the old man closed his eyes, he saw that the soldier would live happily and would be quite popular. But he could also see the day when the soldier would grow older and his looks would vanish. Not only would he lose his friends, but he would be ugly again.

The third soldier was both poor and ugly. He also made his wish, sincerely thanked the old man, and went home. As he left, the old man closed his eyes and saw that this soldier would remain poor and ugly all his life. But he would live in peace, for his wish was simply to be happy with whatever he had.

Today I will no long search for happiness. Happiness can never be found, because it was never lost. Happiness is within me.

Try This On for Size

"People may doubt what you say, but they will always believe what you do."
—NANNIE HELEN BURROUGHS, EDUCATOR AND CIVIL RIGHTS ACTIVIST

Many of us languish under a consciousness of "I'll try." Just two little words; so enabling, yet so inhibiting.

Trying is usually an excuse for not doing. It is a concept employed to justify self-defeat. For example, have you ever "tried" to sleep at night? If you did, you awoke the next morning groggy and listless. Have you ever "tried" to lose weight? If so, the only thing that you probably lost was time. Just "try" to quit smoking. So many smokers do as they light up another cigarette. "Trying to quit" means you're still smoking and working like hell not to. If you "try" to do something, you're expending a great deal of energy on activity, not accomplishment. And accomplishment is the bottom line.

In the real world there are no A's for effort, only for results. If you doubt me, just "try" to sit down—either you do or you don't. I know many college dropouts who "tried" to complete their degrees. Remember, the world will judge you—not "try" to judge you—by your actions, not your intentions.

I will do, not just try.

If I Be Lifted Up

"The only justification for ever looking down on somebody is to pick them up."
—JESSE JACKSON, FOUNDER, THE RAINBOW COALITION

A woman had taken her five-year-old son shopping at a large department store during the Christmas holidays. She knew he would like to see all the decorations, window displays, toys, and of course Santa Claus. As she dragged him by the hand, twice as fast as his little legs would move, he began to fuss and cry, clinging to his mother's coat. "Good heavens, what on earth is the matter with you?" she asked impatiently. "I brought you with me to get into the Christmas spirit. Santa doesn't bring toys to little crybabies."

His fussing continued as she tried to find some bargains during the last-minute holiday rush. "I'm not going to take you shopping with me ever again if you don't stop whimpering," she warned. After she got through with her verbal tirade, she looked down and noticed the boy's shoes.

"No wonder you're upset—your shoes are untied." She knelt down in the aisle to tie his shoes. "You've probably been tripping over your laces all morning." As she knelt down beside him, she happened to look up. For the first time she viewed a large department store through the eyes of her five-year-old son. From that position there were no toys, no treats, no gifts or gaily-decorated tables. All that could be seen from his limited position was a maze of corridors and towering adults, all pushing and shoving, bumping and rushing throughout the store. To the tiny child the scene looked absolutely terrifying. She took her son home and vowed never to impose her version of a good time on him again.

So many petty disagreements could be avoided if we would only look at circumstances from the other person's perspective.

In judging others I will see with my heart as well as with my eyes.

Are You Expecting Someone?

*"It's better to be prepared for an opportunity and
not have one, than to have an opportunity and not
be prepared."*
—WHITNEY YOUNG, FOUNDER, NATIONAL URBAN LEAGUE

Remember what a flurry of activity the phrase *company's coming* used to create? I imagine this scenario was played out in every home across the country. At our house my mother started directing traffic as soon as she caught wind of guests arriving: "Pick up those papers, put your junk in your room, straighten out the sofa, vacuum the carpet, and run to the store to pick up something sweet."

It was a different story if she received a little advance notice. Usually the extent to which preparations were made was in direct proportion to the distance the company was traveling. Walls were washed, windows and blinds cleaned, furniture polished, carpets shampooed, and fine silverware and china cleaned and inspected. My mother left no stone unturned; nothing escaped her eagle eye. She directed each assignment with the finesse of a great conductor before a sold-out symphony crowd.

At last the long-awaited company would arrive. My mother would run to the door outfitted in her apron with a smile as shiny as the spotless house behind her. If I wasn't sitting at my father's knee, I could be found playing with my brother. Both of us had been warned by you-know-who to be on our best behavior.

For most of us our lives mirror a "guess who's coming to dinner" attitude. Hustling, bustling, always engaged in a flurry of last-minute activity. There's nothing wrong with getting the job done, but do we need to do everything at the last minute? In the long run, wouldn't it be better to do a little something every day than to throw yourself into a last-minute tailspin as you attempt to put your best foot forward?

Today I will write a "to do" list and complete my number-one task.

Don't Leave Me Hanging

"A world without dreams and hopes is no world at all."
—ARETHA FRANKLIN, SINGER

One day a wishing well in the center of a shopping mall captured the attention of three small children—two boys and a girl. As they leaned over a guardrail, the shimmering coins in the bottom of the water caught their eye.

"Wow, look at all that money!" one exclaimed. "There must be at least a hundred dollars down there."

"Looks like it's closer to a million," his tiny companion blurted out. "I'll bet we could get some."

"Oh, yeah? How?"

"We can make a chain—we can hang on to each other. I'll hold your feet, and you can grab her feet, and she could lean over and scoop up some of the dimes and nickels."

The little girl's face clouded over. She seemed very unhappy about their plans. As one of the boys began to climb over the retainer, she tugged on his shirt and cried out, "Oh, no, you can't do it! Don't you know you'll steal the dreams and wishes of all the people who threw money?"

How often have we sat innocently by and seen friends and family steal the dreams of others? Through words of doubt or negative thoughts we participated in a crime. Do your friends a favor, believe in their dreams.

Today I will call a friend and share their hopes and dreams.

Rhythm Nation

"Not all black people can sing and dance."
—NIARA SUDARKASA, PRESIDENT, LINCOLN UNIVERSITY

Most people approach life like a TV game show: they spin the wheel, try their luck, and hopefully reach their goal. Playing the "wheel of fortune" is both senseless and a waste of time. Though we cannot control what happens to us, what others do to us, or where we start in the race of life, we can control our reactions to experiences. We can allow circumstances to bury us, or we can choose to rise above them.

Hattie McDaniel, the first African American to capture an Oscar, told an aspiring black actress, "You cannot control the length of your life, but you can certainly control what you do and what you accomplish."

Many people feel that they have little control of their lives. They work for a boss who is a tyrant, they live with a domineering mate, or they feel their finances place heavy restrictions upon them. It's true that we have little influence over many things. However, it is also true that we have the control to change the course of our lives.

Sometimes, as you set out to seize your destiny, it seems as if everything around you is conspiring to keep you from reaching your goal. But there is a certain rhythm and harmony to life. The secret is to pick up on that rhythm and harmony and take advantage of the momentum it provides.

I will open myself to the divine flow of life.

I Am Somebody!

*"I'm articulate. I'm thoughtful. I care about my
work and my standards are very high."*
—AVERY BROOKS, ACTOR

I may never be an artist like Romare Bearden or Margaret Taylor Burroughs, but I've painted the interiors of several homes that I'm proud of. You and I may not be the king or queen of a royal court, but we are special in our own right. Wouldn't it be wonderful if everybody felt special?

Of all the judgments we pass in life, none is as important as the one we pass on ourselves. How we feel about ourselves affects every aspect of our lives, from the way we function at work, to the way we operate as parents, to how high in life we rise.

"How few people realize," wrote the historian Charles Wesley, "their success in life depends more upon what they are than upon what they know. It is self-esteem that has brought the race this far." Marcus Garvey concurred. He said, "The man who lacks self-esteem won't possess anything else." And supermodel Beverly Johnson drives home the same message. She says, "Youth and beauty may fade, but esteem always endures."

Our responses to the circumstances in our lives are shaped by who and what we think we are. The higher our self-esteem, the more inclined we are to treat others with respect and goodwill. The more positive our self-esteem, the more joy we experience. Self-esteem holds the key to understanding ourselves and other people. Positive self-esteem is a cardinal requirement of a fulfilling life.

Today I will take a few moments to list my qualities and strengths. I am special!

The Night Shift

"Black folks need to blow out the dim lamp of poverty and turn on the beacon light of hope."
—T.J. JEMISON, PRESIDENT,
NATIONAL BAPTIST CONVENTION

Some years ago, on returning from a business trip, a man brought his wife some souvenirs. Among them was a matchbox that would glow in the dark. After giving it to her, he turned out the light, but the object was not visible.

"This must be a joke!" she said. Disappointed, the husband commented, "I've been cheated!" Then his wife noticed a few words written in French on the bottom of the box. Taking it to a friend who knew the language, she was told that the directions read, "If you want me to shine at night, keep me in the sunlight during the day." So she placed her gift in her bedroom window. That evening when she turned out the light, the matchbox had a brilliant glow. Her surprised husband asked, "What did you do?"

"Oh, I found the secret," she replied. "Before it can shine at night, it must be exposed to the light."

This tale has a deeper meaning. Before you can shine in all types of circumstances—before you can reach your full potential—you must be exposed to the light: *You must place yourself in situations where opportunity is possible.* How do you ask the sun for sunlight? By getting out into the sun. How do you ask electricity for light for your lamp? By turning on the switch. How do you ask the Creator for what you want? By placing yourself in the Divine flow. All light, all power, all energy, flows to the individual who places himself or herself in situations where opportunities are possible.

I will make it a point to walk in the light.

Can't Touch This!

"Wake up. The hour has come to be more responsible. Change this world by starting with yourself. The world is not going to change until you change."

—DR. BETTY SHABAZZ, EDUCATOR AND WIDOW OF
MALCOLM X

I receive many letters from men and women across the nation who say they want to be successful but don't know how. They've tried following all sorts of involved principles, yet they only need one. The following story provided a clue.

There is an African ritual that is used as a rite of passage for males bridging from youth to adulthood. The young boys of the village are instructed to find the most valuable thing in the world and to return to show it to the elders.

One young enthusiast raced for the snow-capped mountains of Mount Kilimanjaro, which fascinated him immensely. He climbed higher and higher, up through the hinterland, to experience the feel of snow for the first time. There, among the clouds and frozen turf, he plunged his hand into the stinging coldness and clutched a handful of snow in its marvelous purity. With his hand held tightly closed, he raced back to the village. The villagers were assembled as the elders inspected the eye-catching treasures the other youths had discovered: jewels, silks, and various wonders of nature.

Suddenly the young boy broke into their midst. "What have you brought us?" they asked excitedly.

"See!" he cried triumphantly, as he opened his hand. But his hand was empty. The villagers saw nothing. Only the young boy knew the meaning of what had happened.

"The most valuable thing in the world," he said, *"cannot be held by the human hand. It's an idea!"*

Today I will begin to list all my ideas and set a timetable for putting at least one into action.

Ghosts of the Past

"I'm ready to close this chapter of my life."
—BILLIE HOLIDAY, JAZZ SINGER

Life moves on inexorably. Much as you might want to relive the past, to recapture a rare moment of delight, you cannot do it. You can recall the memories of past moments of glory, but you can never relive them. You can revisit scenes of your childhood, but you cannot reexperience bygone days. The aura has changed. There are no voices to hear, no old associations to relive. Everything is different. You are looking back through the haze of memory. Satchel Paige, the great pitcher from the historic Negro Leagues quipped, "Don't look back, someone could be gaining on you."

You can't go backward. Life is a forward impulse; the past is gone. You can only live in the here and now. But there are compulsive people who insist on looking backward. Rigid, attempting to stay within boundaries as though wearing blinders, they look to a past that cannot be relived or experienced again. They fail to understand that, at best, all they can do is react emotionally or intellectually to the past. They can never turn back the clock.

Living in the past means clinging to nonproductive attitudes and remaining in situations that hinder your personal growth and development. Take an honest inventory of yourself. Be frank in your appraisal. Are you hanging on to relationships that aren't rewarding? Do you become involved with people or circumstances that drag you down? Do you find yourself thinking about the way things might have been? If so, then you are living in the past.

Today is a day of renewal. I will finally release those negative experiences in my past. They will no longer hold me back.

Better Homes and Gardens

*"There is only one source—the spirit of God.
There's no need to search any further."*
—BARBARA KING, PASTOR, HILLSIDE INTERNATIONAL
TRUTH CENTER

Philosophers, wise men, and poets are nearly unanimous in their conclusion that the ultimate goal of life is to be happy. Yet happiness, for most of humanity, is a butterfly that, when pursued, is always just beyond our grasp. Why? What is there about happiness, which is free to all, that makes it so rare?

Success and happiness are often coupled as goals, as if the attainment of the first automatically guarantees the second. Not so. All of us know successful individuals who are miserable. I know a man who thought he would be happy if he accumulated $100,000 by his fortieth birthday. This he did, rather easily. He then set a goal to become a millionaire several years later. This he did also. Was he happy? Not in the least. He couldn't rest; he wanted more and more. It seems as if we are all seeking better food, better clothing, better cars, better homes and gardens.

Perhaps the ultimate purpose of life itself is the testing of the human spirit, to develop it into something better. The ultimate success of the individual, then, is not to be found in the material results of his labors, for entire civilizations have been buried in the sands and dust of antiquity chasing this elusive goal. Success can only be found in the human spirit itself. Each of us has been entrusted with a fragment of that human essence, to spark our own existence from birth to death. *It's not what you have in your wallet that makes you special, it's what you have in your heart.*

You will be rich when you enrich the life spirit within you.

A Command Performance

"We can't all be great, but we can attach ourselves to great causes."
—CAMILLE COSBY, PHILANTHROPIST

It's amazing how an actor will perform at his peak when he knows an important person is in the audience. More than one athlete has knocked himself out because he knew that his family was sitting in the stands.

There's a story of a college football player who was comfortable playing for the second string. Yet his father never missed a game. After his father's death the son, with tears in his eyes, approached his coach and said, "Please let me start tonight. I want to play for my dad."

The coach, knowing that the boy's father had never missed a game, agreed. The young man's performance on the field was outstanding. When asked to explain his phenomenal play, he said, "Coach, I played this game for my dad. My father never missed a game, but he never saw me play—until tonight! You see, my father was blind."

With a similar type of emotion how much better could you perform in the game of life? Our Creator is in a front-row seat watching your performance. He is applauding the moment you move into the scene. *What previously untapped levels of energy, creativity, and accomplishment will you reveal?*

I admit I can do more than I have done. Today I will operate at my peak level.

Field of Dreams

"A person never knows what he can do until he does it."
—GORDON PARKS, SR., FILMMAKER

In his book *The Heart of a Champion* Bob Richards tells the story of Olympic champion Charley Paddock. While speaking before a group of students in Cleveland, Ohio, Paddock challenged the audience to think big. "If you think you can, you can," he coached. "If you believe a thing strongly enough, it can come to pass in your life!" Before Paddock concluded his remarks, he lifted his hand and said, "Who knows, there may be an Olympic champion sitting among us." No sooner did he utter those words than a spindly-legged child approached him.

"Mr. Paddock," he said excitedly, "I would give anything if I could be an Olympian just like you." It was the boy's hour of inspiration. From that moment on his life would change. In 1936 the skinny kid traveled to Berlin and turned in four electrifying performances capturing gold medals in the process. His name: Jesse Owens.

During a victory tour through the streets of Cleveland, Owens stopped to sign autographs. A tiny child pressed against his car, looked his idol in the face, and said, "Gee, Mr. Owens, I'd give anything if I could be an Olympic champion just like you." Jesse reached out and replied, "You know, young man, that's what I wanted to be when I was a little older than you. If you will work and train and *believe*, then one day you'll hit your goals."

Twelve years later, at Wembley Stadium in London, England, six sprinters exploded out of the blocks in the 100-meter-dash finals. The sprinter in the outside lane burst into the open, drove down, and broke the tape first. His name: Harrison "Bones" Dillard. You say that's a coincidence? You say that it will never happen again? *You're wrong.* It will happen again and again to the person who captures a vision and backs it with action.

I believe, I act, and I will succeed.

Family Feud

"We will band together and survive or live apart and die as fools."
—SUSAN TAYLOR, EDITOR-IN-CHIEF, *ESSENCE* MAGAZINE

An African prince had four sons who constantly bickered with each other. Their father often told them how much easier life would be if only they could learn to cooperate.

One day in his frustration the prince sent his sons into the fields to find a piece of wood. When his sons returned with the wood, the father tied the four sticks into a bundle and asked the oldest to break it. Try as he might, the boy couldn't break the tightly bound bundle of wood. His father then untied the string and separated the sticks. "Now try," he ordered the boy as his brothers looked on. The lad broke each stick with the greatest of ease. "Do you all see my point?" he asked. "It is the same with you. If you stand together, nothing can defeat you, but if you remain divided, you will become vulnerable."

As we continue to march toward full participation for the American dream, Black America could benefit from such a message. In our zeal to grab a collective slice of the pie called opportunity, many within the ranks have taken a less-than-unified approach. Though other groups ventured to these shores under various flags, ours is the only ethnicity that shares a common history, landmass, and destiny. And make no mistake about it—wherever and in whatever conditions you may find us—we, Black Americans, *are all in the same boat*. No matter our individual background and preferences—some of us are rich, while others are poor—*we're all in the same boat*. Regardless of the level of education—some may have attended Morehouse, while others went to "no house"—*we're all in the same boat*. Whereas some may tout impressive qualifications, boasting a Ph.D., J.D., M.B.A., M.A., D.D.S., or B.S., while others slide by with "any ol' mess"—*we're all in the same boat*!

Samuel L. Gravely, America's first black admiral, once

commented on the benefits of teamwork and unity. Admiral Gravely said, "The boat won't go if we all don't row."

No one lives on an island. We could all benefit from the cooperation of others.

Let's Do Lunch

"What you see is what you get."
—FLIP WILSON, COMEDIAN AND ENTERTAINER

Do you believe in fate? Do you believe that you are a pawn in the game of life, doomed to failure no matter what you do? Are you dissatisfied with the conditions in your life, but convinced there is nothing that you can do about them? This type of thinking reminds me of the story of two construction workers, Tom and Dave, who ate lunch together every day. Each day at the stroke of twelve they sat in shade of the building project and opened their lunch boxes.

On Monday Tom carefully unwrapped his sandwich. Picking up the top layer of bread, he peeked inside. "Peanut butter again!" he said with a look of disgust. Dave continued to eat without uttering a word.

On Tuesday Tom again examined his sandwich and with even greater annoyance exclaimed, "No, not peanut butter again!" Again Dave refrained from comment as Tom went ahead and ate his lunch.

On Wednesday, when the same routine was repeated, Dave could no longer keep silent. "If you don't like peanut butter, why don't you tell your wife?" he said.

"Now, listen," replied Tom, "you leave my wife out of this. I make my own sandwiches!" I wonder how many of us are putting up with something that annoys us, thinking that we have no control over it. What kind of "sandwiches" are you making for yourself?

You are not at the mercy of fate. You can control your life.

The Fish That Got Away

"I never forget who I am. If I give up, who is going to do it, as far as minorities and women are concerned?"
—PHYLLIS TUCKER VINSON, TELEVISION PRODUCER

True prosperity is an awareness of the abundance of life. To *prosper* means "to flourish; to succeed; to thrive; to experience good or favorable results." Your measure of prosperity is particular to you. Therefore to prosper does not necessarily mean to possess a great fortune, although earning large sums of money can well be one of the by-products of a prosperity consciousness. True prosperity is infinite. It starts with an inner dominion that causes one to prosper at every level of his experience. It includes right mental attitude and complete fulfillment. The law of wealth could care less who you are, what your background is, or your race or gender. It works entirely through consciousness.

For example, two weekend fishermen sat in a boat with their lines cast in the water. For the third time one of the men took a large rainbow trout off his hook and threw it back into the lake. With the next cast he caught a tiny flounder no bigger than his index finger. With a broad smile he took it off the hook and stuck it in his basket. His fishing buddy said, "You caught three nice trout and threw them all back, but now you keep this tiny fish not much larger than a sardine. I don't understand it. What's going on?"

"I've got a small frying pan," he replied.

This story points up a great truth. Too many of us continually sell ourselves short because we have a small evaluation of our capabilities, of our own self-worth, of how much we could earn in our lifetimes. *How many wealth-creating opportunities have you thrown back into the water because you did not believe yourself worthy?*

Society takes us at our own value. We are worth only what we think we're worth.

So What?

"Honey, eighty percent of the people could care less about your problems, and the other twenty percent are glad that you have them."
—JACKIE "MOMS" MABLEY, COMEDIENNE

There are times in everyone's life when plans go awry, when anticipated profits fail to materialize, when illness or accident breaks into the normal flow of daily activity. At such a time we all need something to fall back on, inner resources that strengthen our resolve.

A psychiatrist listened one day to a patient recount—in great dramatic detail—the tragedies of her life. After a short period the woman paused, fully expecting her doctor to become involved in her troubles, to brilliantly analyze her plight, and to solve her problems. Instead he looked at her and simply said, "So what?"

The question caught the woman completely off guard. She reviewed all that she had shared. "Yes," she finally admitted, "so what?" With this one question, her attitude shifted and her altitude lifted. So what? is a question that can help us enjoy life. We can use it to feel lighter, less attached to the burdens of life, to free ourselves from the ups and downs of others.

There's nothing wrong; we know that life at times can be indifferent. So if things go awry, if your dreams don't pan out, if you can't get that break that would put you over the top, you can start this very moment to create for yourself circumstances that you truly desire. And in the future if things fail to work out, put your problems in perspective. Sit down, lean back, and say, "So what?"

I will put my problems in perspective and move on.

The War on Poverty

*"I grew up so poor that plenty of nights I had sleep
for dinner."*
—DAMON WAYANS, ACTOR AND COMEDIAN

Before her death in 1934, entrepreneur and publisher Maggie
L. Walker gave her prescription for black progress. In a
lengthy newspaper column she wrote, "God helps those who
are doing, striving. Ours is a poor lot, but our spirits must remain full and rich." Though faced with poverty, Walker was
more concerned with the spiritual side of prosperity. Lack,
limitation, or poverty is simply a state of consciousness. An
empty pocketbook may spell poverty to millions of people, but
it is only because they have lost sight of the true picture. Opportunity abounds whether one sees it or not. A wealthy man
may fall asleep and dream that he is poor. In his dream he has
all the experiences of poverty, but it is still only a dream. Finally he awakens and he is wealthy again. The only effort required in this frightening experience is the awakening. In a
very real sense your need in the face of apparent lack is to
awaken and realize that you live and breathe in a sea of abundance.

"The kingdom of Heaven is at hand." Your miracle of
abundance is ready for you. Awaken from the illusion of limitation. Lift up your eyes; turn away from empty pockets. You
can find unlimited opportunity where you stand. The place to
overcome lack—unemployment and financial strife—is in the
state of your thinking. The person who has a consciousness of
limitation, whose cup is upside down under the faucet of prosperity, will always experience hardship in tough times. We
must change the "war on poverty" to a program of "education
for abundance."

**From this day forward I will be spiritually attuned to the unlim-
ited prosperity that lies at my feet.**

Equal Opportunity

*"If there is any equality now, it has been our
struggle that put it there. Because they said, 'All
people are created equal.' They said 'all' and meant
'some.' They meant 'white.' All means all,
sweetheart."*
—BEAH RICHARDS, ACTRESS

We are not all born equal. Some of us are more blessed than
others. Some individuals are born with much more going for
them: wealthy parents, a thriving and supportive community,
and a nurturing environment. Yet some individuals who hail
from the most backward, discouraging beginnings have grown
into outstanding examples of achievement in spite of the odds.
Attitude is the answer. Your attitude toward your potential is either the key to or the lock on the door of personal achievement.

Some of the world's greatest men and women have risen
above adversity. Force him to shine shoes and you have a James
Brown. Place her in a wheelchair and you have a Barbara Jordan. Confine them to a prison cell and they become a Malcolm
X and a Nelson Mandela. Bury him in the frigid snows of the
North Pole and you have a Matthew Henson. Raise him in ab-
ject poverty and he becomes a Booker T. Washington. Tear out
his roots and you have an Alex Haley. Blind him and find a
Stevie Wonder. Allow sexual and physical abuse to ravage their
bodies and they become Maya Angelou and Oprah Winfrey.
Tell her she's "ugly" and she becomes a Cicely Tyson. Tell her
she can't write and you have an Alice Walker. Force him to the
back door and he becomes a Thurgood Marshall. Call him a
"slow learner" and you have a Benjamin Mays. Write him off
as another fatherless black male and he grows up to become a
Benjamin Carson. Conceal his history and you have a Carter G.
Woodson. Spit on him and he becomes a Marcus Garvey. Steal
his dream and he becomes a Martin Luther King. In my study
of those who have pulled themselves up, an attitude of success
is the common denominator.

I can become great by developing an attitude of greatness.

For Women of Color

"I refused to be discouraged, for neither God nor man could use a discouraged soul."
——MARY MCLEOD BETHUNE, EDUCATOR

Several years ago fifty-four women from every part of the country toured the nation. Some of the women have famous names; others are unsung. Some remember when racial integration and women's liberation were almost unimaginable; others were barely aware when circumstances began to change. Yet all dared to dream of a world where character and accomplishment would conquer color and gender. A photographer captured the project in black and white, he said, because it allowed him "to weave images together in a way that color does not allow." The result was a moving photo essay entitled *I Dream a World.* These women acted on their dreams and changed America in the process.

Professional storyteller Jackie Torrence recounts the days that few remember. As a child she secretly tested "whites-only" water fountains "to see if the water came out white." Other testimonies recalled the highs and lows of the civil rights movement, when women took the first steps of civil disobedience to challenge discrimination. Some, like Myrlie Evers, widow of civil rights activist Medgar Evers, warned that all those hard-won gains could be lost: "I feel as though I should shout from the mountaintops, 'Don't you see what's happening? *Don't let history repeat itself!*' "

Many face the continuing battle with remarkable good humor. Chicago teacher Marva Collins, confronted with an illiterate, seventeen-year-old white student's racist epithet, responded, "Sweetheart, when you learn to read, write and spell *jungle bunny*, Mrs. Collins will take offense to it." Another powerful subject was Marian Wright Edelman, who called this group of fifty-four achievers "ordinary women of grace." Let us all take a few moments to recognize our sisters, "women of color" who struggle on our behalf.

Today I will praise all women of color who struggle against the odds to make this a better world.

You Ain't Seen Nothing Yet

"Know thyself, believe in God, and dare to dream."
—JOHN SALLEY, NBA STAR

This morning I spoke to a man who had overcome discouragement. He told me that a year ago things looked dark and without hope. It seemed as though everyone in his life had begun to take advantage of him. Judging by appearances, he had every right to be discouraged. But he had remembered what the Master admonishes: "Judge not according to the appearance, but judge righteous judgment." My visitor began to follow this advice.

According to appearances, he had no money, but he told me he held to the truth. That he had more than his pockets could hold. He worked on the premise "Nothing is against me—not even poverty." Through self-talk he told himself, "God is ever present. There is nothing but God, therefore if God is for me, who can be against me?"

Today he has proven to himself and to his friends that all things work together for good for those who love good. By holding to the true idea "nothing is against me," he has developed a successful business. Though lacking in material resources, he invested spiritual capital and accomplished the "impossible," drawing to himself the people and contacts who were needed.

This truth applies to each of us. A belief in sickness, lack, or ill will is really a feeling that somewhere in life something is against us. Nothing in life is against us. There is no power on earth that could limit our good. Therefore there should be no room for discouragement.

I will remember today and every day that nothing is against me. I am walking with God, poised in his presence, secure and unafraid.

Roots

*"If we would just support each other—that's ninety
percent of the problem."*
—EDWARD GARDNER, FOUNDER, SOFT SHEEN PRODUCTS

On a recent trip to San Francisco I learned a valuable lesson
about mutual support from California's majestic redwood trees.
Redwoods are inclusive trees—as they grow, they incorporate
into their basic structure objects around them, including rocks
and other plants. Although redwoods have shallow roots, they
are noted for their strength and longevity because they share
their roots with others. Each individual tree is invited into the
whole and in turn helps support the entire group. This adaptation appears to have worked, for redwoods are among the oldest living species of vegetation on earth.

Black America could learn a lesson about surviving and
thriving from the redwoods. We must continue to share our
roots and heritage with each other, to ask for encouragement
and support when we need it, and to stand ready to give the
same to those who come to us. Harold Washington, Chicago's
first African-American mayor, remarked rather proudly, "Sure,
I'm pro-black. If we don't support and give to our own, who
else will do it? We must use whatever power or position that
we have to ensure that no one is left out."

By sharing our roots of support, resources, and compassion,
we uplift the race and ensure that the whole is greater than the
sum of its parts.

I will support my own, including people, businesses, and ideas.

Scared Straight

*"Every day I run scared. That's the only way I can
stay ahead."*
—JOHN H. JOHNSON, FOUNDER,
JOHNSON PUBLISHING COMPANY

As more and more of us leap into the choppy waters of the
business world, we face the challenging prospects of failure.
Will we succeed or fail? Do we have what it takes to capital-
ize on our knowledge, market our wares, and stay afloat in a
sea of black, not red, ink? Because of the ever-present possibilities of failure, many of us are afraid to take the risks that
success requires. One of the best ways to overcome our fears
is to analyze the ingredients of failure:

F: Fear, frustration, futility, falling short
A: Anger, anxiety, adversity
I: Impatience, indifference, impulsiveness
L: Lethargy, laziness
U: Unworthiness, uselessness
R: Regret, remorse, resentment
E: Envy, egotism, emotionalism

We're probably familiar with some of these characteristics.
But the only way to overcome them is to force these culprits
into the open and no longer deny them. From looking at them
deeply we realize that these characteristics are remnants of old
inadequacies and beliefs from the past. Now here's our chance
to blast through them.

Do you have a dream? Is there a business you have secretly
longed to launch? Are you avoiding starting your business because of the fear of failure? If you answered yes, learn to analyze the fear of failure and begin to overcome it.

**I will encourage myself to face failure. I accept this risk as a part
of doing business.**

Fly High!

"It's the struggle that makes you great."
—DARRYL L. MOBLEY, FOUNDER, MOBLEY PEAK
PERFORMANCE INSTITUTE

A constant struggle, a ceaseless battle to bring success from inhospitable surroundings, is the price for all great achievements. The man or woman who has not borne the scars and who has not shed the tears does not know the highest meaning of success.

A young boy confined to bed because of a lingering illness watched a cocoon of a beautiful butterfly on his windowsill every day. As nature took its course, the butterfly began its struggle to emerge from the cocoon. But it was a long, hard battle. As the hours went by, the struggling insect seemed to make almost no progress. Finally the little boy, thinking that "the powers that be" had erred, took a pair of scissors and snipped open a larger hole. The butterfly crawled out, but that's all it ever did—*crawl*. The pressure of the struggle was intended to push colorful, life-giving juices into the butterfly's wings, but the child in his supposed mercy prevented this process. Because the boy stopped the butterfly's struggle, it would never fly on rainbow wings above the beautiful gardens. It was condemned to spend its brief life crawling in the dust.

Malcolm X once mentioned to a young, struggling student who searched for the keys to success, "If you want one year of prosperity, grow trees. If you want ten years of prosperity, grow grain and trees. But if you want prosperity for a lifetime, then grow people." In other words, the key to success is personal development. Our Creator has a divine plan for each of our lives. It's a fact that you can depend on him—even when it seems the struggle is hard and meaningless.

I will continue to struggle and press forward.

The Level of Your Conviction

"In my line of work, people have too many opinions and not enough conviction."
—DANIEL "CHAPPIE" JAMES, FIRST AFRICAN-AMERICAN
GENERAL, U.S. AIR FORCE

In May 1990 Derrick Bell, Harvard Law School's first tenured black professor, announced he was taking an unpaid leave of absence to protest the school's failure to grant tenure to a woman of color. Despite Bell's walkout and numerous student protests, Harvard has not altered its hiring policies. Due to a deep level of conviction Professor Bell refuses to be silenced.

Testing, challenging, and measuring our own limits requires conviction. Pride, dignity, and self-respect grow out of conviction. We don't always win all our personal contests, but through our attempts we come to know the boundaries of ourselves.

Bishop Desmond Tutu offered the final word on conviction when he said, "It's important that people know what you stand for. But it is equally important that they know *what you won't stand for.*" When it comes to testing levels of conviction, some people are like wheels—they don't work unless they're pushed. Some people are like trailers—they have to be pulled. Some people are like kites—always up in the air, and if you don't keep a string on them, they'll fly away. Some people are like canoes—they have to be paddled. Some people are like blisters—they don't show up until the work is done. Some people are like balloons—always puffed up and so full of themselves. Some people are like flat tires—they have to be jacked up. Some people are like lights—always switching off and on. But, thank goodness, some people are like Derrick Bell—committed, always on time, dependable, quietly busy, and full of good works!

Today I will test, challenge, and measure my level of conviction as I pursue my goals.

Sharing Your Gifts

"Our aim should be service, not success."
—BARBARA SMITH, FORMER FASHION MODEL AND
RESTAURATEUR

Surely one of the saddest experiences in life is to hear someone say, "If only I could run, jump, sing, dance, or write like him or her." The message is, "If I just had someone else's ability, I'd be a star!" But this simply isn't true. You're fooling yourself if you believe that you would utilize someone else's ability if you are not using your own. The truth of the matter is *you already possess the ability and tools necessary for success*. But you must use *your* gifts and your ability. And the most effective way to share your gifts is through service.

A guest in a hotel restaurant motioned to the head waiter one morning and said, "I want two boiled eggs, one of them so undercooked that it's runny, and the other so overcooked that it tastes like rubber. I would also like an order of grilled bacon left on the counter to get cold, burnt toast that crumbles as soon as you touch it with a knife, butter so cold that it rips the bread as I spread it, and a cup of very weak coffee, lukewarm."

"That's a complicated order, sir," replied the bewildered waiter. "It might be a bit difficult."

The guest shot back, "Oh, but that's exactly what you gave me yesterday!" Unfortunately far too many of us don't bother to use our gifts to the best of our ability. Complacency and indifference can be found anywhere. Be sure not to fall into this trap.

Say it with deeds, and words will become unnecessary.

Life Is Short, So Play Hard

"My top priority is to align myself with the Father of creation."
—JAYNE KENNEDY OVERTON, TELEVISION PERSONALITY

A man had been hospitalized after an abdominal attack. A preliminary examination indicated a tumor, which he was warned could be malignant and in his case incurable. For several days he lived under a cloud of gloom and fear, awaiting the outcome of an exploratory operation and a biopsy. One morning the doctor came into his room, put a hand on the man's shoulder, and said, "Friend, you are going to live."

This man felt like he had just come out of a dark tunnel into bright sunlight. He heard music in the sound of the birds that he had never heard before. The sky outside his window was a richer blue; the clouds were more beautiful, as were the flowers on his nightstand. His family and friends suddenly seemed more important, more beloved than ever before. Lying in bed during the days of his convalescence, this man did some deep thinking. He began to see that he had been living on the surface. His life and attitude had lacked depth. For the first time he seemed to understand what life really is—not a transient experience between birth and death but a spiritual encounter with God. He was a man reborn and in tune with the Infinite.

Every day we have an opportunity to be reborn, to draw closer with the Infinite. Let's refocus our priorities and rejoice in life.

Today I will spend a few minutes to center my thoughts on the infinite spirit that rests within me.

The Eyes Have It

"In search of my mother's garden, I found my own."
—ALICE WALKER, PULITZER PRIZE-WINNING AUTHOR

The lady was small, old, and frail. She had just lost the sight of her eye and had to have it removed. When she learned it had to be replaced with a false eye, she said to the doctor, "Be sure to choose one with a twinkle in it."

How wonderful it is to know that we can be transformed, healed, and revitalized "in the twinkling of an eye." Miracles become apparent when we open our eyes to a new dimension of life.

The next time you feel weak, tired, lifeless, or down in the dumps, affirm for yourself, *"I am radiant with life and vitality."* Even as you speak, know that you have a life that is larger and deeper than the one you are experiencing. Speak these words repeatedly and joyously. Then give them true meaning by acting as if you really believe them to be true now. In so doing you will open the floodgates, allowing more of life to pour in.

My eyes are the windows of my soul. I see only perfect pictures.

Return to Sender

"I tell Michael, 'Let them know what your priorities are: God, family, doing right, respect.' These are the things that are important in life."
—DELORIS JORDAN, MOTHER OF MICHAEL JORDAN

The way we hope others will respond to us is the manner in which we must express ourselves. Life is a mirror that reflects your expressions. If you smile, you'll see people with cheery dispositions. If you are irritable, you'll find a true picture of your contemptible self. You will find nothing in the world that you will not find in yourself. Nature takes on your moods. If you rejoice, the world rejoices. If you trust, you are trusted. If you love, you are loved. If you hate, you are hated. You will cast your own reflection.

A prosperous young Wall Street broker met and fell in love with a rising young actress. He frequently escorted her about town, hoping to secure her hand in marriage. But being a cautious man, he decided that before proposing to her, he would have a private investigator check her background and present activities. After all, he reminded himself, I have both a growing fortune and my reputation to protect against a marital misadventure.

The young man requested that the agency not reveal his identity to the investigator filing the report on the bride-to-be. In due time the investigator submitted his findings. It said the actress had an unblemished past, a spotless reputation, and her friends and associates were of the highest repute. The report concluded, "The only shadow is that she is often seen around town in the company of a young broker of dubious business practices and principles."

In his effort to uncover her shortcomings, the young stockbroker exposed his own. Life will send back your own reflection.

Today I will give love, joy, and happiness and await their return.

With That in Mind . . .

"Thoughts have power; thoughts are energy. And you can make your world or break it by your own thinking."
——SUSAN TAYLOR, EDITOR-IN-CHIEF, *ESSENCE* MAGAZINE

Within you, at this very moment, is something urging you on to greatness. It is the same "something" that pushed Hannibal across the Alps, that delivered Harriet Tubman to freedom, and drove Ernie Green to endure a year of hardship and strife in order to desegregate Arkansas's public schools. This "something" within keeps telling you that you can do anything you want to do, be anything you want to be, and have anything you want to have. But you need a one-track mind to achieve your goal.

A boss commented to his secretary about one of his men: "John," he said, "has such a one-track mind, it's a wonder he remembers to breathe. I asked him to pick up a newspaper on his way back from lunch, but I'm not so sure he'll remember." Just then John burst through the door, brimming with enthusiasm. He exclaimed, "Hey, boss, guess what! At lunch I ran into Tom Johnson. He hasn't given us an order in seven years, but before he left the restaurant, I talked him into a million-dollar contract!"

The boss sighed and looked at his secretary. "What did I tell you? Since John is always thinking about business, he forgot the newspaper."

If you could have one wish, what would you wish for? Wealth? Fame? Fortune? What one thing do you desire above everything else? Whatever it is, you can have it. Whatever you desire wholeheartedly and with singleness of purpose—you can possess. But, first and foremost, you must know exactly what you want. *And you must develop a one-track mind until you get it!*

A single-minded approach is the only way I will achieve success.

Father's Day

"I'm a man of great faith. I have no army behind me except the army of God. There's nothing behind me except the faith and belief that the walls will come down."
—LEON SULLIVAN, PRESIDENT, OPPORTUNITIES INDUSTRIALIZATION CENTERS

What does the future hold? As long as freedom rings and dreams continue to flourish, the future is glorious. When my father was born in 1921 in eastern Ohio, our country had a very modest means of living. We hadn't yet developed commercial air travel, traffic lights, transcontinental telephones, television, refrigerators, talking pictures, color film, antibiotics, a cure for polio, insulin for diabetes, plastics, frozen foods, photocopiers, calculators, genetic engineering, or nuclear energy. The uniform wage for unskilled labor was ten cents an hour. Yet today, those Americans who live within the "limited" means of public assistance experience a life-style far more comfortable than that of 40 percent of the free world.

We now enjoy prosperity greater than ever imagined. With less than a fraction of 1 percent of the world's population, Black America holds *more than 5 percent of the world's wealth*. We should be overwhelmingly grateful to have been born in this century. The slow progress of the prehistoric ages is over, and now great possibilities are miraculously brimming forth. If you don't often count the many blessings which your Father has given to you, then you just haven't seen the big picture.

I thank the Father for all that I have.

Global Warming

"As we make it, we've got to reach back and pull up those left behind."
—JOSHUA I. SMITH, FOUNDER, THE MAXIMA CORPORATION

In 1977 *Guidepost* magazine reported the story of a man hiking in the mountains. He was taken by surprise by a sudden snowstorm and quickly lost his way. Since he was not dressed for the dropping temperature, he knew he needed to find shelter fast, or he would freeze to death. Despite all his efforts he failed to find shelter, and his hands and feet became numb. He knew his time was short.

As he wandered in the frozen landscape, he tripped over another man, who had succumbed to the bitter cold. The hiker had a decision to make: continue on in the hope of saving himself or try to help this stranger in the snow. In an instant he made his decision. He threw off his wet gloves, knelt beside the man, and began to massage his arms and legs. The man began to respond, and together they were able to push forward and find help. The hiker was later told that he had helped himself by helping another. The numbness that had stricken him vanished while he was massaging the stranger's arms and legs.

On the way to personal fulfillment others have already helped you or will help you—many whom you couldn't possibly repay. An old saying comes to mind: Don't repay a kindness, pass it on. Chances are, after fulfilling our dreams, we will be called upon to pass on some of what we have learned to others.

Jesse Hill, president of Atlanta Life Insurance Company, remarked, "The reason why I stand so tall is because I stand on the shoulders of those who have gone before me." This is equally true of each of us, no matter where life may find us. It's always nice to give others a helpful boost. Every day I become more convinced that the surest way to reach the summit of my life is to help others reach their summits first.

Today I will find and help someone in need of my support. By helping others I will help myself.

The Crab Mentality

"We must turn to each other and not on each other."
—JESSE JACKSON, FOUNDER, THE RAINBOW COALITION

Some people don't like to see others succeed because it reminds them how shallow their lives are. They will do anything to diminish your hopes, even if they don't know what they are talking about. While staring at an owl on its perch, one such naysayer said, "That owl isn't stuffed right! Its head is twisted; the body isn't poised correctly. Its feathers are shaped wrong. If I couldn't stuff an owl any better than that, I would get out of the taxidermy business!" Just then the owl moved. The cynic had been criticizing a live owl!

When others try to talk you out of your dreams, they are really talking themselves back into their comfort zone. Some people will do anything to pull you back to the pack.

The animal kingdom illustrates this point perfectly. For example, I know of a type of crab that is agile and clever enough to escape any crab trap by itself. And yet these crabs are caught by the thousands every day. A fisherman puts bait in a wire cage and lowers the cage into the water. One crab enters the cage and begins to dine on the bait. Soon a second, then a third crab join in. When all the bait is gone, you'd expect each crab would easily climb up the side of the cage and out through the hole on the top, but they don't. They stay in the cage long after the bait is gone.

Should one of the crabs attempt to leave, the other crabs will converge to stop it. They will repeatedly pull it off the side of the cage. If the crab is persistent, the others will tear off its claws to keep it from climbing. If it persists further, they will kill it. The crabs—by force of the majority—stay together in the cage. The cage is eventually hauled in, and the crabs are all eaten. All too often we resemble these crabs.

Instead let's uplift each other. Let's support each other's dreams and hopes, and when one of us makes it, let's reach back and help another climb out and experience a better life.

I will keep my dreams away from the dream stealers.

Present and Accounted For

*"If Black America doesn't do something to change
the current state of affairs, our goose will be
cooked!"*
—RON DELLUMS, CONGRESSMAN

There was a man who traveled the seven continents searching for a rare bird. This bird was special because it could speak five languages. The man found the bird at a pet store and told the owner to deliver it to his home. When he arrived home at the end of the day, he said to his wife, "Dear, did the bird come today?" She smiled and answered, "Yes."

He then asked, "Well, where is it?" She replied, 'It's in the oven."

"You've got to be joking," he said with disbelief. "You put that bird in the oven? Don't you know that bird can speak five different languages?"

Unimpressed, his wife curtly replied, "Then why didn't it speak up?"

At different stages in our lives we resemble that bird. Feeling bored or overwhelmed may mean that we approach life like an apathetic child going to school—not present or speaking up with enthusiasm but attending in a fog of indifference. If we play hooky from life by automatically doing what has to be done but savoring nothing, we are robbing ourselves of the chance to feel and live life vigorously. We are not answering, "Present!" when life calls the roll.

In order to feel alive and live up to our creative potential, we need to make a commitment to being present and speaking up in our lives, not just slumped in the back row apathetically waiting for the bell to ring. Otherwise our goose will surely be cooked!

I give myself the gift of sitting up front in life. Today I will answer, "Present," and will speak up.

Superwoman

*"Everything in the household runs smoothly when
love oils the machinery."*
—WILLIAM H. GRIER, PSYCHIATRIST AND AUTHOR

The economics of our time are such that in many households
one income is not enough. Two incomes are necessary to survive. What does that mean to the family?

It means that someone's feelings can easily fall through the
cracks. It means that Mom is tired when she comes home from
work, faced with more work—cooking, cleaning, and laundering. It means that Mom is wrung out and probably not able to
be emotionally nurturing after waiting on customers, balancing
account sheets, tending to patients, or fighting traffic. After a
full day of work she still has to pick up the kids at day care,
dump her work on the kitchen counter, kick off her heels, pull
dinner out of the fridge, and get the kids to bed or plop them
in the tub while she does the dishes and the laundry. That's
just for starters.

Is it fair to ask her to provide emotional support to the rest
of the family? To her husband or significant other or to her
children? To read poems, to listen to their problems, to play
games, to provide understanding, or to offer advice? *Is it fair
to her?*

We all need encouragement. We all need understanding. We
all need someone to listen. *But so does she!* Even Superwoman's batteries need recharging. She needs to be nurtured and
coddled. She needs compassion and pampering. Sometimes
Superwoman's cape needs washing and pressing, and it's best
when her family *shows its love and does it.*

Today I will renew my love for my mate. On this day and in the
future I will tend to her needs.

What's the Bottom Line?

"I above all believe in work—systematic and tireless."
—W. E. B. DUBOIS, EDUCATOR AND SCHOLAR

A sign on an employee bulletin board read, IN CASE OF FIRE, FLEE THE BUILDING WITH THE SAME RECKLESS ABANDON THAT OCCURS EACH DAY AT QUITTING TIME.

In his classic best-seller *The Prophet*, Kahlil Gibran admonishes, "When you work, you fulfill a part of the earth's furthest dream, assigned to you when that dream was born, and in keeping yourself with labor, you are in truth loving life, and to love life through labor is to be intimate with life's innermost secret."

The Reverend T. J. Jemison, of the National Baptist Convention, said, "God gives us the ingredients for our daily bread, but he expects us to do the baking." *Get busy and work with all your might!* There is no such thing as failure for the willing, ambitious worker. Work is the greatest teacher, the most effective mentor.

An unknown writer gave the following prescription for work: "If your health is threatened, *work*. If disappointments come, *work*. If you inherit riches, continue to *work*. If your faith falters and you become a bundle of nerves, *work*. If your dreams are shattered and the star of hope begins to fade on your horizon, *work*. If sorrow overwhelms you or your friends prove untrue and desert you, *work*. If you are joyous, keep right on working. Idleness brings doubt and fear. No matter what ails you, work. *Work as if your life were in peril, for it is!*"

Whoever is the most persistent and works in the truest spirit will usually be the most successful. The capacity for hard work is an element of genius.

My career is important to me. Today I will give it an added push.

You Bet Your Life

"When you face a crisis, you know who your true friends are."
—EARVIN "MAGIC" JOHNSON, AIDS ACTIVIST AND FORMER
NBA STAR

A true friend has been defined as a person who shows up when the whole world has disappeared. Value a friend who, for you, finds time on his calendar—but cherish the friend who, for you, does not even consult her calendar.

We should always remember the story of the young soldier who asked his commanding officer if he might brave the gunfire to rescue his wounded comrade. "You can go," said his superior, "but it's not worth it. Your friend is probably dead, and you might throw your own life away in the process."

But the man went. Somehow he managed to get to his buddy, hoist him onto his shoulder, and bring him back to safety, but not without injury. As bullets whistled over their heads, the two of them tumbled into the bottom of the trench. Their officer looked at the rescuer and said, "I told you it wouldn't be worth it. Your friend is dead, and now you are badly wounded."

"It was worth it, sir," he responded.

"How do you mean, 'worth it'?" replied the officer. "I told you your friend is dead."

"Yes, sir," the young soldier answered, "but it was worth it, because when I got to him, he was still alive, and his last words were, 'John, I knew you would come.'"

The main business of friendship is to sustain and make bearable each other's burdens. We may do more of that as friends than we do anything else.

Today I will do something for a friend and express my gratitude that he or she is my friend.

A Real Shoe-in

"There ain't no man who can avoid being born average. But there ain't no reason why a man has got to be common."
—LEROY "SATCHEL" PAIGE, NEGRO LEAGUE HALL-OF-FAMER

First place doesn't go to the most talented man or woman but the individual who believes he can succeed! A powerful idea is this: Determination, drive, and a consuming desire will easily compensate for limited talent.

San Francisco's Potrero Hill is still the poorest section of town. When he was born in 1947, it was a real ghetto. He was born with rickets, a poverty-related disease attributed to malnutrition, to a single mother. His vitamin-deficient diet weakened his bones, and his legs began to bow under the weight of his body.

Too poor to afford braces, his mother reversed his shoes to correct his pigeon-toed condition. She then taped a metal bar across the tops of his shoes to keep his feet pointing forward. Six years later his bones had hardened but his legs were permanently bowed. His playmates nicknamed him Pencil-legs. At thirteen he joined a street gang, which led to a few scrapes with the law. On more than one occasion his mother had to get him out of jail. A neighbor who was watching his life spin out of control exposed him to sports, where he excelled. He ran track, played baseball and basketball. But it was in football that he would make a name for himself.

As a member of pro football's Hall of Fame, he rubs shoulders with achievers from all walks of society. His name? O. J. Simpson. Although poverty and adversity pushed him at every turn, O.J. pushed back. *And so can you!*

Who says you're not tougher, smarter, more creative, or harder working than people are willing to give you credit for? It doesn't matter what "they" say. What matters, the only thing that matters, is if you say it.

I am focused, I am determined, and I will continue to push forward!

Hold on to Your Faith

"Mountain, get out of my way."
—MONTEL WILLIAMS, TALK-SHOW HOST

Faith is the prerequisite to power; it gives you perspective and the confidence to forge ahead. Faith lets you see the invisible, believe the incredible, and receive the impossible. Great men and women have never found the easy road to triumph. It is always the same old route—by way of hard work and plenty of faith.

The drought of the past winter threatened the crop in a village of southern Africa. A farmer told the villagers, "There isn't anything that will save us, except a special prayer for rain. Go to your homes, fast during the week, believe, and do not be discouraged. Rain will come." The villagers heard him, fasted during the week, and visited his farm on Sunday morning for more prayer. But as soon as the farmer saw them, he was furious. "Go away," he said. "I will not pray with you! You do not believe."

"But, sir," they protested, "we fasted and we believe."

"Believe?" he retorted. "Then where are your umbrellas?"

It's not what we eat but what we digest that makes us strong. It's not what we gain but what we give that makes us rich. It's not what we read but what we practice that makes us wise. And it's not what we know but what we believe that makes us successful.

"Faith helps us face the music," preaches Bill Gray, former executive director of the United Negro College Fund, "even when we don't like the tune."

I will keep the faith.

Speaking in Tongues

*"Practicing the Golden Rule is not a sacrifice, it's
an investment."*
—BYLLE AVERY, FOUNDER, NATIONAL BLACK WOMEN'S
HEALTH PROJECT

The Golden Rule is the same for all believers:

Judeo Christian: "Therefore, whatever you want men to do
to you, do also to them, for this is the Law of the
Prophets."

Islamic: "Let none of you treat his brother in a way he himself would dislike to be treated."

Confucian: "What you would not wish done to yourself do
not unto others."

Buddhist: "One should seek for others the happiness one
desires for oneself."

Hindu: "The true rule of life is to guard and do by the
things of others as they do by their own."

Husia: "He sought for others the good he desired for himself. Let him pass on."

Since the Creator wound the hands of time, mankind has
constantly preached the Golden Rule. When you select the rule
of conduct by which you will guide yourself and your affairs,
you need to realize that you are unleashing a power that will
run its course back to you. You may deal with others as you
wish. But if you understand the law upon which this simple
key is based, you will know that its application spells success
in any language.

The Golden Rule will be my guiding law of life.

Living Life Triumphantly

"I still have much more to achieve. If I had already achieved it all, I'd go home and sew."
—CLARICE D. REID, PHYSICIAN AND SICKLE-CELL ANEMIA RESEARCHER

In a previous meditation we examined the components of failure. Let's take a look at the qualities that make up triumph:

T: Teachability, truthfulness, thankfulness
R: Responsibility, respect, resourcefulness
I: Integrity, imagination, ideals
U: Understanding, usefulness, uplift
M: Motivation, mind, morality
P: Passion, persistence, patience
H: Hope, happiness, harmony

Just knowing the qualities that comprise triumph is not sufficient. We must use them. "What we want," said Benjamin O. Davis, the first African American promoted to the rank of general in the armed forces, "is to return to our families *triumphantly!*" The eminent heart surgeon Daniel Hale Williams told a group of struggling interns, "The *triumphant* life belongs to the individual who narrows the gap between *what he is, what he appears to be, and what he longs to be.*"

When it comes to living life triumphantly, a spark of an idea can cause an explosion of possibilities. To fan the flames, we need to be enthusiastically supportive of our dreams, no matter how crazy or farfetched they seem. A triumphant life occurs when we pursue worthy goals and ideals. The only way that we can triumph is through the successful realization of our goals.

I understand what it takes to be triumphant. I can see that success is possible for me.

Doesn't It Blow Your Mind?

"All of the attention over my career as a pilot is nice. But I know if we put our minds to it, there isn't anything we cannot do."
—SHIRLEY TYUS, FIRST AFRICAN-AMERICAN FEMALE
COMMERCIAL-AIRLINE PILOT

Each of us has unlimited power and potential. High-achieving men and women know how to use their gifts. You, too, are in possession of this power. But will you convert it into actual power to achieve your life's desires?

You've heard it said that a mind is a terrible thing to waste. It's true. The greatest machine that was ever conceived—so awesome that only God himself could create it—is the human brain. Your human computer. Do you use it? Could you put it to better use? Millions of dollars have been spent on the development and improvement of electronic computers. Millions more have been spent to train people how to use them. Men and women have spent untold hours using them. Think of the potential if the same amount of time and money were spent to improve the use of our human computers—our brain.

Human and electronic computers are similar in many respects. The main difference is that the brain possesses infinite powers. An electronic computer, on the other hand, doesn't possess the physical characteristics that allow it to live and grow. Its powers are finite.

You will never reach your maximum potential; no one ever does. But as you strive to convert your potential power through the use of knowledge and experiences, you will become more successful in reaching your goals.

Today I will center my mind on what is truly possible. I will write down all the ideas that surface from this introspection.

Raising Your Voice

"No life will ever be great until it is dedicated and disciplined."
—PETER C. B. BYNOE, FIRST AFRICAN-AMERICAN OWNER OF
A PROFESSIONAL BASKETBALL TEAM

How do you unleash the power of self-discipline? By habit. It's been said, "Sow an action and you will reap a habit; sow a habit and you will reap a character; sow a character and you will reap a destiny." In the simplest of terms, self-discipline is taking control of your mind, your habits, and your emotions. Until you master self-discipline, you will be unable to master anything else. The following story demonstrates the power of self-discipline.

He was abandoned, along with his twin brother, when he was three weeks old, classified "educable mentally retarded," and placed in special-education classes. His adoptive mother's friends advised her to send him back to the Department of Welfare. This may sound like a living nightmare to many, but not to Les Brown, one of America's most sought-after motivational speakers. Brown's route to the top was circuitous, to say the least. After graduating from high school he became an unpaid gofer at a Miami radio station, always intent on working his way up and living his dreams. He eventually became a disc jockey, a state representative, and now a television talk-show host. At each step along the way he was aided by his relentless self-discipline.

"Discipline was the only thing that kept me from failing," he attests, "and it might be the difference in your life as well. Whenever life knocks you down, get back up and demand the best out of life. Each of us could live our dreams if we'd only master our habits. The disciplined person is not a spectator in life *but a participant in it.*"

Today I will use the power of self-discipline to lead me toward my goals.

The End of Hatred

"Why hate when you could spend your time doing other things?"
—MIRIAM MAKEBA, FOLKSINGER

During a recent "King Day" holiday celebration, U.S. congressman John Lewis asked, "Wouldn't it be nice if we could rid ourselves of hatred for just one day, or one hour, or even one minute?"

The world would be a better place to live if society could turn from thoughts of fear, anger, and hatred to the loving and pleasing emotions that are found in the heart of our dreams. You can't hate when you experience the birth of a child; throw a coin into a wishing well; try out for an Olympic team; enter a road race; sink your life savings into a business; peek into your children's bedroom in the middle of the night and watch them as they lie sleeping; become a beauty pageant contestant; strike oil; restore an old jalopy; search for a cure for cancer; practice medicine in a less developed country; enjoy a candlelight dinner; take a cruise; start a diet two months before attending your class reunion; become an astronaut; join Alcoholics Anonymous; finance your own college education; adopt a child after a number of failed attempts; overcome drug dependency; hit the lottery; gaze into Tiffany's window; put a tooth under your pillow; become an organ donor; learn how to read after a lifetime of illiteracy; train for a marathon; use the Heimlich maneuver at a restaurant; stroll along a sandy beach; open your first savings account; graduate from college; crack open a fortune cookie; feed a starving child; read a book; go hot-air ballooning; climb Mt. Everest; get married; dig for gold; walk through an automobile showroom; find a treasure map; sit before a cozy fireplace on a rainy winter's night; paint a picture; visit Paris in the springtime; or blow out birthday candles.

It's impossible to hate when you're so busy dreaming.

Today I will reserve some time just to dream and remove hatred from my heart.

Mule-headed

*"The greatest pleasure in life is being pleased with
your own efforts."*
—BLAIR UNDERWOOD, ACTOR

Pioneers in every field have faced the critical laughter of jealous observers. The first American steamboat took thirty-two hours to travel from New York City to Albany. People laughed. The horse and buggy passed the early motor car as if it were standing still. Again people laughed. The first electric light bulb was so dim that people had to use a kerosene lamp to see it. Once more people laughed. The first airplane was airborne for only fifty-nine seconds. As expected, people laughed. If you try to tackle a big job, or if you have new ideas, expect criticism.

There once was an old man whose grandson rode a donkey while they were traveling from one city to another. The man heard people say, "Look at that old man suffering on his feet while that strong young boy is sitting."

So the old man rode the donkey while the boy walked. However, he heard someone say, "Look at that, a healthy man making the poor young boy suffer."

So the man and the child both rode the donkey, until they overheard a bystander say, "Would you look at those two men making that poor animal suffer?" So they both got off and walked, until they heard someone say, "Look at that—a perfectly good donkey not being used." In the end the boy decided to walk while the old man carried the donkey.

Pleasing yourself will draw you much closer to your goals than pleasing everybody else.

I am not afraid to lift my head above the crowd, though I may draw criticism.

Cliff Notes

"I've got my faith, and that's all I need."
—NELSON MANDELA, SOUTH AFRICAN HUMAN RIGHTS
ACTIVIST

Some people put their faith and trust in their wealth, others in their intellect, and even fewer in the Creator himself. There are people who say, "I earned my wealth by working hard," which is true in a limited sense. But who gave them the ability to work hard and as a result live a life of comfort? Our Creator. Ultimately we must call on him for solutions to our problems.

A tourist came too close to the edge of the Grand Canyon, lost his footing, and plunged over the side, struggling to grasp the cliff's edge to save himself. After he slipped out of sight of the others, he managed to latch on to a thin bush, which he desperately held with both hands. Filled with terror, he called out toward the skies, "Is there anyone up there?"

A calm, powerful voice came out of the sky: "Yes, there is."

The tourist pleaded, "Please, can you help me?"

The calm voice replied, "Yes, I can. What is your problem?"

"I fell over the cliff and I'm dangling in space holding on to a branch that is about to give out. Please help me!"

The voice from above said, "I'll try. Do you believe?"

"Yes, yes, I believe!"

"Do you have faith?"

"Yes, yes. I have strong faith."

The calm voice then said, "Well, in that case simply let go of the branch and everything will turn out fine." There was a tense pause, then the tourist yelled, "Is there anyone else up there?"

We never know when or how our help will come. Sometimes we can help ourselves by *just letting go of our problems*. Our only duty is to have faith.

I have the faith and trust to reach my goals.

Right On!

"I was just trying to stay alive."
—RODNEY KING, VICTIM OF THE BEATING THAT
PRECIPITATED THE LOS ANGELES RIOTS

As a black male I know how difficult it is for black men to feel valued and strong when each day of our lives we are viewed negatively and reacted to as potentially threatening. I know that life for black men in America continues to be a perilous ordeal. Trying to stay afloat in a less-than-sympathetic society can be life-stunting—mentally and spiritually crippling. But there is hope, and there is an answer. The greatest gift we can give the black male is to encourage him, affirm his presence, and help him if he needs to right his life.

A young business executive took some work home to complete for an important meeting the next day. Every few minutes his small son would interrupt his train of thought. After several such interruptions the young executive spotted the evening paper with a map of the world on it. He took the map, tore it into a number of pieces, and told his son to put the map back together again. He figured this would keep his son busy. However, in a few minutes the boy excitedly told his dad he had completed the task. His father was astonished and asked the boy how he had done it in such short order. The boy replied, "There was a picture of a man on the other side, so I just turned the paper over and put the man together. When I got the man right, the world was right."

When we help our men "get it right," Black America will be right. We need to be enthusiastic about the hopes and aspirations of our males. We must encourage them and show them that we believe in their ability and power. Our future is not at the mercy of outside conditions. Our destiny lies within us. Let's help our black men get it right.

When I see a young brother on the streets, I will affirm his presence. I will smile and say, "How are you doing, Brother? *We need you.*"

Wait Watchers

"Wait means never!"
—MARTIN LUTHER KING, JR., CIVIL AND HUMAN RIGHTS
ACTIVIST

Several years ago a college professor and his wife were visiting the West Indies, when the professor noticed a man sitting by the side of a river. Every time he passed this spot, he saw the same man. One day the professor's curiosity got the best of him, and he asked the man why he spent all of his time in such a manner. The West Indian replied that he believed in reincarnation. According to his belief, we have all lived many times before and we will live many times again. And then he said, "This life I'm sitting out."

What happens to a person during his lifetime is in direct relation to the way he passes his days. Many of us wait for miracles from above. I've heard a number of people say, "Well, I'm ready. I'm just waiting for a sign from above. I'm ready to do God's will—I'm just waiting on the Lord." If these souls were indeed "ready," they would be busy fulfilling their mission on earth.

While cleaning out his desk, a man found a ten-year-old shoe-repair ticket. Figuring that he had nothing to lose, he went to the shop and gave the ticket to the repairman, who began to search the back room for the unclaimed shoes. After several minutes the owner reappeared and gave the ticket back to the man. "What's wrong?" asked the man. "Couldn't you find my shoes?"

"Oh, I found them," replied the repairman, "and they'll be ready next Friday." Like the above story, the repairman felt like waiting. The main thing that comes to the person who waits is regret for having waited.

Don't join people who watch and wait—you'll lose nothing but time!

Keep on Pushing

"Keep on going, keep on pushing, keep on fighting injustice."
—MARY CHURCH TERRELL, FEMINIST AND CIVIL RIGHTS
ACTIVIST

Have you ever noticed how some people seem to be constantly excited and enthusiastic about their lives? They seem to experience one success after another. Their achievement level continues to escalate and climb. How do you explain it? These individuals use every ounce of their potential and are self-motivated.

But there are times that we don't know the limits of our potential until an external stimulus forces us to test them. This is why people who dread their jobs often perform poorly and why those who love their work do so well. One is motivated to perform, while the other is not. People who possess a burning desire to accomplish a goal attain it; while others, lacking the necessary motivation, fail. The following story illustrates the power of motivation. Years ago an old gentleman took a cruise on an ocean liner. When a storm blew up at sea, a young woman, leaning against the ship's rail, lost her balance and was thrown overboard. Immediately someone plunged into the waves beside her and held her until a lifeboat came to their rescue. To everyone's astonishment the hero was the oldest man on the voyage—well past eighty. That evening he was given a party in honor of his bravery. "Speech! Speech!" his fellow passengers cried.

The old man rose slowly and looked around at the enthusiastic gathering. "There's just one thing I'd like to know," he said testily. "Who pushed me?"

Don't wait to be pushed! The secret to real motivation has been known for years: *The people who succeed are those who give themselves a little nudge just when they need it.*

No one needs to push me toward success. I am self-motivated.

Fourth and Long

"I used to want the words 'she tried' on my tombstone. Now I want 'she did it!'"
—KATHERINE DUNHAM, PRODUCER AND CHOREOGRAPHER

The word *impossible* is a dangerous word. Too often progress has been delayed or even halted by people who used that word. Transplant a human heart? *Impossible!* Put a man on the moon? *Impossible!* Place a black man or a woman in the White House? *Impossible!* But are any of these missions truly impossible? As Earl G. Graves, publisher of *Black Enterprise* magazine remarked, "Over time, the impossible becomes the possible."

When uttered aloud, the word *impossible* has a devastating effect on our subconscious mind. Thinking stops. Progress halts. Doors slam shut. Effort comes to a screeching halt. Projects are abandoned. Hopes are dashed. Dreams are discarded. The light of imagination goes dim. The best and the brightest of the creative brain cells die in some dark corner of the mind. And the result? Possibilities are rejected.

Now, let someone utter the magic words "It may be possible! I don't know how or when, but it might be possible." Those stirring words rally forth hopes yet unborn. Buried dreams are resurrected. Enthusiasm begins to build. Sparks begin to fly. Dusty files are reopened. Lights go on. Once-closed factories are retooled. Ideas are developed. Markets begin to open. Telephones begin to ring. The drought ends.

Never allow anyone to get by with the judgment that something is impossible. That is one word that blocks all human progress. Possibility thinkers see every problem as a possibility, every obstacle a challenge.

I won't allow anyone to tell me what is impossible. I will define my own limits.

Call It the Way You see It

"Hey, man, tell me what you really see!"
—WALLY "FAMOUS" AMOS, ENTREPRENEUR

The bumper sticker on the automobile in front of me read A BLIND MAN DRIVES THIS CAR. "Oh, yeah?" I thought as I watched the driver comply with all the traffic signals. The driver was not blind—at least not physically. Physical blindness is just one form of blindness. As great a handicap as physical blindness is, it may not be nearly as debilitating as spiritual, intellectual, or moral blindness—or any combination of these.

An eight-year-old boy looked forward to Saturday because his father had promised to take him fishing, weather permitting. But Saturday morning dawned rainy and dreary, and it appeared that the rain would continue throughout the day. The child moped around the house, peering out the windows and grumbling, "Seems like the Lord could've chosen a better day to make it rain." His father tried to explain to him how badly the rain was needed. But his son was adamant. "It just isn't right," he repeated.

By mid-afternoon the rain had stopped. The boy and his father quickly loaded their gear into the car and headed off to the lake. As anticipated, the fish were biting, and both returned home with a stringful of big fish. At dinner, when some of the fish were served, the boy's mother asked him to say grace. He did—and concluded his prayer by saying, "And, Lord, if I sounded grumpy earlier today, it was because I couldn't see far enough ahead."

Just like this little boy, so many of us suffer from spiritual blindness because we can't see with our hearts far enough ahead. When we visualize our good, anticipate it, and trust in our Higher Power, we avoid the most debilitating form of blindness.

To avoid spiritual and moral blindness, I will keep my eyes, my mind, and my heart open.

Sesame Street

*"All of us are born in a state of ignorance, and
many of us never change residence."*
—EFFI BARRY, WIFE OF MARION BARRY, FORMER MAYOR OF
WASHINGTON, D.C.

It's remarkable how much you have to know before you realize how little you know. We are where we are because of what we know. If we hope to experience more of what life has to offer, we'll be forced to take in additional information.

Life is for learning. In the first five years alone we learned to walk, talk, eat, and interact with playmates and family. From five to ten we learned to read, write, and do arithmetic. We also learned more about friends, relatives, supporters, and detractors. And so our learning continued.

Most people continue to learn until the age of fifteen or twenty. Then the growth slows, or in some cases stops. Most people then declare their formal education over. They feel they have nothing else to learn, which means *they have a lot to learn*.

An ancient African proverb offers excellent advice: "He who knows not, and knows not that he knows not, is a fool—*shun him*. He who knows not, and knows that he knows not, is a child—*teach him*. He who knows not, and knows not that he knows, is asleep—*wake him*. He who knows not, and knows that he knows, is wise—*follow him*."

I now know that it makes a big difference in life whether I live and learn or just live.

Are You Still Doin' Drugs?

"Sometimes I just feel so good all over."
—STEPHANIE MILLS, SINGER AND ENTERTAINER

We have the ability to accept emotional and physical pain as a part of our lives, to adjust to it and learn to live with it. And any support we need in making the adjustment is easily available to us. We live in a society where there is a pill for every pain. We can always find something, over-the-counter or prescribed, to dull any discomfort and keep us going. But where are we really going? On to serious illness, disease, and an early grave. What's in our medicine cabinets is a good indication of the state of our health.

Good mental and physical health is our natural state of being. It's what our Creator intended for us. Mental and physical health is born of spiritual health. When we make our spiritual well-being our priority, the natural outcome is strength, beauty, harmony, and a healthy mind and body. The opposite is also true. Discord and unhealthy, negative behavior offend the spirit and create the space for illness to take root. The main focus in our lives should be to monitor our moment-to-moment thoughts, feelings, and actions to ensure that they are in agreement with our spirit and our values.

What must I do or eliminate from my life to be in perfect health? The answer is obvious. We must place our physical bodies in order. We must eat the appropriate foods and exercise our bodies regularly. Identifying what we must do to have optimum health is simple; permanently adopting the behavior that ensures it is difficult. But a plan has already been developed for us: *We can summon the Infinite Intelligence that is part of each of us—that power that created, supports, and orders the universe—to help support and guide our lives.* When we live in accordance with this one power, the inevitable result is perfect health.

Today I will develop a health consciousness and begin to enjoy the benefits of sound health.

How Soon We Forget

*"I never wanted them to forget Babe Ruth. I just
wanted them to remember Henry Aaron."*
—HENRY AARON, BASEBALL HALL-OF-FAMER

I remember what it was like as a child attending church every
Sunday morning with my family. My favorite hymn was "The
Lord Is on Our Side." At the time the words to that song were
just words. But today they fall upon my ears with new meaning. After struggling many years, after encountering a host of
setbacks, after coming to the stark realization that the world is
tough and that life can sometimes be difficult to swallow, I
welcome the soothing words "The Lord Is on Our Side."

Just as they have done in my life, these words have sup-
ported black achievers throughout the ages. *The Lord is on our
side.* "Amen!" shouts Mari Evans, the award-winning writer
who knew nothing but poverty and lack throughout her childhood. Today her résumé includes teaching stints at Purdue,
Cornell, and Spelman.

The Lord is on our side. "Thank you, Jesus!" cries Beverly
Johnson, the first black model to grace the front cover of
Vogue magazine. Fresh out of college, she knocked on every
agency door on Madison Avenue, only to have those doors
slammed in her face. But today it is Beverly Johnson who is
the standard by which all models are judged.

The Lord is on our side. "Word up, Brother!" exclaims
Stanley Burrell, better known as M. C. Hammer. And the Lord
had to be on his side after being rebuffed by every major recording studio in the country. Since the industry giants
wouldn't sign Hammer on, he signed up himself by launching
his own private record label. He now reaps millions.

As I look back on my own journey, I think about the countless jobs I held in college, the all-night study sessions, and
raising three children as I completed a Ph.D. I begin to feel
self-made, believing that I shaped my own destiny. How soon
I forget. *The Lord was on my side!*

When I succeed, I will remember that the Lord was by my side.

What Goes Around Comes Around

"Forgive, forget, and move on."
—DR. LOUIS SULLIVAN, FORMER SECRETARY, U.S.
DEPARTMENT OF HEALTH AND HUMAN SERVICES

Wellington Webb, Denver, Colorado's, first African-American mayor said, "It's better to forgive and forget than to hate and remember." He who does not forgive others burns before him the bridge to God's forgiveness. Forgiveness is a language that even the dumb can speak and the deaf can hear.

A young employee secretly misappropriated several hundred dollars from his firm's bank account. When this infraction was discovered, he was told to report to the senior partner of the firm. The young man was heavy-hearted as he walked up the stairs toward the administrative offices. He knew he would lose his job. He also feared the possibility of legal action. He felt his whole world was collapsing.

His superior began to question him about the affair as soon as he arrived in the office. He asked the young man if the allegations were true. He nodded his head. Then the senior partner asked this question: "If I keep you in your present capacity, can I trust you in the future?" The young man brightened up and said, "Yes, sir, you surely can. I've learned my lesson."

His boss then responded, "I'm not going to press charges, and you can continue in your present job." He then concluded the conversation by saying, "I think you ought to know, however, that you are the second man in this firm who succumbed to temptation and was shown leniency. *I was the first.* What you've done I did. The mercy you are receiving I received." When a friend makes a mistake, don't rub it in. *Rub it out.*

From this day forth, when I forgive, I will forget.

Give It Up!

"The key to my success has been to give up everything for my dream."
—JOHN H. JOHNSON, FOUNDER, JOHNSON PUBLISHING COMPANY

In one single, sweeping sentence our Creator gives us the key to help us unlock our possibilities: "Cast your bread upon the waters and it shall return to you." If we release our talents, our time, our gifts with a feeling of hope and positive expectancy, they will return to us in the form of multiplied blessings.

When I began to study this verse, I came to the conclusion that it didn't make much sense. If you throw bread upon the water, it will get soggy and dissolve. If it does return, neither of us would care to eat it.

The text doesn't make much sense until you realize that the phrase was originally spoken in a culture where fish was the basis for economic survival. If you throw bread upon the water, the bread itself will not be edible, but it will attract fishes to the surface so you can net them. That's what the author of this biblical verse had in mind. If you're hungry, take your bread and give it up! Throw it into the water. You'll lose your bread, but you'll gain a meal fit for royalty!

Likewise a seemingly insignificant, "crazy" idea can deliver enormous potential. When you give forth your talents, time, and gifts, your "bread" will return to you multiplied.

I will concentrate on giving my talents and gifts. In due time my good will return.

Seven-Eleven or the Two-Minute Drill

*"My family keeps me centered. They tell me when
I need to turn the dial down."*
—EARL G. GRAVES, FOUNDER, *BLACK ENTERPRISE*
MAGAZINE

A day after his checkup a man called his doctor to get his results. The doctor said he had bad news and worse news for him. Which did he want to hear first? The man decided he'd rather hear the bad news first. His doctor said, "The bad news is that you have only twenty-four hours to live." As expected, the man became distraught. He shouted into the phone, "Twenty-four hours to live? I can't believe this, it's incredible! What could be worse news than this?" The doctor replied, "The worse news is I was supposed to tell you yesterday, but I forgot."

The Bible says, "Thou wilt keep him in perfect peace, whose mind is stayed on Thee; And he that ruleth his spirit, than he that taketh a city." This is a great thought, but have you ever felt just a little frustrated with these words of truth—especially when it's so difficult to keep your mind focused on your objectives? In our preoccupied and sometimes hectic lives, we need the patience of a saint to "think on these things" all the time.

So what's the key? How do you stay focused in the midst of turmoil? Each morning I take just a few precious minutes to mentally set the tone for the entire day. This mental conditioning helps to slow me down or buoy me up—depending on my needs. These golden moments incite me to enthusiasm and calm me with tranquility. Just a few minutes each day can work wonders. By taking time to center ourselves we can approach life in a peaceful state of consciousness. We can laugh at the absurdities of our fears and at the incongruities of life.

Today I will take a few moments to relax and center my thoughts.

Diamond in the Rough

"I always had only one prayer: 'Lord, just crack the door a little bit, and I'll kick it open all the way.'"
—SHIRLEY CAESAR, GOSPEL SINGER

Many years ago, within the bowels of a once-closed African mine, a diamond of immense proportions was discovered. The stone was presented to the king of England to be set in his crown. The king sent the gem to Amsterdam to be cut and polished, and it was placed in the capable hands of a very talented jeweler. But the jeweler did something very strange. He took the priceless stone and cut it in two. Did the jeweler do this out of carelessness or blatant disregard? Not at all. For days and weeks he had studied and carefully planned the procedure. Drawings and models had been made of the jewel. Its quality, defects, and lines of cleavage had been studied in great detail. The man to whom it was committed was one of the most skilled jewelers in the world.

Everyone wanted to know why he broke the diamond. Was it a mistake? Did he cut the stone at the wrong angle? No! This process was the climax of the jeweler's skill. When he struck that blow, he did the one thing that would bring the gem to its most perfect brilliance and splendor. That blow that seemed to destroy the precious stone was in fact its redemption. From those two halves were wrought two magnificent diamonds, which only the skilled eye of the jeweler could see hidden in the rough stone given him months before.

Sometimes our Creator lets a stinging blow fall upon our life. Our blood spurts; our soul cries out in agony. The blow seems to be an appalling mistake. But it's not. Our moments of despair and tribulation bring out our perfect brilliance and redeeming qualities.

I will not pray for an easy life; instead I will ask to become a stronger person.

On the Right Track

*"Some people dream of great accomplishments,
while others stay awake and do them."*
—CONSTANCE NEWMAN, DIRECTOR, THE SMITHSONIAN
INSTITUTE

Attitude has many facets. For example, the student who studies for high grades alone will probably receive them. However, the pupil who studies for knowledge will not only achieve high marks but will gain considerably more knowledge in the process. Conversely if you work for a salary alone, you'll draw a paycheck. But if you work to improve the quality of the organization, not only will you draw a paycheck but you will also gain the recognition and respect of your colleagues, placing you in line for even higher pay. The following story says it quite well.

Several years ago a railroad crew was laying tracks. Suddenly their work was interrupted by a slow-moving train. When the train came to a stop, a man peered out of a window and yelled, "Bill, is that you?" Bill Johnson, the crew chief called back, "Sure is, Tom. It's really good to see you." With that pleasant exchange Tom Wilson, president of the railroad, invited his longtime friend Bill Johnson for a visit. Then they exchanged tales, shook hands, and went their separate ways.

Bill Johnson's crew was shocked that he knew the president of the railroad. Bill then explained why their lives had traveled along different paths after the two had begun working for the railroad on the same day. With that, one of his crew members asked him why he was still a crewman laboring in the hot sun while Tom Wilson had become president. Rather wistfully Bill explained, "Twenty years ago I was laying tracks, but Tom Wilson was building a railroad."

Given the opportunity, you should build and not bow. You should excite and not just exist.

Today I will tackle my task with drive and commitment. I am excited and enthusiastic about the possibilities for my future.

The Electric Slide

"Man, nothing happens until somebody cuts on the juice."
—LOUIS ARMSTRONG, MUSICIAN

Electricity is a name we give an invisible power that we do not fully comprehend. Nevertheless we try to learn all we can about the principle of electricity and how its power can be harnessed.

The scientist cannot see an electron, yet he accepts it as a scientific fact. We cannot see life, but we know we are alive. We are all a part of this great electrical charge that empowers the universe.

The man or woman who believes that the earthly cycle of birth, youth, maturity, and old age is all there is to life is indeed to be pitied. Such a person has no anchor, no hope, no vision, and to him or her life has no meaning.

This type of belief brings frustration, stagnation, and a sense of hopelessness. If you cannot walk as fast or as far as you once did, or if your body has slowed down, remember life is always clothing itself anew.

Every age has its own glory, beauty, and wisdom. Peace, love, beauty, happiness, wisdom, goodwill, and understanding are qualities that never grow old or die. Your character, the quality of your mind, and your faith are not subject to decay but to this vast, powerful, ever-present force throughout the universe. Now, go forth, and put a charge into your life!

I am a part of this great life force. With this positive force I empower my dreams.

Get the Picture?

"We can finally say that we're in love."
—WHITNEY HOUSTON AND BOBBY BROWN, NEWLYWEDS

August Wilson, the highly acclaimed playwright, wrote, "All you need in the world is love and laughter. That's all anybody needs." Vanessa Williams, the former Miss America agrees. She says, "Love is the fairest flower that blooms in God's garden." Everyone needs love. The more you give, the more comes back to you.

A wealthy man died, apparently without leaving a will. Consequently, according to law, the estate was to be divided up among his cousins, who were his next of kin. Also as prescribed by law, the deceased's household goods and personal belongings were to be converted into cash at a public auction. During the sale the auctioneer tried to sell a framed photograph, but no one bid on it. Later a shabbily dressed old woman approached the auctioneer and asked if she might purchase the picture for a dollar, which was all she had. She said it was a photograph of the deceased man's only son.

She went on to say that she had been a servant in the deceased's household when the boy lost his life trying to rescue a drowning person. She had loved the son very much. The auctioneer accepted the dollar and the woman went home and placed the photograph on a table beside her bed. One evening she noticed a bulge in the back of the frame. She pulled the picture apart, and there, to her amazement, was the rich man's will. The instructions in the will were simple: "I bequeath all my possessions to the individual who cares enough for my son to cherish this picture." Love is an unusual game. There are either two winners or there are none.

I am loved and I give love freely.

Not Just Another Pretty Face

"Everything comes from within. The beauty is within me."
—KENYA MOORE, MISS USA 1992

"Judge not, that ye be not judged. For with what judgment ye judge, ye shall be judged; and with what measure ye mete, it shall be measured to you again." A study of this verse and the application of its inner truth represents the real key to harmonious relations.

A man and woman had been corresponding by mail several years before they fell in love. They agreed to meet at the airport. Since they had never seen each other, they devised a plan that would help them recognize each other. The woman was to wear a green scarf, a green hat, and a green carnation pinned to her coat.

When the man got off his plane, he immediately began searching for his pen pal. Suddenly, he saw a woman with a green scarf, hat, and carnation, and his heart sank. She was one of the homeliest women he had ever seen. He was tempted to board the plane without approaching her. Nevertheless he walked over to the woman, smiled, and introduced himself. Immediately the woman said, "What's this all about? I don't know who you are. That woman over there," she continued, "gave me ten dollars to wear this outfit."

When the man looked over to where she pointed, he saw one of the most beautiful women he had ever seen in his life. After approaching her, the woman explained, "All my life men have courted me because of my beauty. I want someone to love me not just for my outward appearances but for what I am on the inside." If you're going to judge by appearances, be sure to look at the heart.

I will not be trapped by outward appearances. I will look beyond to the deeper possibilities.

All Dressed Up and No Place to Go

"It ain't what's on your head, it's what's in it!"
—H. RAP BROWN, HUMAN RIGHTS ACTIVIST

A wise man said, "If you work for a man, in heaven's name work for him. If he pays you wages that supply you your bread and butter, work for him, speak well of him, think well of him, stand by him, and stand by the institution he represents."

One of life's worst nightmares is to have no purpose, no destiny—nothing useful to do. The person who hasn't experienced the joy of hard work or, even worse, has confused activity with accomplishment, has lived in vain.

Although Jim had been content with his sales job, he had been just going through the motions for years, thinking about his next promotion. The new position meant a huge raise, and he and his wife began planning things they could do with the extra income. For three months they had pored over travel folders outlining a trip to Hawaii. So when Jim was called into the president's office on the morning following the retirement party for the former vice president, he wore his best suit and a smile to match.

After the president winced through the cheerful "good morning" from his senior salesman, he looked him straight in the eye and said, "Jim, I have to tell you that the executive committee has awarded the position of vice president in charge of sales to Bill Mitchell." There followed a deep silence. After a few moments Jim finally managed to protest. "But Bill has been with the company only five years. I've been here twenty-five years!" But in the weeks and months that followed, it finally dawned on him that he had confused seniority with accomplishment. Jim didn't really have twenty-five years' experience with his firm; he had one year's experience repeated twenty-five times!

When I do my best, when I go the extra mile, and when I give superior service, opportunities will come my way!

"CP" Time

"Honey, it's so easy to talk a good game. What we need are folks who will do something!"
—MAXINE WATERS, CONGRESSWOMAN

A concert pianist once gave a performance before a large audience. Afterward, over coffee, an admirer said to the virtuoso, "I'd give anything to play as you do." The pianist took a sip of her coffee and said without blinking an eye, "Oh, no you wouldn't!" A hush fell over the table, and the admirer squirmed with embarrassment. "If you would give anything," continued the artist, "you could play as well as I do, possibly better. But you'd give anything to play as I do except time—the one thing that it truly takes!"

Most of us want to play the piano, not learn the piano; speak a foreign language, not study it; enjoy success, not earn it. We want our dreams to come true ahead of time and without too much effort. We don't want to accept the *becoming* that comes before the *being*.

But success is built on time, not wished into the moment. And in spite of our daydreams, success is always earned the hard way—by putting in the time! Time is ours to use.

But in the past what if you promised yourself to quit smoking or lose those extra pounds—and failed? Don't sweat it, you've got more time. Reset a new deadline and try again. Have you failed a second time to make a dreaded phone call? Try a third time. Has the ladder to success slipped out from under you again? Maybe your goal will require more time. After all, you've got the time. Once you arrive, no one cares how long it took for you to get there.

When it comes to my dreams and goals, I will be on time by putting in the time.

Did You Set Your Alarm?

"Isn't it a shame? A black man invented the clock and we still have black folks who don't know what time it is."
—JEWELL MCCABE, FOUNDER, 100 BLACK WOMEN

We are told in Genesis that "a deep sleep fell over Adam"—but nowhere does it say in the Bible that he woke up! In essence all the events that followed Adam's falling asleep are a part of his dream.

Many of us possess an "Adam" mentality. Far too many have entered into a deep sleep. Many have never realized, or even worse, have forgotten, our true identity. Each of us was created for success. An honest look at the troubles we have created for ourselves as a people reveals that we have painfully lost sight of the visions that once painted our future. What began as a happy dream seems to have spun into a nightmare of fear, deprivation, and unhappiness. These clouds have hidden the great origins of our history.

But nightmares always end with an awakening. While the dream may seem overwhelming as you experience it, it becomes nothing the moment you open your eyes. If you are passing through such a dream, take comfort in knowing that this type of experience is important. When planting a garden, the earth must be turned over, tilled, and smoothed out before new seeds can grow. In the same way, before a new building can be erected, the old, useless structure must be leveled and cleared away. We must make space for something new and better to enter our life.

While it may seem that sometimes we are spinning dangerously out of control, we are not alone. The Creator is ever present. Such a time calls for faith, the knowing that somehow everything will work out for the best. It is not your world that is shattering, it is your illusions.

I know what time it is. It's time for me to realize my true identity and to reach my goals.

Did Someone Get Hurt?

"This is a tough game. There are times when you've got to play hurt, when you've got to block out the pain."

—SHAQUILLE O'NEAL, BASKETBALL SUPERSTAR

I know that life can be difficult. Sometimes so difficult, it hurts. But real achievers make the best of their circumstances.

I remember riding through a tough section of Detroit, seeing boarded-up houses lining the street. Nearly all had broken windows and a pervading sense of urban blight. Several were vacant and overrun by drug dealers.

Then I saw something that lifted my spirits. In the middle of one desolate block stood a house that lacked the look of decay. It stood out because it was in perfect condition—no boards on the windows, no cracked glass, no weeds growing in the front lawn. I was especially touched to see little planter boxes at each side of the doorway in which fresh flowers were blooming. On the porch of this cozy home sat the lady of the house. She waved and smiled as I drove by. What a contrast. In the midst of an ugly neighborhood she made her home comfortable and a showcase. What was her secret? She had discovered the possibilities in her situation. She had found a way to overcome life's hurts.

How will you react to your hurts today? You can react negatively and *curse* your hurts, blaming others or blaming yourself. You can *nurse* your hurts, tenderly keeping them alive, indulging in self-pity, and asking yourself, "Why did this happen to me?" You can even *rehearse* your hurts, by going over them again and again. Or you can *reverse* your hurts by allowing your difficulty to become an opportunity, your adversity an asset. Allow your problem to become a new project, then get busy!

Life's bumps and bruises don't bother me. I can blossom anywhere. I can shine under any circumstance.

Aid to Families with Dependent Children

*"If you can't hold children in your arms, please
hold them in your heart."*
—CLARA "MOTHER" HALE, FOUNDER, THE HALE HOUSE

Staggering amounts of manpower and money are devoted each year to discovering, understanding, and harnessing the forces of nature. Almost everyone agrees, however, that one of the greatest forces on earth is love. The real wealth of a nation does not come from mineral resources but from what lies in the hearts of its people.

Several years ago a grief-stricken mother sat motionless in a New York hospital with tears streaming down her cheeks. She had just lost her only child. Down the same hall where her daughter had died sat a little boy. The woman did not notice him. A head nurse who saw both the mother and the child saw an opportunity and took it. She approached the woman and pointed out the small child.

"That little boy's mother," the nurse confided, "was brought in by ambulance a week ago. She was in a car accident and lies in a coma. Every day her son sits here from sunup to sundown with the hope that his mother will pull through. The two of them are the only family they have."

The woman stopped her tears long enough to listen. The nurse continued. "Just a few minutes ago his mother died. Now it is my responsibility to tell this little fellow that his mother is gone. It'll break his heart." The nurse paused, then turned to the woman and said, "I don't suppose that you would tell him for me? I know it's a part of my job, but I just can't bear to do it." The grieving woman stood, dried her eyes, walked through the corridor, and put her arms around the tiny child and took him home.

So many of our own children are found in the same situation. Let's embrace them and give them a home.

Today I will volunteer my time to be a big brother or big sister to one black child.

I've Got Just the Ticket

"Success doesn't mean the absence of failure; it means the attainment of objectives."
—ROY ROBERTS, CORPORATE EXECUTIVE,
GENERAL MOTORS

My friend Ed won two million dollars in the New York State lottery. But before he could collect the money, he had to do three things: First, Ed had to buy a ticket. He had to take action in order to win the prize. In other words, you can't be dealt a "royal flush" if you're not in the game.

Second, Ed had to read the newspapers and watch the local lottery show on television to see if his number was drawn. You must be vigilant for your good. You must look for the outward signs that your desired good is on its way.

Finally, Ed had to show up at the lottery office and claim his prize. You must claim your good. To claim it is to state exactly what you want and ask for it with authority. You have the right to say with power and feeling, "This is mine, and it is my divine right. I will not do without it!" There is no need to fight or struggle for your good. The moment you recognize that you deserve your good, the fight will be over. This is one mental law we all must learn.

Today I will spend thirty minutes to think of new and different ways to reach my goals. I will prioritize these plans and take action.

It's a Brave New World

"Courage is being brave when you know something isn't going to happen to you."
—WILLIAM H. GRAY, FORMER PRESIDENT,
UNITED NEGRO COLLEGE FUND

Have you ever stopped to think about how much more people could have, know, and do if they would only try? When timidity erects walls between us and the things we would like to have or do, we need the courage to leap over our self-imposed barriers and achieve our desires.

Courage is often a matter of simple logic. I remember a story about a man running toward a river. As he reached the dock, he increased his speed and threw himself as far out over the river as he could. He landed in the water about ten feet from the dock, swam back, and climbed out. A bystander asked him why he jumped into the river. He answered that a friend had bet him a thousand dollars that he couldn't jump across the river. After thinking about the money, he just couldn't walk away without trying.

Many things that appear impossible from a distance become quite feasible once we muster the courage to make an attempt. If we step out solidly, there's always a way to reach every desirable goal. If the man who tried to jump across the river had courageously swum to its source, he would have found that he could step across it and win his bet. There's only a slight difference between keeping your chin up and sticking your neck out, but it's worth knowing.

We cheat ourselves of the lives we could live because we're afraid to try. If we knew ourselves better, we would fear less and accomplish more.

Today I will generate the courage to tackle my number-one fear. I know what it is, and I will finally confront it.

The Glass Ceiling

"Did I pay my dues? You bet. Was it tough? Without a doubt. But I was determined to find out how high is high!"
——HALLE BERRY, ACTRESS

Experts in psychology say you cannot change your whole personality. Yet regardless of the personality you have, you can be content with yourself and your world. The way to achieve this peace of mind is to develop yourself as fully as possible.

Each of us has a ceiling of performance. This ceiling is high in the areas in which you excel and low in the areas in which you have little or no aptitude. Your peace of mind or dissatisfaction is directly related to how far you develop your own abilities and skills. If you knew how to exploit your talents fully, you would know complete contentment. Your discontent reflects your unfulfilled potential.

Just how much of your potential are you using? Fifty percent? Thirty percent? How about twenty? A man who spends his Saturdays constructing a summer home or chasing a remote idea is usually much happier than the man who spends his weekends lying on his couch. As a rule the person whose job makes him work close to his potential is a much happier person. The tougher the task, the more fulfilled the individual. Contentment comes to us when we become fully engaged with our powers and potential.

It is important that each of us maintain a mental picture of the person we want to become. This blocks boredom and stifles any feelings of inferiority caused by working too far below our potential. Self-fulfillment comes to those who work full-blast, fully extended. Only then can we experience the satisfaction of a job well done.

Today I will ask, "How much of my potential am I using?" I will begin to exploit my talents.

Head for the Hills

"There are gems of inspiring thought which we all can use. You must search for them."
—ETHEL WATERS, SINGER, DANCER, AND ACTRESS

From time to time you may hear, "You know, those people who got in on the ground floor were really fortunate. They're the lucky ones. Just think of those who stumbled upon fortunes in the oil fields during the Depression or those who traveled West and discovered gold in the foothills of California. When I was younger, we used to dream of days like that!"

Try to get a mental picture of a gold mine or an oil field before it was discovered. No busy traffic, no noisy machinery, no crowds wandering through. Just barren land covered with prairie grass stretching as far as the eye can see. However, beneath that vast stretch of land are minerals and deposits worth millions. But you would never know that they were there.

Before these rich deposits were mined, thousands of people walked and rode over them without realizing that riches beyond their wildest dreams lay beneath their feet! But somebody had to come along looking for them. Somebody had to be willing to dig for them. Somebody had to be willing to risk his or her existence upon the gold or oil being there. Somebody had to turn away from all the negative people who thought he or she was crazy. *Somebody had to believe!*

Perhaps you never thought much about it, but each of us has our own private gold mine just waiting to be developed. People who have succeeded have followed their dreams to their gold mines. Let's head for the hills of our minds and mine out a healthy and prosperous life.

I will not belittle the dreams of others, for they are the forerunners of civilization.

The Door Is Unlocked

"Every new idea is an impossibility until it is born."
—RON BROWN, SECRETARY, U.S. DEPARTMENT OF COMMERCE

Nothing is impossible. Nothing is beyond your reach unless you allow a barrier to stand between yourself and your dreams. The bricks of such a menacing wall are forged with thoughts of doubt and "I can't." "Impossible" is a concept that exists only in the mortal mind; it is not a part of the world formed by our Creator. His world is one of endless possibilities. If we perceive a dead end to our potential, we have wandered into a perilous room of illusions. Never agree that limitation is real.

For example, engineers analyzed the bumblebee and, upon review of its wings, size, weight, mass, and strength, came to the conclusion that flight is impossible for such a creature. The structure and strength of the bee's wings, scientists tell us, cannot support its body. Thank God no one told the bumblebee.

We must turn our minds in the direction of possibility thinking. To see the potential rather than the problem is the all-important difference between those who ride the crest of life and those who flounder in the waves. The great question is, Do you want the problem or do you want the solution? The door to all the power in the universe is in your mind. When asked where lies the key to the universe, a guru answered, "I have good news and I have bad news: The bad news is that there is no key to the universe. The good news is that the door has never been locked." Your vision is the key that opens the door to your destiny. Success is your birthright.

The most important ingredient of success is belief in myself.

Watch Your Language!

*"Thousands of people can speak at least two
languages—English and profanity."*
—JOE CLARK, FORMER HIGH SCHOOL PRINCIPAL

Profanity is a bad habit. It's disappointing to hear anyone use profane language of any kind because we don't know—when or if—they'll stop. For example, a dear old woman wanted a parrot that could talk. She searched in several shops before finding the right one. The owner told her, however, that the parrot was previously the pet of a bartender and was liable to say anything—even use profanity. Nevertheless the woman purchased the bird with the hopes of teaching it to use acceptable language. Everything went well for nearly a month. But one day she forgot to feed her pet. When she walked into her house, the bird cursed at her. She grabbed it and said, "I'll teach you never to use those words again." She put the parrot in her freezer to punish it. A few minutes later she removed the bird and asked, "Have you learned your lesson?" The bird shivered and replied, "Yes, ma'am." She asked, "Are you going to use those words again?" The parrot shook its head and said, "No, ma'am."

A year went by without further incident. Then one day the woman forgot to feed the bird again. When she returned home, the parrot was cussing up a storm. She grabbed her feathered friend by the neck and put it back in the freezer. When she finally took him out, he said, "I thought I had a filthy mouth until I listened to that turkey in the icebox."

I find it difficult to believe that anyone—for example, the turkey—has positively influenced another person by using profanity. But I know of many instances where friendships were disrupted, sales were lost, and opportunities were missed because of the slip of a tongue. *Profanity is the use of strong words by weak people.* You'd better watch your language, because you never know who's watching yours.

I am too sharp and articulate to express myself profanely.

Chance of a Lifetime

"We've already won! What were the chances of us making it beyond slavery?"
—JOHN LEE HOOKER, BLUES SINGER AND GUITARIST

Dr. Hugh Gloster, past president of Morehouse College, delivered a commencement address before nearly two thousand graduates and guests. Dr. Gloster's remarks were charged with emotion and inspiration. He spoke of the power of chance.

"Men, now that you've graduated," Dr. Gloster asked, "what chance do you have? The same chance that anyone has. But it doesn't mean a thing unless you take it. Sitting in these seats were young men just like you—aspiring leaders who approached life with little more than high hopes and a briefcase full of ambition. What chance did they have?

"For example, society took one look at a shy, young writer from Jackson, Mississippi. The boy attended the city's segregated schools and was barred from using its libraries. When told of his desire to write, others laughed and said, 'No chance.' But racism was no deterrent. Today Lerone Bennett is executive editor of *Ebony* magazine, and it is his words that mold and shape the images of Black America.

"Who would have thought that one of our own would direct the same city that withheld so many of its opportunities from him. With degree in hand as he searched for employment, Maynard Jackson was told that he had little chance because of his race. But fired by a lofty purpose, Jackson convinced southern voters to take a chance on him and he became Atlanta's first black mayor.

"Upon arriving in Montgomery, Alabama, the sight of women being beaten and children being bitten by dogs turned his stomach. 'Oh, Lord,' he thought, 'how could one human being do this to another?' But turn an oppressive hatred into love? Fat chance! With no organization or influence, a young, unproven Baptist preacher taught a nation to look beyond race. Because he took a chance, Martin Luther King's place in history is assured."

It's been said that the individual who never had a chance never took one. *Success is never won by chance but by choice.*

There's no way to succeed unless I take a chance. Today will be the day I take my big chance.

You Deserve a Break Today

"Let's face it. Much of our community is tension filled. Without adequate methods to relieve this stress, many of us exist within a time bomb."
—M. JOCELYN ELDERS, SURGEON GENERAL

Everything we do is either goal achieving or tension relieving. If a person is not happy with his progress, he should take a good, hard look at everything he does during the course of the day. As he approaches his tasks, he should ask himself, "Is this goal achieving or tension relieving?" We all need to relieve our tensions, but if we are doing too many things for escape and too few for achievement, we are going to hold ourselves back.

Wouldn't it be interesting if we surveyed the average individual to determine how much time is devoted to goal-achieving acts? We might be amazed to discover what a small amount of time we actually spend preparing for the future. A doctor, for example, might spend twelve hours a day in the presence of his or her patients. Every minute with a patient would have to be labeled "goal achieving." Time spent consulting with other physicians, however, would be labeled "tension relieving." A teacher would consider time driving to and from school or in the cafeteria or the teacher's lounge as tension relieving. But preparing the next day's lesson over the kitchen table would be categorized as goal achieving.

There is of course a time to be idle—tension relieving—and a time not to be idle. The success of a person in any undertaking will hinge directly upon his making certain that he relegates his tension-relieving acts to a secondary position. This gives our lives balance as well as a much-needed break from the routine.

Today I will find the delicate balance between pursuing my goals and relieving stress.

Boomerang

"Of all the qualities necessary for success, none comes before character."
—ERNESTA PROCOPE, CEO, E. G. BOWMAN COMPANY

A young woman preparing to entertain guests went to a small grocery store to buy food. She stopped at the meat counter and asked the butcher for a large chicken. He reached down into the cold-storage compartment, grabbed the last chicken he had, and placed it on the scale. "This one weighs four pounds, ma'am," he said.

"I'm not sure that will be enough," the woman replied. "Don't you have something bigger?" The attendant put the chicken back into the compartment, pretended to search through the melting ice for another one, and then brought out the same bird, discreetly pushing his hand gently on the scale. "Ah," he said with a smile, "this one weights six pounds."

"I'm still not sure that's enough." the woman said with a frown. "I'll tell you what—wrap them up. I'll take them both!"

The dishonest person is his own worst enemy, and he is, in the end, his own victim. When a person does something dishonest, he is essentially tossing a boomerang. How far it will travel, no one knows. Only time will tell how great or how small a circle it will traverse. But eventually it will come back swift and unseen to the person who released it.

The same principle holds true when a person conducts himself in an honest and forthright fashion. Good results from good acts are just as certain as bad results from bad acts. Each act is an unfailing boomerang.

Honesty pays. This may be the quickest way to build your fortune.

Between a Rock and a Hard Place

"I've benefited from many scholarships. A number of people paid a lot of dues for me to do what I do. I feel it's my responsibility to give back."
—WYNTON MARSALIS, JAZZ TRUMPETER

A young boy was doing his best to lift a rock that was too large for someone his size. He huffed and puffed as he tried in vain to lift the huge stone. In spite of his efforts the rock wouldn't budge. His father walked by and, after watching his son's struggle, asked if he was having trouble. The boy answered, "Yes, I've tried everything, and it won't move!" The father replied, "Are you sure you have used every resource at your disposal?" The boy looked up, frustration filling his face, and blurted out, "Yes!" Kindly his father bent over and said softly, "No, my son, you haven't. You haven't asked for my help."

Have you ever heard someone say, "I don't need anybody. I'll go it alone." In my younger years, when I had more ambition than common sense, I vaguely recall saying those words. We can't go it alone. We need and must depend upon each other.

A rich man, feeling that he was alone, said the he would divide his fortune among his friends if only he knew who they were. Years passed, and the man died. His death occurred in the midst of a blizzard. His last request was that his funeral be held at four o'clock in the morning. But only one man and a poor old woman turned out to pay their last respects. When the rich man's will was read, they learned that his vast estate was to be equally divided among those who attended his funeral.

A friend steps in when others step out. In life and death we all need friends.

Today I will take a few moments to begin new friendships.

C'mon, Get Real

"Your goal should be out of reach but not out of sight."
—ANITA DEFRANTZ, OLYMPIC CHAMPION AND MEMBER,
INTERNATIONAL OLYMPIC COMMITTEE

It's fun to watch a magician pull a rabbit out of an empty hat or to see him produce a coin out of thin air. If we were to believe what we see, we would think that he had really materialized these objects.

So it is with life. When driving along a country road the trees in the distance seem to move along with us, while the shrubbery close by moves swiftly past us in the opposite direction. It would appear that the entire landscape was moving in one direction, while we are standing still.

There are other times when we accept appearance as reality. For example, we see poverty and sickness and, judging by their appearance, we come to the conclusion that these images are real. But our Creator instructs us "not to judge by appearance, but to judge by righteous judgment."

Righteous judgment is the judgment that comes from right thinking, and right thinking comes from God. And God is *real* and *good*! When we judge righteously, we know that as real as sickness and poverty may seem, they are only appearance, not truth. These negative conditions have no real substance except that which we give them by our thoughts. As long as we accept them at face value, they will appear real and we will suffer the consequences until we change our thinking.

The first step in overcoming any negative circumstance is to look beyond these temporary conditions and frustrations of the material world.

Today I will look for what's real. I will set my sights beyond negative conditions or circumstances for the true picture.

Finding Your Key

"The best way to develop any career is heart first."
—MALCOLM-JAMAL WARNER, ACTOR

During a recent orientation at the Clark Atlanta School of Business, I was introduced to a student who had quit college several years ago to try his hand in investment banking. The young man failed miserably and finally had to face up to the fact that he wasn't going to succeed in his chosen field. In an effort to find direction he went back to school. One night during a party he had an interesting conversation with a young coed majoring in fashion design. As the fashion major talked, the former financial planner found himself completely engaged. As a result of that evening he enrolled in several fashion-merchandising courses, even though he had never given a thought to the clothing business. Completely enthused, he was like a bird released from a cage. He immediately set a goal to launch a custom T-shirt business.

This story shows the importance of giving yourself a chance to discover the type of work that is right for you. If you like your work, you'll succeed. People who work at jobs they don't like are unsuccessful. Millions of people go through life without being "turned on" by what they do. They never find the key to the right field—the field that could offer them a career of interest, challenge, and rich rewards. It's never too late to get into the field that is right for you—*and there is a field right for you*!

You'll find the key when you begin to chase the dreams in your heart!

I will concentrate on the field that I love. I will match my interests with my career.

Race Issues

"I'm in my prime. There's no goal too far, no mountain too high."
—WILMA RUDOLPH, OLYMPIC CHAMPION

It's hard to win a race if you start off fifty feet behind. Yet that's just the handicap that we face in our quest for success. Because of racism and discrimination, just getting to the starting line is an exhausting effort for us. It doesn't seem fair, and it isn't. But the fact is that we can only take off from where we are.

We who have heard "You can't win" or "You'll lose, so there's no sense trying" all our lives have to shake off those muddy messages before we can run free. All the resentment and self-pity in the world, understandable though it may be, won't turn what is into what ought to be. The mud is there. Until we commit ourselves to cleaning our shoes—doing our best and concentrating on the race at hand—our running shoes will be heavy. So what if others are better prepared than we are? So who cares if others have better trained coaches? It doesn't matter. All that happened yesterday, not today. *And today's race is the race that counts*!

Those of us who start out with handicaps, who begin several feet behind, need to give ourselves credit for running the race at all. We need to stop resenting where we are and start loving ourselves for the daily courage it takes to suit up and show up. We deserve to win, and we can win if we stop looking backward.

What's been done is done. Today I will press on to my goal.

Health Food

*"When it comes to food for thought, some of us are
on a hunger strike."*
——DICK GREGORY, ACTIVIST

Your mind is extraordinarily complex. Yet it works in a simple, three-step manner. First, it takes in information—what you see, hear, smell, taste, and feel. Second, it processes these data—how does this information relate to me? Third, after processing the information, your brain tells you what action to take. In building a life of success or failure, your mind takes in information, processes it, and then tells you what to do.

A cliché of modern times is "garbage in—garbage out." In other words, if incorrect or bad data are absorbed—garbage—the processed information will be misleading. As a result the action taken on the processed data will also be incorrect—or "garbage."

A woman walked into a bookstore one day to buy a computer guide. When asked what type of handbook she wanted, she cavalierly replied, "Oh, just anything—any book will do." So the clerk handed her an out-of-date manual. She rapidly flipped through the text, and then said, "This looks good. I'll take it."

Half an hour later the same woman arrived at a meat market and demanded prime rib. She scornfully refused the first cut, as well as the second, insisting upon "the best that you have." When she finally received the most expensive cut, she announced, "I am particular about what I eat." How unfortunate that so many people feed their bodies with the best that money can buy while their minds get by on "just any old thing."

Start a health-food diet by feeding your mind healthy, uplifting thoughts.

I will be very particular about what I feed my mind.

Do the Right Thing

"The real problem is not the bad guys, it is that the good guys have gone to sleep."
—MAYNARD JACKSON, MAYOR, ATLANTA, GEORGIA

A young boy and his father were excited about fan-appreciation night. They wanted to get one of the souvenir baseballs that are thrown into the stands. As they hurried toward their seats, they saw a man drop a ten-dollar bill. The boy picked up the money.

"Hey, mister," he said loudly. The man in front of him turned around. "You dropped this." The boy handed him the money.

"Thank you," the man said. The boy returned to his father. Just as he and his dad reached their row, a ball came sailing toward their empty seats. A fan in the row behind reached forward and caught it. The little boy swallowed hard.

"I know, son," said his father, looking the boy straight in the eye. "But you did the right thing."

For his effort the child will bring home a souvenir far more lasting and valuable than a baseball or a ten-dollar bill. He will know the bittersweet feeling of making a sacrifice to do what is right.

There is a power for good in the universe greater than you will ever know. You can use this power to transform your life whenever you wish.

Today I will ask, What sacrifices have I made to do what is right?

Cultural Diversity

"In our complete darkness we are all the same, it is only our knowledge and wisdom that separate us. Don't let your eyes deceive you."
—JANET JACKSON, SINGER

We may have an inner circle of support, but we are also part of a larger community. Humanity is interconnected. The keynote of harmony throughout the universe is: We are one. The buzzword is "unity."

Regardless of race, creed, or color, unity is the basic theme. The word *universe* is derived from two Latin words meaning "to turn into one." It depicts one coherent, cooperating, system, achieving unity out of diversity. *We are one!* Each of us is a single cell in the great mind of God. We are part of a complex and loving system that binds us together. Our Creator instructs, "Behold, how good and how pleasant it is for brethren to dwell together in unity."

Unfortunately many people practice a belief in separation or *dis*-unity without being aware of it. For example, goodwill is unity; ill will is separation. Love is unity; hate is separation. Hope is unity; fear is separation. The following tale demonstrates the benefits of unity.

One day a little girl from an African tribe wandered off into the tall jungle grass. She couldn't be found, though the tribe searched several days. Then a little boy got an idea. He suggested that everyone hold hands and walk through the grass together. Surprisingly the girl was found, but due to her exposure to the damp evening air she died. In his anguish and through tears, her little playmate cried, "If only we had held hands sooner."

Today I will extend my hand in friendship or offer a hand of support to someone of a different background.

Tears in Heaven

"It's better to walk in the dark with God than to run in the light alone."
—BOBBY JONES, GOSPEL SINGER

Life is a gift from our Creator. Life constantly unfolds before us and takes on different forms throughout different periods in our lives. No power in heaven or on earth could stop this forward-moving process called life. Life is. It can never stop.

We are told that we are born with a will to live. Unfortunately many are born with an almost equal will to die. The following story amplifies this point.

Two years before his death a man began to make preparations for his demise. He bought a cemetery plot that he visited weekly. He planted grass, and watered and mowed it regularly. On Memorial Day he placed flowers on the gravesite, thinking, "I want to see the flowers now. When I'm gone, I won't be able to see them." He even visited a funeral home and picked out his casket, saying to himself, "That's where I'll rest one day."

One evening he invited his family and friends to dinner. After a hearty meal he began to dispense with his personal effects. Then he handed a nephew his will. As he did so, he dropped dead of a heart attack—a victim of his thoughts! His guests stood in stunned silence. Everyone except his nephew. As a matter of fact a smile appeared on the boy's face. Sensing their uneasiness, the boy shook his head. "My uncle made a huge mistake," he shared openly. "For most of his life he was an atheist. But now he knows the truth!" Life is a piece of happiness that God gives to us.

Today and every day, I will cherish this special gift called life and the power that created it.

The Land of Milk and Honey

"I had crossed the line. I was free, but there was no one to welcome me to the land of freedom. I was a stranger in a strange land."
—HARRIET TUBMAN, CONDUCTOR,
UNDERGROUND RAILROAD

Harriet Tubman was a woman who devoted her life to helping slaves escape their bondage. In her youth she had been hit on the head. As a result, she suffered dizzy spells for the rest of her life. In spite of her affliction, and at great risk to her own life, she guided many slaves on the Underground Railroad to freedom.

Freedom from slavery is different today but just as necessary. It may mean freedom from being a slave to what others think of us, freedom from drug abuse, freedom from jealousy, freedom from trying to force others to do what we want them to do.

We are free to be the very best people we can be. Our own freedom can be even more fulfilling when we welcome others enthusiastically into that land of freedom by allowing them the room to be themselves without fear of judgment. This is the "land of milk and honey." In this way, by freeing ourselves, we free one another.

Today I will free myself by freeing others of my unrealistic expectations of them.

Role Model

*"Simply having children does not necessarily make
a woman a mother."*
——MARY FUTRELL, EDUCATOR

A young mother set her foot on the path of life. "Is the road long?" she asked. Her guide replied, "Yes. The road is hard and long, and you will be old before you reach the end. But the end will be better than the beginning."

One day, while on her journey, a storm arose and the path was dark. Her children shook with fear. Their mother drew them close and covered them with her love. Her children said, "Oh, mother, we are not afraid, for you are near." When the storm subsided, the mother said, "This is better than the brightest day, for I have taught my children courage."

With the coming of a new day a steep hill appeared on their path. The children climbed and were exhausted. Though she was weary, too, the mother continued to inspire them. "Just a little bit longer," she said, "and we will be there." So the children continued to climb, and when they reached the top, they looked back and said, "Mother, you motivated us. We could never have reached the top without you." As the stars fell, the mother said, "Today is better than the last, for my children have learned the meaning of patience and persistence in the face of adversity."

The next day strange clouds darkened their path—clouds of hatred and evil. As a result the children groped and stumbled. "Look up," coached the mother. "Walk tall. Don't bow down to anyone. Lift your eyes to the light; you are worthy!" And the children searched above the clouds and saw the true idea. It guided them to safety. Her children said, "Mother, you have inspired us to continue on in spite of our difficulties." That night the mother said, "This is the best day of all, for I have shown my children God—Creator of the universe, and now I have given them everything." The guide was right: The ending was better than the beginning.

Today I will recognize the efforts of the women who struggle to raise their children during these difficult times.

One Moment, Please

"Great opportunities come to those who make the most of small ones."
—DEMPSEY TRAVIS, ENTREPRENEUR

Once a famous artist was hired to put stained-glass windows into a cathedral. His eager young apprentice pleaded for the chance to design just one window. The master artist feared that an experiment on even a small window would prove costly, but his persistent apprentice kept up his pleas. Finally the master agreed that he could try his hand on one window if he furnished his own materials and worked on his own time.

The enterprising apprentice began gathering bits of glass that his master had discarded and set to work. In short order the church was finished. When the cathedral doors were opened, parishioners stood in awe before the apprentice's stained-glass window, praising its beauty.

Our lives are like this. If we take the time to gather together the moments and opportunities we, too, often discard and waste, we find we can shape them into something of value and beauty.

Today I will take a long look at the moments I waste. What can I make of these moments?

Cross Training

"God is!"
—REVEREND CALVIN BUTTS, PASTOR,
ABYSSINIAN BAPTIST CHURCH

It was written, "He has achieved success who has lived long, laughed often, and loved much. Who has gained the trust of pure women, the respect of intelligent men, and the love of little children. Who has filled his niche and accomplished his task. Who has left the world better than he found it, whether by an improved poppy, a perfect poem, or a rescued soul. Who has always appreciated earth's beauty and never failed to express it. Who has always looked for the best in others and always given the best he had. Whose life was an inspiration, whose memory a benediction." This moving statement, besides providing a spirit-filled soliloquy, sets the stage for the following story.

Several years ago a child wanted to enter a Sunday-school class in Philadelphia, but was told there was not enough room. She began saving her pennies to "help the church build a bigger class."

Two years later the girl became ill and died. Family and friends who cleaned out her belongings found a small book under her pillow. Within the book were fifty-seven pennies and a piece of paper that read, "To help build the 'Little Temple' bigger, so more children can go to Sunday school." One Sunday the pastor told this story to his congregation, and a newspaper picked up the lead. The story soon spread across the country. Soon the pennies grew, and the outcome can be seen in Philadelphia today. Thanks to a little girl's tiny seed, there is a church that seats nearly four thousand members. Thanks to her humble efforts, Temple University was founded. And thanks to her mighty gift, the Temple Sunday school was constructed. And it all began with a tiny child who wanted to make the world a better place for others.

Today I will make a contribution to help make this world a better place to live.

Good Hair

"Aunt Jemima is the black woman who cooked and cleaned, struggled, brought up her own family and a white family. And if I'm ashamed of Aunt Jemima— her head rag, her hips, her color— then I'm ashamed of my people."
—MAXINE WATERS, CONGRESSWOMAN

It's hard not to compare ourselves—our looks, our capabilities, our accomplishments—with "paragons of perfection." We know who they are. We see them every day—in magazines, in music videos, on television—models, actors, and celebrities of one kind or another. No matter where we turn, we are bombarded with their images and all the adjectives that go with them: "Oh, such and such has a beautiful complexion," or "Did you see you-know-who's hairstyle? I wish my hair was like that."

Needless to say, we fall short in these comparisons. For most of us falling short may not be devastating, but it certainly can result in a subtle and steady erosion of our self-image and self-confidence. If we persist in comparing ourselves to these standards, we will always be "too dark" or "too light" and our hair will be "too short" or "too nappy."

In order to strengthen our self-image, we have to develop respect for our own uniqueness and individuality. The culture may define beauty in terms of a particular body shape or facial structure, but what qualities do we possess that are equally attractive? What about traits other than physical ones?

The point is, you need to define and aspire to your own sense of beauty. Right now you are the "right" color, and your hair is "good"! You need to determine and hold fast to what is right for you individually.

I am unique and attractive. I am beautiful in the mind of God.

It's as Clear as Day

*"It was clear as day. I saw myself beating the odds,
coming back to play again."*
—BO JACKSON, PROFESSIONAL BASEBALL PLAYER

There are two types of birds that fly over the California desert—the hummingbird and the vulture. The vulture, with its outstretched wings, makes a silent sweep until it spots the carcass of a dead animal and torpedoes down upon it. The tiny hummingbird, on the other hand, flies over the same terrain never noticing the carcass. Patiently it hovers near a cactus and spots a plant in full bloom. The bird spears the plant, drawing out the honey with its long, thin bill. Each creature, in its own way, puts on mental blinders and finds what it is looking for.

This is a parable for life: *You will find what you look for.* One day a group of friends went swimming, and one of them lost a ring in the bottom of the lake. Everyone started diving from different directions to find it until they stirred up so much mud and sand that no one could see a thing. Finally everyone decided to clear the water and waited patiently on the shore for the mud and sand to settle. When it finally cleared, a single swimmer dove in and picked up the ring.

When we are confused about something in our lives, we often receive answers and advice from different directions. Our friends will tell us one thing and our subconscious another, until we're mixed up. If we look away from our problem and let patience and time do their work, the mud inside us will settle and clear. And like a bird searching for food, we will find what we are looking for.

I will begin to block out everything that is not in line with my goals.

Friends in High Places

"We'd better pull together before the forces pull us apart."
—WILLIE BROWN, SPEAKER, CALIFORNIA STATE ASSEMBLY

When ducks migrate, they can be seen flying in a V-shaped formation. If you watch them, you will see that the lead bird—who was doing most of the work by breaking the force of the wind—will drop off and fly at the end of the formation. This bird then gets to rest while another one takes over. By cooperating—working together, supporting each other—the geese can safely complete long migrations.

"Few burdens are heavy when everybody lifts," attests civil rights pioneer Charles Evers. "When I look at my brothers and sisters, I am really looking at myself," said Hazel Johnson, the first female African-American general in the U.S. Armed Forces. "We will achieve greatness together or failure apart." Through friendly support and a spirit of cooperation, we all benefit.

A story is told of two artists who were putting the finishing touches on a painting high on a scaffold in a church. The younger artist stepped back to admire his work and became enraptured with the beauty of what he had created. His partner saw with horror that in the emotion of the moment his co-worker was inching toward the edge of the scaffold, and would, in another moment, slip to his death. Fearing he would frighten his partner by a warning cry, the man deliberately splashed paint across the mural. His friend lunged forward in disbelief and cried out, "Why did you do that? Look at what you have done!"

When he saw that his partner had saved his life, his anger and confusion melted into tears of thankfulness. As we travel through life, let's share the burden that comes with being the lead bird—let's support each other.

Cooperation is an asset that can only be gained by giving.

A Journey of a Thousand Miles

*"Man, you can't be tired. You haven't done
a thing yet."*
—J. BRUCE LLEWELLYN, ENTREPRENEUR AND
PHILANTHROPIST

It's interesting that people who have goals tend to live longer than people who don't. It's as if they extend their lives simply because they have something to do. For example, there are old ships that are beautifully maintained, still navigating the seas. They have weathered hundreds of storms and have success-fully docked at thousands of ports. After each trip these ships are better equipped to handle the next assignment. Goal-oriented people are like these vessels. They always have some-thing to look forward to, and each goal, successfully reached, finds them better equipped to set the next goal. Each goal is a bit more demanding and fulfilling than the one before. In a few years they find themselves accomplishing, with surprising ease, goals that would have been impossible for them when they first began setting objectives.

Years ago, during the Depression, a young man was hitch-hiking around the country. He struck up a conversation with an older man who had offered him a ride. The older man asked him what his goal in life was. The young man replied that his greatest desire was to be a millionaire. "Oh, no it isn't," the old man said. "If that were true, you wouldn't be wasting your time bumming rides around the country. *You would be hard at work trying to make your dream come true.*"

Goals are important. When a person knows where he or she is going and is engaged in getting there, the most amazing co-incidences begin to take place. When we know where we're going and are occupied on our journey, it seems as if all the forces, whatever they are, come to our aid. And by using these forces, we find our desires. *Another goal is reached!*

The purpose of life is a life of purpose. Today I will develop a clear vision of what is important to me.

The Discover Card

"The person who is self-centered is off-centered."
—SIMON ESTES, OPERA SINGER

It's no secret that business is always on the prowl for new money. Many times it is found in our community. Everyone wants to know how we, Black Americans, spend our money. Ken Smikle, publisher of *Target Market News*, says, "With the introduction of more and more products specifically geared to African Americans, it's clear that Madison Avenue recognizes the growing importance of this segment of the population."

Madison Avenue is a power that has dictated our lifestyle to a great extent. Provocative copy and images advertise and encourage our buying. We are constantly bombarded with messages telling us that in order to amount to anything, we have to dine at the right restaurants, drink the right beverage, drive the right car, wear the right clothing, live in the right house, and shop in the right stores. If we don't, then we are missing out on life. We have made names like Gucci, Mercedes, Fendi, Nike, Starter, Giorgio, and Mont Blanc rich, powerful, and well known.

Madison Avenue advertisers should not be the power that dictates how we run our lives or how we feel. We need to understand that high principles and a spiritual approach to life are far more rewarding than the drive for money, property, and prestige. With this approach we can discover a whole new life!

Today I let go of all useless status symbols.

Learning Disabled

"It took me ten years to write my first book. I learned more about this business when I was stumbling than you could ever imagine."
—JAMES BALDWIN, WRITER

Speaking before a Houston, Texas, high school, all-pro quarterback Warren Moon made the following point: "There are a lot of ways to become a failure, but never taking a chance is the most successful. *There is something to be gained from just about everything, even failing.*"

Once there was a little girl who was trying to learn to walk, but her mother wouldn't let her fall down. Every time she took a step and was about to fall, her mother would rush behind her and catch her.

It quickly became apparent that she wouldn't learn if she wasn't permitted to fall. But the child was too young to correct her mother's ways. The mother thought she was helping her daughter, when in fact she was inhibiting the learning process. Allowing the little girl to fall would have shown trust in the child, trust that she could master the process and walk like everyone else.

Sometimes we resemble this mother, protecting each other from life's important lessons. We have to stop. This doesn't mean that we allow someone to get seriously hurt, but that we permit each other the freedom to learn and grow in individual ways.

I will allow others to learn at their own pace.

You Can Dish It Out But You Can't Take It!

"Your hair is so short that if you stood on your head your hair still wouldn't touch the ground!
—KIM WAYANS, COMEDIENNE

It's hard to know how to react when we are being teased, or when we are the target of someone's cynical humor. We may be terribly hurt or offended yet remain silent because we don't want to appear overly sensitive. We may want to lash out at the person who is needling us, or we may simply want to flee because we feel vulnerable and anxious as we wait for the next barb.

If teasing, sarcasm, and innuendo affects us in these ways, why do we sometimes dish it out ourselves? In all honesty most of us do. We joke insensitively about someone's hairstyle or weight or "mama," and then say, "Just kidding!" We mock another person's speech and then make it worse by saying, "C'mon, talk right!"

The next time we are tempted to tease someone or shoot a sarcastic quip, we should recall what such jibes have done to our own well-being when we've been on the receiving end. We should also remind ourselves that this sort of so-called humor drives people away, and eventually extinguishes love. If you must talk about someone's speech, weight, or family, then do it in a positive, edifying manner.

Today I will be sensitive to the feelings of others. I will rely on the language of love and kindness.

I Heard It Through the Grapevine

"I think the public is too hungry for gossip. There are things more important than who slept with whom."
——ED BRADLEY, *60 MINUTES* COHOST

The television program *60 Minutes* once reported on a widely read tabloid and interviewed people who were buying the paper at grocery store checkout counters. "Do you believe what you read in this paper?" the reporter asked. "No," came the reply, "but we like to read it anyway." Gossip holds a strange fascination for all of us.

There is a legend that drives home this point. A man with a troubled conscience asked the village priest for advice. The man had repeated some gossip about a friend and had later found his words to be untrue. He asked the priest what he could do to make amends. The priest told the man, "If you want to make peace with your conscience, you must fill a bag with feathers, go to every house in the village, and drop a feather on each doorstep." The man did as he was told. He then went back to the priest and asked, "Is this all I need to do?"

"No," the priest replied. "Take your bag and gather up every feather. The man left. After a few days he returned, saying, "I could not find all the feathers, for the wind had blown them away." The priest then said, "So it is with gossip. Unkind words are so easily given but difficult to take back."

Gossip is like mud thrown on a clean wall. It may not stick, but it always leaves a dirty mark.

The most useless thing in the world is idle gossip. I refuse to be part of it.

Hands On

"All mothers are handicapped. They only have two hands."
—ENOLIA P. MCMILLAN, FIRST WOMAN EXECUTIVE DIRECTOR
OF NAACP

Opening ourselves to others is a beautiful pattern that we can weave. Lending a hand and an empathetic ear can lift the spirits not only of the person in need but also of the person serving. We need to remind ourselves constantly that each of us can serve, and through our service we increase our self-worth.

A man broke his left hand. One night, as he lay in bed, he imagined a dialogue between his right and his left hands. His right hand said, "Left hand, you're worthless. Everybody's glad it was you that was broken and not me. You're useless." His left hand asked, "Why are you superior?"

His right hand replied, "Why, my owner cannot write a letter without me." His left hand said, "But who holds the paper on which he writes?" The right hand came back with, "Who swings the hammer?" The left hand asked, "Who holds the nail?" Then the left hand continued, "When our owner shaved yesterday, you held the razor, but his face was cut because I wasn't there to help. When our owner's watch stopped, you couldn't wind it because I wasn't there to hold it. You can't even remove money from his wallet unless I'm there to help. Our owner can do very few things without me."

We, Black Americans, resemble both hands. We live in a sometimes difficult world. We can do very little without the support of each other.

I open myself to others and, in turn, I support my own.

Growing a Tail

"Responsibility develops some individuals and ruins others."
—ROBERT WOODSON, FOUNDER, NATIONAL CENTER FOR NEIGHBORHOOD ENTERPRISE

It's very important for us to learn to ask for help and be willing to receive it, but it is even more important that we learn how to help ourselves. We are our constant companion and we know, better than anyone else, what is good for us and what we want and need.

The phrase "God helps those who help themselves" is a sound and practical philosophy, but I also love the lighter approach taken by the African proverb, "God will not drive flies away from a tailless cow." We all know "tailless cows": people who always look outside of themselves for solutions and are adept at never taking responsibility for their own lives.

During the trauma of a divorce a friend regressed to a helpless state in which, at first of necessity and then out of habit, he hung on to his friends for support while lamenting his situation. We were willing to be there for him for a while, but finally his "tailless" state caused another friend to confront him about his lack of self-help. Although the confrontation was painful, it opened his eyes and he began accepting responsibility for his part in the divorce and finding ways to take charge of his life. My friend grew a tail.

Being able to rely on yourself is the major responsibility of adult life. As we learn to trust and support ourselves consistently, our "tails" lengthen and the flies that have been persistently pestering us disappear.

I am willing and able to help myself. I take responsibility for my actions and reactions.

The Today Show

"You never know which key unlocks the safe."
—BRYANT GUMBEL, MORNING NEWS HOST

Success can be achieved only by those willing to persevere beyond the point where the majority stop and turn back. Few of us realize how long it takes in the early days to succeed in an extraordinary way. There are difficult steps to be taken.

A story is told of a scuba diver and fortune hunter who spent fourteen years searching for a sunken Spanish galleon off the Florida Keys. Each day the crew kept looking for this elusive ship. Many wondered if they would ever find it or if the ship was even there. The captain of the expedition had a motto that kept the crew inspired: "Today's the day!" He had T-shirts and signs printed bearing that maxim. Then one day *today was the day!* The crew found the sunken treasure, turning each crew member into a millionaire in the process.

Anita Baker, the talented female vocalist, was turned down by numerous record companies and reduced to tears before she signed on with Elektra Records. *But today is her day!* Film producer Mattie Rich made more than one hundred presentations to potential investors before he secured the funding to produce his first movie, *Straight Out of Brooklyn. But today is his day!* And dancer and choreographer Judith Jamison began her quest for the bright lights when she was six. Many days she danced on aching legs and bleeding feet. *But today is her day!* Today she is labeled America's premier dancer.

Today is your day! Today is the day for you to take another step closer to your goal. Often it is just a single step that makes the difference.

Today, and every day, I will continue to step toward my goal.

Getting Over

"It's not the load that breaks you down, it's the way you carry it."
—LENA HORNE, SINGER

An overburdened and overworked ant was told to carry a piece of straw across a large slab of concrete. The straw was so long and heavy that the tiny insect staggered beneath its weight. Nonetheless the ant was committed to completing its task. Finally, as the stress of its burden began to take its toll, the little creature was brought to a halt by a gaping crack in its path. The ant saw no way of getting across or around the deep divide. Then a thought suddenly struck. Carefully laying the straw across the gulf, the ant walked over it and safely reached the other side. The ant's heavy load had become a helpful bridge because he was committed to his task.

The preceding story is one of commitment. *Commitment is a key ingredient in the success of any endeavor.* Both husband and wife must be committed to each other in order to develop a happy marriage. The successful salesman must be committed to his product. If we're committed, we will always find a way out, a way to move ahead, even if we're sidetracked or temporarily delayed. The simple value of commitment is that life works better when you do what you say you are going to do. Living up to your word will bring you great inner strength.

Because I am committed to my goals, my burdens can be overcome.

The Last Word

*"The older he grew, the less he said, and the more
he spoke."*
—BENJAMIN E. MAYS, EDUCATOR

To see what you are asking for, look at what you are receiving.
We get exactly what we ask for—no more and no less. If life
does not seem to be supplying you with your needs or desires,
it's not because the universe is malfunctioning; it is because
subconsciously you are asking for or expecting something
other than what you believe you want.

Day by day we write our own destiny. Thoughts are causes,
and conditions are effects. If you've ever wanted to know the
status of your thoughts, you need only to look at your conditions. One of the greatest messages ever given to mankind is
written in the Scriptures: "Whatsoever a man soweth, that
shall he also reap." Translated, it means that whatever you
send out in word, thought, or deed will sooner or later return
to you—and with astounding accuracy. In practical terms, if
you crave friendship, affirm friendship. Do you want love?
Speak loving words to others. If you want the confidence of
others, show confidence in others. You have the power to do
whatever you wish, but you must *think and speak* it into action.

A hunter rasied his rifle and took careful aim at a large
black bear. When he was about to pull the trigger, the bear
said in a soft, soothing voice, "Isn't it better to talk than to
shoot? What do you want? Let's talk about it." Lowering his
rifle, the hunter replied, "I want a fur coat."

"Good," said the bear, "we can compromise. I only want a
full stomach. Let's negotiate the matter." They soon sat down
to bargain. After a brief period the bear walked away alone. In
the beginning was the word, and the word gives power to our
universe. Use it to create the type of world you desire.

I direct my life. I only think and speak exactly what I want.

The Conservative Party

*"I don't give a damn what others say. It's okay to
color outside of the lines."*
—JIMI HENDRIX, GUITARIST

Many of us bristle like porcupines if anyone dares to tell us
what to do. We're insulted by the very idea that we need advice or guidance of any kind. Allow ourselves to be bossed
around? Never! Thank you very much, but we'll make our
own decisions.

Yet the vast majority of us are followers at heart. Our dress,
talk, tastes, and habits are almost always styled by the dictates
of one group or another. In our need to fit in, we have formed
and shaped ourselves very carefully to be "a part" rather than
"apart."

Business executives and college professors may criticize the
peer pressure that has young people wearing unlaced gym
shoes and Starter jackets. But what of all those pinstripe suits
and wing-tip shoes marching in lockstep? What of all those
rumpled tweed jackets and baggy wool sweaters? Isn't that
conformity? Are we afraid to break out of the pack? In a sense
we all conform, and to a degree we are all conservative.

Most of our waking hours are spent following guidelines
that are not of our own making. We go along to get along,
keeping pace with our associates as best we can. The fact that
we do conform is unquestionable. To ask ourselves why we so
hotly proclaim otherwise is the real question in our search for
greater self-awareness.

I may follow the crowd in terms of dress and style, but not in
terms of my thinking.

Wheel of Fortune

"For some, self-help is too much to ask."
—TONY BROWN, JOURNALIST AND TALK-SHOW HOST

The grandest fortunes ever accumulated began with energy, intellect, and will. From Frederick Douglass, the great abolitionist, to Oprah Winfrey, America's number-one talk-show host; from W. E. B. DuBois, the founder of the National Association for the Advancement of Colored People, to the acclaimed writer Toni Morrison—the story is the same. Those who have won must have relied mostly upon themselves.

Surely one of the saddest creatures around is the one labeled the "prisoner of hope." This is an individual who hopes that someday a wealthy relative will die and leave him a fortune. The prisoner of hope hopes that someday, while walking down the street, he will see bags of money that will contain his life's fortune, or at least enough to give him security. He's the kind of person who goes to the shore to see if his ship is coming in, when in reality he knows that it has never left the port. The prisoner of hope hasn't discovered that if you really want to find a helping hand, you should look at the end of your own sleeve.

Each of us must set in motion the words of Booker T. Washington, who urged us all to "start where you are with what you have, knowing that what you have is plenty enough!"

There is no free lunch. I plan on working for everything I get.

Teach Your Children Well

*"Strive to make something of yourselves, then strive
to make the most of yourselves."*
—ALEXANDER CRUMMELL, MINISTER AND PAN-AFRICANIST

Anyone who has raised a child knows times of intense frustration. I remember hearing an angry father shout at his twelve-year-old son, "Why don't you grow up?" After a short pause, while fighting back tears, the boy replied, "That's what I'm trying to do." Raising children is like pouring concrete. Before concrete can be laid, a solid base must be prepared. Once the concrete is poured, the mixture must be shaped and molded before it sets; once it sets, change is possible only after you have removed what has already been laid down. If done properly, a well-poured footing will last a lifetime. If done incorrectly, the surface crumbles, the structure cracks, and the walls and floors shift. The analogy is obvious.

The following thoughts express the influence that parents exert on their children: If a child lives with criticism, he learns to condemn; if a child lives with fear, he learns to hate; if a child lives with pity, he learns to feel sorry for himself; if a child lives with praise, he learns to be appreciative; if a child lives with acceptance, he learns to love; if a child lives with honesty, he learns truth; if a child lives with sincerity, he learns to have faith; if a child lives with love, he learns that the world is a wonderful place in which to live.

Children are fast learners. Let's be patient and teach them well.

Today I will spend time with a child or children. I will instruct them on the true values of life.

Head Case

"The mind is the standard of the man."
—PAUL LAURENCE DUNBAR, WRITER AND POET

It can be infuriating to hear someone say that a very obvious, concrete issue we're struggling with is an "attitude problem." When we're pounding away at some unyielding difficulty, the last thing we want to hear is, "It's all in your head." Such comments make us feel that our intelligence, not to mention our sanity, is being discounted. We resent the oversimplification of what seems to us a very complex dilemma.

The truth may well be that our problem is as real and as hard to crack as a slab of stone. Yet it may also be true that some attitude we're bringing to the problem is wearing us out more than the problem is! After all, our attitudes are the tinted glass through which we see our problems. So, of course, our attitudes always precede our actions.

A creative attitude transforms many setbacks and disappointments into learning experiences. A receptive, sensitive attitude lifts the cloak off the mundane and routine so that we may see the beautiful sights and amusing events. A roll-up-the-sleeves, can-do attitude is the best problem solver there is.

Today I will examine the power of my attitude. If my problems are in my head, then the power of my attitude is greater than the power of my problems.

The Juice Man

"A river can't rise beyond its source. What's in the seed determines the fruit."
—T. M. ALEXANDER, ENTREPRENEUR

There was a strong man who traveled with a circus. One of his more memorable stunts was to take a lemon and squeeze every last drop of juice out of it. He would then offer a thousand dollars to anyone who could manage to squeeze as much as one additional drop from the fruit. He boasted about his feat from city to city, but no one was able to win the money. One day he came to a small town and pitched his offer. A small, frail woman stepped forward and accepted the challenge. She took the crushed lemon and squeezed several drops of juice from it. The man couldn't believe his eyes. "How did you do it?" he asked. The woman shrugged and said, "My husband has been out of work for nearly a year. I do this all the time."

When it comes to pushing ahead and using our talent, we must squeeze out every drop. When presented with the heroic challenge of carving out a better life, many who faced barriers have managed to squeeze every drop from their ability. Think of how Marian Anderson became the first African American to perform at New York's Metropolitan Opera House, Charles Drew perfected blood plasma, John Baptiste du Sable established Chicago, Jackie Robinson shattered baseball's color line, Richard Allen founded the African Methodist Episcopal Church, Phillis Wheatley became the first African-American poet, Garrett Morgan created the traffic signal, Millie E. Hale built one of the first black hospitals in the country, "Wild Bill" Pickett became the "king of the rodeo," and Crispus Attucks was the first man to die defending our nation's freedom during the Revolutionary War. These men and women exemplify the best that is in us.

Our time and place is now, and we have the opportunity to do all the pioneering we've ever dreamed of. As in all other times we need only courage and determination to squeeze out every last drop.

I will use all my untapped abilities.

Pour Me a Cup

"We deserve everything we can get. We spilled the blood. We shed the tears. No one has given more than us, and now it's payback time."
——CHARLES RANGEL, CONGRESSMAN

A friend of mine attending a conference was surprised to notice that everyone at the breakfast table had coffee but him. He felt a little miffed and said, "Why didn't I get coffee?" A guest at the table answered, "Your cup is upside down. You have to turn your cup over." When it comes to receiving all that life has to offer, we must turn our cup over.

Why do we have such qualms about anticipating and accepting abundance? Maybe it's due to the role that Black Americans have been forced to play in society. Historically we have rendered services that were largely taken for granted. Years of slavery and discrimination have taken their toll on our psyche. We learned to give to others but expect nothing for ourselves. In order to invite abundance into our lives, we need to feel worthy of the myriad blessings life has to offer: peace and harmony, health and energy, supportive relationships, a decent education, and satisfying careers, to name a few.

Whatever the reasons for our hesitancy in accepting all forms of prosperity, it is important now that we change any limiting beliefs and awaken to the realization that we deserve to live abundant lives. We need to turn our cups over and allow abundance to pour in until they overflow!

I deserve to live abundantly. I am worth every blessing life has to offer.

Labor Day

*"The only place where success comes before work
is in the dictionary."*
—S. B. FULLER, ENTREPRENEUR

One day a preacher drove down a country road and came upon the most magnificent farm he had ever seen. The farm stood out like a diamond—it sparkled. While it was by no means a new farm, the house and surrounding property were finely constructed and freshly painted. The garden around the house displayed an array of beautiful flowers. The fields were uniformly tilled, and an impressive herd of cattle grazed in the pasture.

In his unabashed gazing, the preacher noticed the farmer on a big, shiny tractor hard at work. Upon noticing his visitor the farmer stopped his tractor, shut off the engine, and shouted a friendly hello. The preacher then said, "My good man, God has certainly blessed you with a magnificent farm." There was a pause as the farmer removed his cap and wiped the perspiration from his face. He studied the preacher for a moment and replied, "Yes, he has, and I'm grateful. But you should have seen this place when he had it all to himself!"

As he drove off, the preacher thought about the fact that every farmer along this road had been blessed with the same land, the same opportunity, and each worked according to his pleasure. He understood that every farm was the reflection of the people who lived there. Furthermore, he also knew that the land we are given comes not in the form of acres or lots but in terms of the life we are blessed with; that's our plot of land. And what we do with it is our business. Finally, the preacher realized that though the farmer was grateful for what he had, he knew that what he did with it spelled the difference between success and failure.

Luck may help you get to the top, but it takes hard work to keep you there.

I welcome hard work. It is the shortest path to success.

Spirit in the Dark

"In spite of everything that was done to me and my race, in spite of the adversity and the bitter moments, again we rise!"
—MAYA ANGELOU, WRITER

To ask, "What is the role of attitude in a person's success or failure?" is like asking, "What is the role of water in the Atlantic Ocean?" Attitude comes very close to determining success or failure. With a great attitude a person can succeed, though he may start with little else. Attitude makes the sale or loses it.

One evening a young man took a shortcut home through the cemetery. As luck would have it, he fell into an open grave. He screamed and desperately tried to climb out, but to no avail. With no one to hear his pleas, he settled down in a darkened corner of the grave to wait for morning. A short time later another man strolled along through the cemetery, taking the same shortcut home, and he, too, fell into the same grave. He started clawing and shouting, trying to get out just as the first had done. Suddenly the second fellow heard a voice out of the black corner of the grave say, "You might as well give up. You'll never get out." *But he did!* The most powerful thing you can do to change your circumstances is to change your attitude. It is *attitude*, not aptitude, that governs altitude.

We are not born with a drive to succeed. That quality comes from learning or experience or both. But we are born with exuberance and curiosity, and when these qualities are combined with motivation and positive expectations, we can expect great results. Attitude helps to explain why some of the least likely people succeed beyond all expectations. This is why the timid young girl becomes a leading actress, or the boy with terribly burned legs becomes a world-class track star, or the kid with a low self-image goes on to make millions and carve a name for himself in industry and finance. On the other hand, our colleges and universities are filled with sharp, articulate students who unfortunately will never reach their full potential because they lack the most vital ingredient of all: *attitude—the great craving to suc-ceed.*

I free myself from a negative or self-limiting attitude, and I welcome the opportunities that will come my way.

Something Worth Leaving

"It's not what you take but what you leave behind that defines greatness."
—EDWARD GARDNER, FOUNDER, SOFT SHEEN PRODUCTS

Reluctantly Mary McLeod Bethune left her comfortable old house in Florida for the railroad station. She had promised to speak at a dinner in Washington and did not want to disappoint her friends.

As a champion of human rights, she wore the title of "the most powerful Negro in America" with dignity and respect. Now her battle was nearly over. She was almost eighty. As the train and her life neared its final destination, she pulled an envelope from her purse, thought deeply for a few moments, and made some notes for her speech:

"If I have a legacy to leave my people, it is my philosophy of living and serving. . . .

"I leave you love. Love builds. It is positive and helpful. *I leave you hope.* Yesterday our ancestors endured the degradation of slavery, yet they retained their dignity. *I leave you the challenge of developing confidence in one another.* This kind of confidence will aid the economic rise of the race by bringing together the pennies and dollars of our people and plowing them into useful channels. *I leave you thirst for education.* Knowledge is the prime need of the hour. *I leave you a respect for the uses of power.* Power, intelligently directed, can lead to more freedom. *I leave you faith.* Faith in God is the greatest power, but great, too, is faith in oneself. *I leave you racial dignity.* I want Negroes to maintain their human dignity at all costs. *I leave you a desire to live harmoniously with your fellow man. I leave you, finally, a responsibility to our young people.* The world around us really belongs to our youth, for our youth will take over its future management." Let's leave the next generation our greatest gifts.

When my journey comes to an end, I will give future generations something worth leaving—love, dignity, and faith.

What Do You Bring to the Table?

"The roots of happiness grow best in the soil of service."
—RUTH B. LOVE, EDUCATOR

What do you bring to the table? Do you add value to the lives of others? Do you bring peace, understanding, or knowledge? Perhaps you think you can continue to take while providing nothing in return. After all, doesn't everybody do it? It doesn't hurt. You're wrong—it does hurt. The following story proves my point.

An African chief invited the men of the tribe to a great feast. "All the food will be provided," he announced, "but each of you must bring a jug of wine." Ali wanted to attend the feast but had no wine to give. His wife suggested, "You could buy a jug of wine. It's not too expensive."

"How foolish!" Ali cried. "To spend money when there is a way to go free? Rather than wine, I will carry water in my jug. No one will notice. It won't hurt to add one jug of water to the great pot of wine."

On the day of the feast his guests gathered in the chief's home. As each man entered the tribal grounds, he poured his jug of wine into a large earthen pot. Ali carefully added the contents of his container, greeted the chief, and joined the others. When all the guests had arrived, the chief commanded the servants to fill everyone's glass. As the chief blessed the feast, his guests raised their glasses and drank. Suddenly a cry of disbelief arose from the crowd. What they tasted was not wine, but water! Each guest had decided that his jug of water would not spoil the pot of wine.

It is certain—when we take out more than we give, when we sneak by without giving our best, it hurts us all.

Today, and every day, my motto is: Giving more than is expected is always expected.

Think and Grow Rich

"We don't all think alike. In fact, many of us don't think!"
—LEE DUNHAM, ENTREPRENEUR

A man bought a new gadget but couldn't figure out how to put it together even after he read the instructions. Finally he sought the help of a handyman who was working in his backyard. The old fellow picked up the parts, studied them, then began assembling the project. In short order he put it together. "That's amazing," exclaimed his neighbor. "And you did it without even looking at the instructions."

"Fact is," said the old man, "I can't read, and when a man can't read, he's got to think!" Thinking—or creative imagination—will solve all of your problems. How strong is your creative imagination? Can it be improved? Thinking creatively can be applied to anything from raising children to earning additional income.

There's an eye-opening fable that carries this point farther. A wealthy king had passed on, leaving all his possessions to his trusty servant, Omar, with the exception that each of his four sons should be allowed to pick one thing of value to have and hold forever. One son, the eldest, chose the royal palace; another, the crown jewels; another selected the king's land. As each son made his selection, it became evident that the remainder of the vast estate would go to their father's servant. They were such shallow thinkers, except for the youngest. Finally the youngest and the last son stepped forward to make his choice. He said, "I choose to be served by Omar."

Training the mind to become more creative can only be done through use. Be sure to use your creative imagination, the principal source of human improvement.

Today I will practice the art of using my creative imagination.

Something That You Can Use

"The value of our lives depends on how we use them."

—A'LELIA WALKER, PHILANTHROPIST AND DAUGHTER OF
MADAME C. J. WALKER

We all wonder at some point why we've been placed on earth and what the purpose of life is. Of course there are various views on this subject. The first view holds that we should do everything possible to reach our full potential, that we should strive to be the best that we can be. The second view holds that we live to glorify the Creator. The third view holds that we live to serve our fellow man. Jesus of Nazareth, Clara "Mother" Hale, Malcolm X, and Martin Luther King are all examples of people who committed their lives to the service of others.

An elderly woman recently asked me to retrieve a box of letters from her dresser drawer. As I removed the letters, I saw a beautiful quilt in the drawer. When I asked about the quilt, she told me to take it out and look at it. It was a masterpiece! She told me her grandmother had made the quilt as a wedding gift years ago. When I asked her why she did not have it on her bed, she said, "Oh, it's too beautiful to use." How sad she felt her gift was better hidden in a drawer—preserved—than used.

Whether you believe your purpose in life is to reach your full potential, to glorify your Creator, or to serve others, it can only be achieved through personal sacrifice, persistent effort, and cooperation with others. You must find something bigger and grander than yourself, a cause that stirs your emotions like no other. Our Creator gave humanity a beautiful gift, the most beautiful gift in the world. I hope yours is something that you will use.

Today I will analyze my talents and establish goals that make use of them.

The Greatest Show on Earth

"Fear is not a wall but an emotion. And like all emotions, it can be overcome."
—GWEN GOLDSBY GRANT, PSYCHOLOGIST

Fear is not our enemy. Seen rightly, fear becomes our strongest ally. Because there is nothing to fear in our universe, when we experience fear, we have the opportunity to free ourselves from an illusion that has been holding us back from living the life our heart desires.

Many years ago a well-known lion-taming act appeared live on television. The lion tamer walked into the cage to start what appeared to be a routine performance. The door was locked behind him. The spotlights highlighted the cage, the television cameras closed in, and the audience watched in suspense as the trainer skillfully put the animals through their paces. In the middle of the act near-disaster struck—the lights went out! For nearly thirty long seconds—what seemed like eternity—the trainer was locked in the cage with ten man-eating lions. A whip and a small kitchen chair offered meager protection under the circumstances, but he survived. And when the lights came on again, he calmly finished the performance.

In an interview after the show the trainer was asked how he felt knowing these ferocious animals could see his every step but he couldn't see them. He first acknowledged the chilling fear, but pointed out that the lions didn't know that he couldn't see them. He said, "I just kept cracking my whip and commanding them until the lights came on." At some point in our lives each of us will face the terrifying task of fighting lions in the dark. But once we tame our lions, we'll free ourselves from the bondage of fear forever.

Today I will do the thing that I fear, and the death of fear will be certain.

A Stranger in Paradise

"The best preparation for tomorrow is to do your best today."
—LOU GOSSETT, FILM STAR

One of my favorite stories revolves around a sailor who was shipwrecked on a South Sea island. He was seized by natives, hoisted to their shoulders, carried to the village, and set on a crude throne. Little by little he learned that each year the islanders crowned someone king for a year. He was intrigued until he began to wonder what happened to all the former kings. Soon he discovered that every year when his reign drew to a close, the king was banished to an island where he starved to death.

The sailor was moved to action. He ordered carpenters to build boats and told farmers to plant crops on and transplant fruit trees to the barren island. He gave masons the task of constructing houses on the island. When the sailor's tenure concluded, he was not banished to a barren island but to a land of abundance and comfort.

This experience gives us a vivid parable of life. We are all kings and queens, at least for a short period. We are able to choose what we will do with our resources. A part of successfully achieving your goal is not only working hard but working smart. People who reach great heights are those who carefully lay out a definite plan to do so. They not only set a goal, they also establish a course of action to reach their objectives.

I will take a look at my resources and set plans to utilize them.

Giving You the Best That I've Got

*"If we would've given what we should've given, we
wouldn't be in this mess now!"*
—HERMAN B. SMITH, JR., INTERIM PRESIDENT, MORRIS
BROWN COLLEGE

A little girl was given two dollars by her father. He told her
that she could do anything she wanted with one of the dollars,
but the other was to be given in church on Sunday. The girl
nodded in agreement and asked if she could go to the candy
store. With visions of all that she could buy with her dollar,
she skipped to the store holding a dollar in each hand. As she
skipped along, she tripped and fell, and the wind blew one of
the dollars out of her hand and down a storm drain near the
curb. Picking herself up, the little girl looked at the dollar still
in her hand and said, "Well, Lord, there goes your dollar."

The first thing we learn from great men and women is that
giving is a test of maturity. Those who are mature give. The
immature do not. It is wise to practive giving in every area of
life. Give something every day. Give out of the fullness of
your heart. Give your feeling to others. Give money where it
is needed and can truly help someone. Give attention. Give
thoughtful, well-reasoned advice. Give by donating your time.
But most of all give thanks to the Lord for your many blessings. As Reverend Leontine Kelly, the first African-American
female bishop, said so eloquently, "Acquire the giving habit.
Give intelligently and freely. You owe it to yourself to give every day of your life."

**Giving from the heart is a sure path to spiritual and emotional
riches.**

Something in Common

*"A person completely wrapped up in himself makes
a small package."*
—DENZEL WASHINGTON, ACTOR

The power of interdependence is mighty. Life begins with a progression from self-centeredness, or independence, to understanding relationships with others, or interdependence. We aren't mature until we have both the ability and the willingness to see ourselves interconnected, as one among others.

Many years ago two students from Chicago graduated from law school. The highest-ranking student in the class was blind. When he received his degree and honors, he insisted that part of the credit belonged to his best friend, who was born without arms. The two had met on the first day of class. The student who was blind carried the books of his armless friend, while he in turn guided his sightless companion. The acquaintanceship ripened into a lasting friendship and a beautiful example of interdependence. The deficiency of each student was compensated for by the other's ability.

Any deficiencies that we may have can be compensated for by our love and support for one another. As African Americans we are intimately linked to a common history, a common culture, and a common cause. We are connected by language, by race, by land, and by conscience. There is a call stirring within our souls to recognize our heritage, to build our communities, to define our goals, and to unite against those negative forces that seek to tear us apart. Let's rise above any petty differences and focus on the power of interdependence. Let's compensate for our shortcomings by stating a simple affirmation in a single voice: *"I and my brothers and sisters are one!"*

Today I pledge to uplift, affirm, or support a fellow African American.

I'm a Soul Man

"The secret of being a saint is being a saint in secret."
—MARY MCLEOD BETHUNE, EDUCATOR

Many years ago there lived a man so spiritual that angels came from heaven to see how one could be so godly. This kind and gentle soul simply went about his life radiating love. Two words summed up his outlook: He *gave* and he *forgave*. Yet these words never fell from his lips; they were expressed in his ready smile and his kindness, love, and goodwill. Because of his countenance the angels asked the Creator, "Oh, Lord, grant him the gift of miracles!"

God replied, "I consent. Ask for him whatever you wish."

"What do you desire?" cried the angels to this humble servant.

"What can I wish for?" asked the Holy Man. "That God give me his grace? He's already done that."

The angels insisted, "You must ask for a miracle, or one will be forced upon you."

"Very well," said the man. "My wish is that I do a great deal of good without ever knowing it." The angels were even more perplexed. They took counsel together and developed the following plan: Each time the man's shadow fell behind him or at his side, it would have the power to cure disease, soothe pain, and comfort sorrow.

And so it came to pass. As this gentle man walked life's paths, his shadow caused withered plants to bloom and gave clear water to muddy streams and joy to unhappy people. And the people, respecting his humility, followed him closely, never speaking about his miracles. Little by little they came even to forget his name and called him only *the holy man*. By radiating love and kindness, each of us has the power to do good without realizing it.

As I grow older and wiser, I will talk less but say more.

Stand and Deliver

*"The day you take complete responsibility for your
life is the day you start to the top."*
—O. J. SIMPSON, PRO FOOTBALL GREAT

Truer words were never spoken. We live in a society where
many people refuse to accept total responsibility for their lives.
They blame others or circumstances outside their control for
their current situation. They look outward for scapegoats and
seldom look inward to find solutions within themselves.

The victim mentality is detrimental to success and happiness
because it denies the tremendous power within each of us to
substantially direct our lives and destinies. Success is not
something that randomly happens to you; it is not an accident.
Rather success springs from within. It begins with the right
mental attitude and is achieved through persistent action. If
your business, your job, or your life is not going in the direction that you wish, do not point fingers. The problem is not
your boss, your spouse, or your employer. *It is you!* Simply
look in the mirror and you will see the person responsible for
your station in life.

This is not to say that you have control over every facet of
your life. You don't. But you do choose your response to each
event—good or bad. Your present thinking and actions or lack
of actions have brought you to where you are today.

At this point you might begin to blame yourself for all the
opportunities you've missed in life. Careful, now. Blame is
useless and will drag you down. Berating yourself isn't going
to change past experiences. Instead begin with a clean slate
and focus on what you can do *now* to move in the desired direction.

I will now take responsibility for my future.

Put on a Happy Face!

*"Kindness is the language that the deaf can hear
and the dumb can understand."*
—DESMOND TUTU, SOUTH AFRICAN ACTIVIST AND ANGLICAN
ARCHBISHOP

Years ago there lived a cruel and hard-hearted king. After fending off several attempts on his life he suddenly realized how miserable he was and decided to change. He called his royal wizard and asked for help. The wizard pondered for a moment and told the king, "I can help you, but you must carry out my instructions. Wait three days and I'll tell you what I want you to do." Three days later the wizard gave the king a mask. The mask was a replica of the king's face with one exception: Instead of his usual frown and scowling lines the mask was smiling.

"I can't wear that," argued the king. "It's not my face!"

"If you want my help," reiterated the wizard, "you must wear the mask at all times." The king complied, and his world began to change. People began to enjoy his company. His subjects began to treat him with respect. His country began to enjoy the peace it had never known. All was well except within the heart of the king. Although he was overjoyed with the changes in his life, he grew uneasy. He wrestled with discomfort and again summoned the wizard. "I am grateful for the peace within my kingdom, but I cannot deceive my people any longer," he said. "I must remove the mask."

"As you wish," replied the wizard. The king stood in front of a mirror and slowly removed the mask that had changed his life. Drawing forth all his courage, he opened his eyes to look at his scowling face. But he was shocked. Instead of his unpleasant demeanor, he saw a beautiful and joyous visage, even more radiant than the one he had removed. Through his inner transformation the king's face had become a portrait of joy and kindness. To wear a "magic mask" of loving words and deeds is to act in accord with your real nature.

Today I will multiply the emotion of kindness by dividing it.

Do It Now!

*"Many people know how to criticize, but few know
how to praise."*
—ETHEL WATERS, SINGER, DANCER, AND ACTRESS

Why do we find it so much easier to compliment the dead
than the living? At funerals the friends and family members
gathered cannot say enough about the deceased. During life,
however, all those qualities that now draw praise usually went
unnoticed.

On her deathbed, after a lifetime of love and devotion to
others, Ida B. Wells, a journalist and social activist of her day,
left this inspiring message: "Loving praise is the best medicine. Don't wait too late. Be generous with kindness but
cautious with criticism."

Life is as sacred as death. It's appropriate to remember a departed one fondly, but it's even better to say what we have to
say while the person can still hear it. People don't become better or more deserving in death than they were in life. Living,
not dying, is what makes us praiseworthy. It is no small thing
to fall in love, to raise a family, to strive to assist others, to
live each day with all its mundane routines as well as we can.

We need to say all those loving words and express all those
loving thoughts on this side of death. The dead are beyond the
daily struggle and thus beyond any need of encouragement. It
is we, the living, who must depend on each other for mutual
comfort and support. If we have a word of appreciation to offer, let us say it now.

Today I will share my thoughts of love and respect before it's too
late.

A Room with a View

"Don't face the day until you've faced God."
—MAYA ANGELOU, WRITER

George Washington Carver once said, "My prayers seem to be more of an attitude than anything else. I indulge in no lip service, but ask the great God silently, daily, and often many times a day to permit me to speak to him. I ask him to give me wisdom, understanding, and bodily strength to do his will. Hence, I am asking and receiving all the time."

Prayer is need finding a voice. Prayer is embarrassment seeking relief. Prayer is a friend in search of a friend. Prayer is a quest in the darkness of midnight. Prayer is knocking on a barred door. Prayer is communion through both darkness and closed doors.

The Harvard Classics were published on the premise that if an individual would regularly give a few minutes a day to reading and moments of meditation, he or she would be familiar with much of the distilled wisdom of the human race. Spiritual growth, too, requires time each day given to prayer. A young student visited George Washington Carver's laboratory in Tuskegee, Alabama, and noted that the windows were covered with blinds and boards so that curiosity seekers could not spy on him. But the young man learned from Dr. Carver's former assistant that the inventor was not trying to blind prying eyes; rather he was trying to find peace as he knelt beside his laboratory bench for daily moments of prayer.

Our Creator has boundless resources. The only limit is us. Our asking, our thinking, our praying can never be too big.

Today I will pray for the desires of my heart.

Holy Water

"It is not so much what we know as how well we use what we know."
—ERNESTA PROCOPE, CEO, E. G. BOWMAN COMPANY

One of the greatest circulation systems ever designed is the natural recycling process of water. There is no new water on the planet. All there ever was is still here, only recycled. It goes through various stages of course; it evaporates; clouds become saturated; and rain falls. The water you bathe in tonight could be the water that filled the tub of Martin Luther King, Jr. The water you used to wash your car with last week may have contained the very same water that you drank as a baby. And the next bit of water you use may be mixed with the water to be consumed by those who will follow after us.

There is no water shortage as far as the planet is concerned. By storing it and redistributing it inefficiently, we disrupt the natural evaporation process and thereby create circumstances that seem to indicate a shortage, but in reality there is always enough.

To open the valve of plenty, you can use the same system as the water faucet. To get more water through the faucet, you simply open the valve by turning the handle in the proper direction. You remove the barrier that is stopping the flow, and you'll have all the water you need.

The valve of plenty in you can be turned on by turning your thoughts in the proper direction, thereby removing the barriers that are stopping the flow. All the abundance you need is already there for use. Choose your direction.

I will open up the faucet of abundance.

It's a Dirty Job,
but Somebody Has Got to Do It

*"Sooner or later we've got to polish ourselves up,
we've got to let the shine come through."*
—LOU RAWLS, SINGER

It seems to me that we don't have to add anything to our lives; instead we need to take things away. We need to take away the junk. Imagine driving a car with a filthy windshield. The sun is beaming and you can't see a thing ahead of you. The particles of dirt obscure the sun's rays, causing you a real problem. All you have to do, though, is take the dirt off the windows by washing them. The glass is already clear, but the dirt has to be removed.

The same is true of a diamond. All the brilliance, radiance, and beauty of the diamond are released through the facets cut into the stone. Each facet expresses the total vibrancy and beauty of the diamond. And the diamond cannot withhold any of this from the facets. However, when the facet gets dirty or dusty, the radiance of the diamond is hidden until the residue is removed.

You might consider that we are facets of life, and life can withhold energy, health, or love from us no more than the diamond can withhold any of its qualities from the facets— unless we cloud ourselves with fear, self-defeating attitudes, or doubt. Only when these negative qualities are absent can the true nature of our being be exposed to the world.

I will allow my vibrancy to show by removing the junk and dirt—negative habits and negative thinking—in my life.

Just Do It!

*"The only thing worse than failing is being afraid
to try."*
—FRANK MINGO, FOUNDER, MINGO JONES ADVERTISING

Just do it! We see these billboards plastered all over our community. For the sake of physical fitness, a tennis shoe manufacturer urges us to *just do it*. Whether it's tennis, running, cycling, hiking, or slam-dunking, just do it.

For the sake of emotional fitness, that's not bad advice to take. Building a positive self-image is like building anything else; nothing happens until you get started. *Just do it!*

It's a mistake to think that only major achievements count. We don't have to make president of the firm or run a marathon or graduate from college Phi Beta Kappa to significantly boost our self-image. In fact the opposite is true. How we see ourselves is established more by the thousand and one small, daily things we accomplish than by our infrequent moments in the limelight.

So just do it. Speak up at a meeting if that is new for you. Go work on your GED if you were forced to drop out of school. If you're working on standing up for yourself, express an opinion. Call your son or daughter if you're trying to develop a better relationship. Start that business that you have been thinking about. Whatever it is, *just do it*!

Today I will put an end to procrastination and excuses. I'll just do it.

I Wanna Be Like Mike

*"You preach a better sermon with your deeds than
with your lips."*
—CHARLES WESLEY, HISTORIAN

It takes a long time to fill a glass with drops of water. Even
when the glass seems full, it can still hold one, two, three,
four, or five additional drops. But if you will keep at it, one
last drop will make the glass overflow. The same applies to
deeds of kindness. In a series of kindnesses there is at least
one that makes the heart run over.

One of the most difficult things to give away is kindness,
for it is usually returned. Bob Greene, a columnist for the *Chicago Tribune*, relates that one cold night after a game Chicago
Bulls superstar Michael Jordan headed through a large crowd
of fans toward his car. As he opened the car door, Jordan saw
a youngster in a wheelchair some twenty feet away. The boy's
neck was bent at an unusual angle; his eyes could not look directly forward. Jordan walked over to the boy and knelt beside
him. The youngster was so excited that he began to rise out of
the wheelchair. Michael comforted him, talked softly, and
placed his arm around the boy's frail shoulder.

The child's father tried to snap a picture, but the camera
didn't work. Jordan noticed. Without being asked, he continued to kneel at the boy's side until the father was able to take
the picture. Only then did the superstar return to his car. The
boy's eyes were glistening with tears of joy. His dad was already replaying the moment with his son. If nothing good ever
happens again for that little boy, he will always know that on
one night Michael Jordan cared enough to include him in his
world. If we emulate what's best about our heroes, our collective hearts will run over.

Today I will add that one extra drop of kindness that will make
the difference in somebody's world.

Something for Nothing

"Poor is the man who only possesses money."
—T. M. ALEXANDER, ENTREPRENEUR

How much money can you accept? That seems like a loaded question. This "acceptance" seems to be determined by our own consciousness. Most of us know people who are well off, or even financially independent, as well as those who struggle to get by. What's the difference? If a man with virtually nothing is given a large sum of money, it won't be very long before he has nothing again. So many think if they could just get their hands on a bundle of cash, their troubles would be over. They would pay their bills, get out of debt, and have a chance at a new beginning. If you believe in this idea, you might want to consider the following survey.

Several years ago a poll was taken on a number of big-money winners who had landed their fortunes either through the lottery or as the result of television game shows. The majority of those who had won $100,000 or more were nearly penniless five years after their winnings. Their standard of living did not increase. Their lifestyles were the same as before. They had apparently taken the bonanza and squandered it away with no thought of investing.

Merely having money does not raise your consciousness about what to do with it. If you were to take all the people on the planet and give each an equal amount of money, within days you would see some rich and some poor. Take money away from an Earl Graves or a John Johnson today, and tomorrow each would be a millionaire. You are not rich because you have money; *you have money because you believe you are rich!*

Today I will develop a consciousness of wealth, abundance, and prosperity. I realize that believing is half the battle.

From the Back of the Pack

"It's better to look ahead and prepare than to look back and regret."
—JACKIE JOYNER KERSEE, OLYMPIC CHAMPION

After a thrilling come-from-behind win, Georgetown University basketball coach John Thompson was asked by a reporter what he told his players at halftime to spur them on to victory. "I told them that I do not like to lose," Coach Thompson responded. "Defeat, to me, means the failure to reach your objectives. Too many people in business, as well as in sports, are afraid of competition. Competition is a part of life, and if you are prepared, victory will certainly be yours."

Many of us have never been fond of competition, yet we face it every day—as we apply to college, climb the corporate ladder, or face dozens of qualified candidates in a job interview. In these situations the pressure always seems to mount. We feel fragmented, unfocused, and fearful. During these trying moments we can't help but remember similar situations in the past, when we "blew it" because we were not focused. And we can't help but remember how we berated ourselves for not being better prepared, at least emotionally.

It goes without saying that competition is sometimes unavoidable and that we're going to be more successful in some competitive situations than others. But if we prepare ourselves mentally and emotionally for the opportunities that are available, we will certainly have a much better chance of holding our own. Then we could begin to experience our own come-from-behind victories.

Today I feel up to the challenge. I'm prepared for anything that comes my way.

Deal Me In

"There's more power in the open hand than in the clenched fist."
——MARTIN LUTHER KING, JR., CIVIL AND HUMAN RIGHTS
ACTIVIST

One of life's best-kept secrets is that including other people in our goals lends energy and impetus toward reaching that goal. The old stereotype of the lonely, solitary striver grasping for recognition and achievement without regard for anyone else is actually a rare case. The truth is that people who achieve greatly usually share greatly.

There are two types of people in this world: the excluders and the includers. Some people live to get everything they can. They "exclude" as many people as they can because they believe that will leave more of the goodies for themselves. The "includers," on the other hand, include others in everything they do. They share their lives, including their rewards, and because they are so adamant about sharing, they are able to obtain more and give more of what life has to offer.

Sharing is so basic to the human experience. Have you ever noticed how many of the successful people you know enjoy including others in what they do—sharing life with others, giving away with one hand what they've worked so hard to acquire with the other? Regardless of the profession, the truly successful always include others in some form or fashion. For example, top-notch teachers are those who have a compulsion to share what they know with their students. Successful performers are those who reach across the footlights and share themselves with their audiences. Great athletes are those who include their teammates in their achievements. High-achievers are big includers. The act of sharing what they have achieved gives their achievement more meaning.

Today I will share my resources with someone looking for support.

That's Easy for You to Say

"Learn to speak kind words. Nobody resents them."
—CARL ROWAN, SYNDICATED COLUMNIST

Several years ago a publisher shared a profound statistic. He said that the average person uses nearly thirty thousand words each day. If these words were put into print, they would fill a fair-sized book. Over the course of a lifetime these books would fill a college library.

This publisher's thoughts are a bit frightening. They emphasize the fearful responsibility that goes with the gift of speech. Throughout history we can see how words have shaken the world. A few examples are:

"What do we want?" asked Stokely Carmichael to a huddled group of first-time voters. "We want black power!"

"I'm just glad we had it to give," said Camille Cosby to Spelman's president Johnetta Cole with regard to her $20 million gift.

"Let's try to work it out," pleaded Rodney King during a press conference with the hope of ending Los Angeles's deadly riots.

And "I have a dream," preached Dr. Martin Luther King in reference to his vision for humanity.

Words *are* important. The six most important words: *"I admit I made a mistake."*

The five most important words: *"You did a good job."*
The four most important words: *"What is your opinion?"*
The three most important words: *"If you please."*
The two most important words: *"Thank you."*
The most important word: *"We."*

Today and every day I will only include the most important words in my vocabulary.

Set the Record Straight

*"A person is never what he ought to be until he is
doing what he ought to be doing."*
——BUSTER SOARIES, PASTOR

A great violinist stood before an audience and enraptured it
with his playing. Suddenly, in the midst of the selection, he
took the violin from beneath his chin and smashed it into a
thousand pieces upon the floor. The audience sat aghast. In the
silence the violinist walked to the front of the stage and said
quietly, "Don't be alarmed. The violin I destroyed was one I
purchased for a few dollars in a department store. I shall now
play upon my Stradivarius." He took the valuable instrument
from the case, tuned it for a moment, and began to play. The
music was magnificent, but to the majority of those present it
was indistinguishable from the earlier selection. When he concluded, he spoke again.

"Friends," he said, "so much has been said about the value
of this violin in my hands that I wanted to impress upon you
the fact that the music is not in the instrument, it is in the one
who plays upon it."

I am constantly asked by ambitious men and women
whether I think they really have what it takes to achieve success. Without fail, their answer is "yes" if they allow their
music—their talents, potential, and abilities—to flow. I know
you have the ability to succeed, but I don't know if you *will*
succeed. That rests entirely with you. *You can, but will you?*
You say you desire to make your life count, that you are ambitious. Then why don't you blast forward? What are you
waiting for? What holds you back? Answer these questions
and you will have taken the first step toward achievement.
There is only one answer: *you!*

I know that if I wait for favorable conditions or circumstances,
I will do nothing but wait. Today I will set action steps to reach
my goals.

Lethal Weapon

"Either move or be moved!"
—COLIN POWELL, CHAIRMAN, JOINT CHIEFS OF STAFF

One kiloton (KT) is the equivalent to 1,000 tons of TNT. One megaton (MT) is the equivalent to 1 million tons of TNT. The first atomic bomb exploded in New Mexico was nearly 19 KT. The bomb that rocked Hiroshima was 20 KT. The largest hydrogen bomb ever exploded was 100 MT, tested by the Soviet Union in 1960. The force of that bomb measured pressure pulses the world over. Today scientists are discussing bombs of 10,000, 20,000, or even 1 million megatons.

How powerful is a 100 MT bomb? To equal the force of a 100 MT bomb, you would have to drop a 20 KT bomb (similar to the one dropped on Japan) every day of the year for thirteen years! This massive firepower is no comparison to what lies within mankind. Whether we realize it or not, each of us carries around enormous explosive power. Within each of us lies a lethal weapon that can set forth a mighty charge capable of rocking the earth. If you misuse this power, it could blow your hopes, desires, and wishes sky-high. Men and women who have misused this power by inflaming the fears, hatreds, and resentments of others have wreaked untold damage. However, if used properly, this mental dynamite could shake the foundations of your being. It could destroy false concepts and replace them with fresh ideas and ambitions. It could remove fear and worry from your life. It could release your mental brakes, restore your self-confidence, give you a more positive outlook, and enable you to face those challenges you've been avoiding for years.

What is your most powerful weapon? It is your ability to think and to act, and to direct your thoughts to that which you desire most!

Today I will use this weapon to build and grow and not to destroy.

Lethal Weapon 2

"Nothing attracts so much attention as how Black America spends its money."
—TONY BROWN, JOURNALIST AND TALK-SHOW HOST

Money is an important weapon because it is an instrument for good or evil. With a ten-dollar bill we can buy enough liquor to paralyze our thinking, blunt our sense of propriety, and behave like a fool. Or we can purchase the works of Langston Hughes, Claude McKay, or James Weldon Johnson, making available for ourselves the supreme wisdom of the ages. With our wealth—no matter how much we may possess—we can pamper ourselves with creature comforts or we can support the not-for-profit efforts of others. By means of our capital we can back those businesses that exploit human weaknesses and society, or we can support those institutions that serve and lift our own.

We sometimes hear that money talks. If you haven't heard it speak, take my word for it—money does talk! For example, a dollar bill has been known to say, "You hold me in your hand and call me yours. Yet may I not as well call you mine? See how easily I rule you? To gain me, you would all but die. I am as invaluable as rain, as essential as water. Without me men, women, and institutions falter. I go nowhere unless you send me. I keep strange company. For me mankind mocks, loves, and scorns character. Yet I am appointed to the service of saints. I give education to growing minds and food to starving bodies. My power is explosive. Handle me with care lest you become my servant."

Money will reveal two things about a person: how an individual earns it and how he or she spends it. Next to God and your thoughts, money is one of the greatest forces on earth.

Today I will increase my knowledge about money and wealth.

Burn, Baby, Burn

"You're not rewarded for having brains. You're only rewarded for using them."
—MORDECAI JOHNSON, FORMER PRESIDENT,
HOWARD UNIVERSITY

Whenever you buy a plane or train ticket, someone always asks, "Destination, please?" In other words, what's your aim? The universe asks each of us a similar question: "Where are you going in life?" In order to answer this question, you must get SMART about your destination. You must set *S*pecific, *M*easurable, *A*cceptable, *R*ealistic, and *T*ruthful goals. If you engage in the process of becoming "smart," you'll be on your way to reaching your objective. And because you have identified your destination, your personal power will multiply.

For example, on a clear, bright sunny day take a magnifying glass outside and hold it over a pile of crumbled pages of newspaper. Even though you are magnifying the intensity of the sun's rays through the glass lens, you will never start a fire—if you keep moving the glass. But if you hold the magnifying glass still, allowing it to focus the rays in a concentrated beam of sun energy, you will harness the power of the sun and multiply it through the lens—igniting a fire.

The same process could be utilized to start a fire in your affairs. By concentrating on a single goal and focusing your energy, you will harness your personal power and reach your objective. Try it and ignite your ideas.

Today I will identify my destination and ignite my definite purpose.

My Kind of Person

*"God speaks wherever he finds a humble, listening
ear. And the language he uses is kindness."*
—LENA HORNE, SINGER

Kindness is the golden chain by which society is bound together. Every day is filled with the opportunity to be polite and thoughtful instead of indifferent and careless, kind and gentle rather than difficult and contemptible. We can all look back to someone who, through an act of kindness, took special pains to help us.

"A kindness done today," said the famed educator Benjamin E. Mays, "is the surest way to a brighter tomorrow."

"One way to get along better in the world," writes Maya Angelou, "is to be just a little kinder than necessary." Reverend E. V. Hill, pastor of one of the largest black churches in the country, agrees. "Don't expect to enjoy life," he says, "if you keep your kindness bottled up. To be successful means performing acts of kindness."

There is a fable about this idea of kindness. It features the sun and wind, who were engaged in a contest to see who could get an old man to take his coat off first. The wind blows fiercely, trying to loosen the coat, but the old man just pulls his coat tighter around him. Finally the wind gives up and the sun appears. The sun beams a steady warm ray of sunshine down on the old man, who soon takes off his coat to escape the heat.

More and better things are accomplished in the world by kindness than by force. When we find ourselves most frustrated, it is often because we are trying to force certain things to happen. But our own patient and steady desire to grow, fed by the love and kindness of others, cannot be stopped by anything or anyone. Our own kindness is a powerful force in our lives. It is like the tender flower that lifts its petals through the granite.

Today I will perform an act of sincere kindness.

Caution: Adverse Conditions

"Character is what you have left when you've lost everything else."
—PATRICIA HARRIS, FORMER SECRETARY, HOUSING AND
URBAN DEVELOPMENT

A wise man once said, "All of life's experiences are to be either enjoyed or learned from." This is a different perspective from the one we usually hold. We have been conditioned to believe that life is a combination of good and bad and that the price we pay for the good is the bad. Yet there is another way of looking at our experiences.

The hurts and sorrows that we feel in life are not punishments from our Creator; they are messages given to us by a loving God, who is showing us exactly what we need to change in order to grow. Adversity is our friend. It is the driving force that pushes us out of our comfortable nest and forces us to learn to fly on our own. When times are darkest, we develop the fortitude to rally again and win—if we understand the true nature of adversity and life's challenges. Adversity is a gift. Without it our growth is slow; with it we are transformed from fledglings into masters.

Every great person of merit has known adversity. Adversity can forge an immature soul into a powerhouse of strength. Marcus Garvey was spat upon and his very existence as a human being was denied. Rock 'n' roll guitarist Bo Diddley endured years of struggle and strife in dusty Mississippi towns before he captured the ears of talent scouts in New York and California. And we know of the small and stark beginnings of Dr. Dorothy Brown. Though she was abandoned at birth and raised in an orphanage, she became the first African-American female surgeon to practice in the South.

It was not by chance that these achievers faced tremendous adversity—they were in fact made *great by it*. The same demands will be placed upon you. Rejoice and be glad in them.

When circumstances seem bleak, I will redouble my efforts. Adversity will become my greatest asset.

The Great Depression

"Every day that dawns is a reason to say, 'Thank you, Father.' "
—JOHNETTA COLE, PRESIDENT, SPELMAN COLLEGE

Let's face it. There are times when even the best of us get depressed. Times when we feel emotionally bankrupt. Times when nothing seems to work out. Times when we feel like packing a suitcase and going somewhere to forget everything and everybody. Times when pep talks from friends don't seem to help. Times when we feel empty.

During these troubling moments when we begin to search for the source of our depression, we begin to devalue ourselves and list all the things we cannot do: "I can't find a job.... I can't lose weight.... I can't get motivated.... I can't finish school.... I can't start my business.... I can't stop smoking.... I can't quit drinking.... I can't shake this cold.... I can't understand my children.... I can't communicate with my parents.... I can't stand my boss.... I can't get over my grief.... I can't take the racism anymore." Our hearts are torn. No matter how hard we try, we can't find a way to replenish our strength, to uplift our spirits, to overcome our depression.

But hold on, there is a way! There's a way to empower ourselves, to end this confusion and regain our inner peace and tranquility. There's a way to quiet the storms. The answer is prayer!

Prayer is the cornerstone where the weary rest and the dismayed find hope. Prayer is our opportunity to communicate with the source of all inspiration, the fountain of all wisdom. Prayer is the only way we can turn our negatives into positives. It is the remedy that cures the great depression.

I will pray daily. I will affirm my good and give thanks.

Feeding the Masses

"God's part we cannot do; our part he will not do."
—WILLIAM W. SIMMS, MINISTER

All of humanity's guides throughout the ages have taught the principle of service. If you want the key to prosperity, philosophers tell us, then master the art of serving. There is a story about a man who left this earth and was taken on a tour of the inner realms. He was shown a room where he saw a large group of hungry people trying to eat dinner, but because the spoons they were using were longer than their arms, they remained frustrated. "This," his guide told him, "is hell."

"That's terrible," exclaimed the man. "Please show me heaven."

"Very well," agreed the guide, and on they went. When they opened heaven's door, the man was perplexed to see what looked very much like the same scene—there was a group of people with spoons longer than their arms. As he looked more closely, however, he saw happy faces and full stomachs, for there was one important difference—the people in heaven had learned to feed each other.

While we have lofty ideals for social reform and world change, our real purpose in life is to work on ourselves and serve our fellow man. In the long run we will make more of a contribution to mankind when we are clear about our purpose—*to serve*. The greatest service we can offer others is to give of ourselves.

Heaven on earth begins with my ability to give of myself in service to others.

In Living Color

"Different doesn't mean inferior."
—CORNEL WEST, AUTHOR AND COLLEGE PROFESSOR

One of my favorite stories is about an earthworm who pops his head out of the soil and sees a beautiful earthworm just a few inches away. Overtaken by the other worm's beauty, he tells her, "I love you. Will you marry me?" The other worm smiles and answers, "Don't be silly. How can I marry you? I'm your other half!"

Like the earthworm we are one. Behind our nationalities, colors, races, cultures, lifestyles, and histories, we are one. It is this unity, this common bond, that will be the hallmark of a new age.

Mankind is now at a critical turning point. Our choice is the same as it has always been: *Unite or die*. We must learn to cooperate. We must learn to accept. We must build our world on the foundation of *togetherness*, not separateness.

The question is, How big can we expand our idea of "us"? How much can we widen our idea of who is equal to us? Who are we willing to take into our family? As frail, tiny egos, each of us once lived in a limited world, revolving around "me." As our sense of self matured, we expanded to include our immediate family in our sense of "us." Everybody else was "them." One thing was for sure: "They" were different from "us," and "we" had to watch out for "them." As we grew and the world forced "us" to come in contact with "them," experience revealed that some of "them" were really not so bad after all.

Since humanity has now been shown to be one great family, the task before us is: How quickly can we raise our consciousness to "oneness" with all people? Now that we know we are one, the Creator expects us to live as one.

Today I will reach out in friendship to a "family member" of a different race or a different culture.

Our Future Is So Bright, the Light Burns My Eyes

"We make our future by the best use of the present."
—ZORA NEALE HURSTON, WRITER

We often hear predictions about events that will occur in the coming years. Many foretell vast and uncertain changes. We are told that we will have to make sacrifices. We will see the collapse of many of the institutions and ways of life with which we are now comfortable. Whether or not you agree with these predictions is not the issue. But one thing is clear. Those who anticipate the future will control their destiny!

The renowned black writer and publisher David Walker wrote, "Fear of the future is a waste of the present." Paul Laurence Dunbar agrees. He wrote, "The future frightens only those who prefer living in the past." The future belongs to us.

When we see the future, we want to see a life in which men and women of good will live in harmony and brotherhood. To make this day reality, we must all do our part now. We must conduct our lives in the same manner in which we want our future to become. We must live our lives in harmony with the spirit. We must love ourselves as well as each other. We must be strong and compassionate. We must remember who we are—children of a loving God who has planned our bright and prosperous future. We must be proud of and embrace our common heritage. We must serve and respect each other and relinquish any negative thoughts. We must practice what we were admonished to do two thousand years ago: "Love God with all your being, and love one another as yourself." But most of all, we *must* turn toward and embrace the future!

Today I will plot my objectives into the coming year. Future thinking is successful thinking.

Have You Decided?

"If a man hasn't discovered something that he will die for, he isn't fit to live."
—MARTIN LUTHER KING, JR.,
CIVIL AND HUMAN RIGHTS ACTIVIST

A little boy was told by his doctor that he could save his sister's life by giving her blood. His sister was near death, a victim of a rare disease from which the boy had made a miraculous recovery. Her only chance for survival was a blood transfusion from someone who had conquered the illness. After a series of tests the boy was found to be the ideal donor.

"Johnny, would you like to share your blood with Mary?" the doctor asked. The child hesitated, somewhat frightened. Then he smiled, and said, "Sure, Doc—I'll give my blood to my sister." The two children were wheeled into the operating room—Mary, pale and thin; Johnny, robust and the picture of health. Neither spoke, but when their eyes met, Johnny grinned.

As his blood siphoned into Mary's veins, new life seemed to come into her tired body. The ordeal was nearly over when Johnny's brave little voice broke the silence, "Say, Doc, when do I die?" It was only then that the doctor realized what his moment of hesitation meant: Little Johnny actually thought that in giving blood to his sister he was giving up his life! He had made his decision, and he was willing to live by it.

People may think decisions require complex thought. Actually most decision making is simple. The choices we face are not "What should I do next?" but "Should I do this specific thing or not?" Life is mostly a series of small decisions, each decision the natural consequence of earlier choices. For example, Alcoholics Anonymous doesn't counsel drinkers never to take another drink—that's a daunting step. Rather it teaches members to make small adjustments that lead to significant lifestyle changes: Not to take a drink that day. It is often the small decisions that are the most important and lead to the biggest changes and breakthroughs in our life.

I will make strong decisions and stick with them.

Fat Free

*"I've been up and down, and up and down. It ain't
the scale, it's what's in your head."*
—SUZETTE CHARLES, FORMER MISS AMERICA

We step on the bathroom scale in the morning and discover to
our horror that we weigh one pound more than we did yesterday. From that moment on, our day is ruined. We stand before
the bathroom mirror and say, "I'm fat!" Our preoccupation
with that single pound impinges on and influences everything
we do.

We approach our workouts, for example, solely in terms of
"calorie burning," so that they become more remedies for a
problem than the enjoyable life activities they are meant to be.

Those of us who get caught up in the obsessive approach to
weight loss—or life in general—know that it can sabotage our
health and turn us into emotional wrecks. At such times we
need to focus on our overall well-being. The fact is, compul-
siveness is seldom rewarded because it can never be satisfied.
The person who thinks that there is always more to do, that
there can never be enough, is bound to be frustrated.

There are times when enough is simply enough. And when
we perform at this level we remove the fat from our lives. Perhaps we are involved in a difficult relationship and have done
everything possible to make it work. We cheat ourselves if we
hold on to something that reason tells us is unworkable. It's
probably time to remove the fat and move on. When we have
given our all in our job and our efforts still go unnoticed, we
can say, "let's drop the fat," and search for more promising
employment.

There are instances in our life—after we have worked hard
enough, waited long enough, and loved enough—when obses-
sion is counterproductive. At this moment it's better to approach our extra baggage with objectivity, not with dread. It's
better to just drop your burdens and become fat free.

Today I pledge to free myself from burdens in my life.

Life Savers

*"When you knock on opportunity's door, make sure
your bags are packed."*
—DENNIS GREEN, NFL HEAD COACH

A man risked his life by swimming through the treacherous riptide to save a youngster being swept out to sea. After the child recovered from the harrowing experience, he said to the man, "Thank you for saving my life." The man looked into the boy's eyes and said, "That's okay, kid. Just make sure your life was worth saving."

You and I have a life that is calling us. We have a mission that each of us must fulfill in our own way. My life is in my hands, and what you make of your precious time on earth is up to you. Others may show me the way to walk and give me inspiration to walk my path, but in the final analysis only I can do the walking.

When you do not follow your calling to the life you were born to live, there remains a gap in the universe. There will be a space in your heart, a tiny ache calling you to be more, for you know that you are more. There will be a gift to the world left undelivered. In recent years there has been a great deal of attention paid to near-death experiences. There are fascinating accounts of people who have been clinically dead for short periods of time and then returned to life. I think it might be even more urgent to do a study of near-life experiences! The question is not, Is there life after death? The question that begs asking is, Is there life before death? We all need to be present and accounted for in life.

I am alive and well. There's a calling in my heart, and I will make my life worthwhile.

Let's Cut to the Chase

"Do what is required of you and remain a slave. Do more than is required and become free."
—MARCUS GARVEY, PAN-AFRICANIST

A comedian once quipped, "Many of us are at the 'metallic age'—gold in our teeth, silver in our hair, and lead in our pants. Everybody wants to live a long time, but nobody wants to get old."

People who are bored or unhappy can live happy, productive lives—regardless of age—if they take the trouble to find what it is they really want. If they can settle upon a purpose, they will be filled with new vitality. It will seem as though they found the fountain of youth—a way to turn back the clock and experience a life filled with interest, excitement, and fulfillment.

There is an old fable about a dog that boasted of his ability to run at breakneck speed. One day he chased a rabbit and failed to catch it. The other dogs ridiculed him on account of his previous bravado. He replied, "You must remember that the rabbit was running for his life, while I was only running for my dinner." You see, the purpose is so important.

I have met many people who found excitement and youth throughout their lives. I remember my interview with A. G. Gaston, the one-hundred-year-old insurance tycoon from Birmingham, Alabama. People like Dr. Gaston never age. Their minds and interests remain as young and clear at one hundred as they were at twenty, because they've had a singular purpose in life. They have a high degree of empathy with others. They eat and sleep well; they work, play, and love with gusto. Men and women with settled objectives—people who know who they are and where they are going—achieve their goals. There's no stopping them. They are filled with energy, drive, and with too much desire to slow them down. Are you one of these people? *You can be!*

Today I will take a few moments to redefine my goals. It is better that I wear out than rust out.

The Meter Is Running

"You can't build a reputation on what you're going to do tomorrow."
—JOHN ROGERS, FOUNDER, ARIEL CAPITAL MANAGEMENT

Have you ever stopped to figure the cost of the phrase *wait a minute*? For example, if you earned approximately $25,000 a year, every minute you have to wait costs five cents; at $50,000 a year this figure doubles to nearly ten cents a minute. And if you earned $500,000 a year, your time would be worth more than a dollar a minute. Johnson Publishing founder John H. Johnson mentioned that he regarded every hour of his day to be worth at least $1,000. Time is priceless. Indifference to the value of time is a real tragedy. Many a wasted life dates its ruin from a lost five minutes. *Too late* can be read between the lines on the tombstone of many a man or woman who has failed.

A class of sixth-graders had been assigned a term paper to be completed over a two-month period. The day the project was due had finally come. The instructor, a seasoned teacher, was prepared to hear all types of excuses from those who had not been working steadily on their papers. She approached each student to collect their reports. "Where's your report?" the teacher asked the little girl in the last row.

"My dog ate it," the little girl replied through sad eyes. The teacher, who was used to this sort of thing shot the small child a stare of disbelief. But the child insisted, "It's true. I had to force him, but he ate it!"

If we don't begin to put our dreams and desires into action, they will be eaten up by procrastination and inactivity. Don't waste another minute. Read the handwriting on the wall: *Pursue your goals before it's too late!*

Every minute of my time is precious. I will value this irreplaceable resource.

Can You Say "Thank You"?

"You better appreciate what you have before you haven't."
—CECE WINANS, SINGER

What's the secret of a pleasing personality? The following story will provide a clue.

An executive arrived one morning in his office a few hours earlier than usual. No one was there when he arrived except George, the custodian. George was a faithful employee with many years of service to the firm. When his boss walked into the office, George was emptying trash cans, dusting furniture, and cleaning the office. When George's boss noticed him going about his routine, he said, "George, you know, as I look around the building, I can't help thinking what an asset you've been to our organization. You've always kept this place clean and tidy.

"George," he continued, "you're an important part of our team, and I want you to know that I appreciate you and all that you have done."

George paused and then replied, "Thank you, sir," and walked out of the room with his dust cloth in hand. A few minutes passed. Suddenly the office door opened, and in walked George. His eyes were moist, there was a tear on his cheek. His boss didn't understand. He said, "What's wrong? Did I say something to offend you?"

George forced a smile and then replied, "No, sir, you didn't offend me. But I have something I would like to share with you. I've worked for this company for twenty years, and this morning is the first time anyone has ever told me that they appreciated anything I've ever done."

He continued, "I just want you to know that I appreciate what you said more than I've ever appreciated my paycheck!"

The deepest craving in human nature is the desire to be appreciated.

Today I will show appreciation for the people who work tirelessly for me.

Press On

"The road to success runs uphill."
—WILLIE DAVIS, NFL HALL-OF-FAMER AND ENTREPRENEUR

The road to success requires persistence. Little progress will be made if our first concern is to avoid disappointments. In spite of our discouraging past experiences, we need to try again.

There's a story about the California gold rush that tells of two brothers who sold their possessions to prospect for gold. They discovered a vein of the shining ore, staked a claim, and proceeded to get down to the serious business of extracting the gold from the mine. At first all went well, but then a strange thing happened. The vein of gold disappeared! They had come to the end of their rainbow, and the pot of gold was no longer there. The brothers continued to pick away, but without success. Finally they gave up in disgust.

They sold their equipment and claim rights for a few hundred dollars and took the train back home. Meanwhile the man who bought the claim hired an engineer to examine the rock strata of the mine. The engineer advised him to continue digging in the same spot where the former owners had left off— and three feet deeper, the new owner struck gold! Just think, a little more persistence and the two brothers would have been millionaires.

We cannot allow temporary setbacks to be a cause for disappointment. We must press on, press up, and press for success.

Persistence is my passage to reaching my goals. I will persist.

Someone's at the Door

"Opportunity will not only knock on your door; if you're not careful, it will knock you down."
—WALLY "FAMOUS" AMOS, ENTREPRENEUR

There are no hopeless situations; there are only men and women who have grown hopeless about them. When Marian Anderson, the accomplished opera singer, visited the renowned composer Sibelius, the maestro listened to her voice and said with tears in his eyes, "My roof is too low for you!" The world has too low a ceiling for any aspiring individual.

Many of us miss opportunities because our ceiling is too low; unfortunately we live without an expectation of goodness. We believe that something is too good to be true, when in fact blessings are the only things good enough to be true.

There's a story of two salesmen at an outdoor sports exposition, selling motorboats in booths adjacent to each other. Sales were slow and customers were few. A gentleman with sunglasses approached one of the booths and, after a few pleasantries, told the salesman, "I would like to purchase one million dollars' worth of your boats."

The salesman, thinking this customer was too good to be true, became annoyed. "Listen, friend," he grumbled, "come back another time when I'm in the mood for your jokes."

"Very well, sir," the customer replied. "Good day." He walked to the next booth and told the salesman, "I would like to buy one million dollars' worth of your boats."

Without batting an eyelash, the salesman said, "Yes, sir! Which models would you like?" After some discussion the customer took out his checkbook, wrote a deposit check for $100,000, shook the hand of the salesman, and went on his way. As it turned out, the buyer was a wealthy businessman searching for products abroad. The salesman received his standard 10 percent commission—in this case $100,000—because he was willing to accept his good. *Nothing is too good to be true!*

I will accept my good and move on.

Going with the Flow

*"The question is not always where we stand but in
which direction we are headed."*
—MARY FRANCES BERRY, EDUCATOR AND ACTIVIST

Life is showering its gifts upon us at this very moment. A force of love and light is streaming toward you from all angles at all times. All you have to do is allow it to pour in. Blessings are being offered to all of us without condition or limit.

We can look at our capacity through the symbol of the hourglass. God's infinite abundance is above us, waiting for us, waiting to flow down. And, like an hourglass, we have the space to hold it all. Our mind is located at that skinny little juncture of the upper and lower vessels. It regulates how much can come through. If our mind is small, tight, and fearful, only a few meager grains will drop down. However, if our mind is open, free, and expansive, all of God's riches can pour through. We receive as much as we let in.

Positive thinking means seeing the blessedness in everything. It requires a complete revision of the way we view life. It means tearing down our judgments and opinions of what is good and what is bad, what is right and what is wrong. It means having an open mind. And with this open mind we can receive all the blessings that God has to offer.

I open my mind to the prosperity, happiness, and health that God has to offer.

Stuck in the Mud

*"I have a choice. I can sit on my butt and be bitter
about what Hollywood should be doing, or I can
use my resources to do it myself."*
—LONETTE MCKEE, SINGER AND ACTRESS

As we find our way in life, sometimes we are confronted with the question, What are you going to do? Sometimes misfortune strikes and tragedy hits home, and the question begins to surface, What are you going to do? Sometimes sickness and disease flare up or our careers begin to stall, and the question begs asking, What are you going to do? Sometimes we earnestly and sincerely pray, and it seems as if our prayers have fallen on deaf ears. Once again the question confronts us, What are you going to do?

A truck was stuck in mud up to its axles. Three lumberjacks sat in stony silence in the cab. The first man slammed the steering wheel, cursed, and stormed out of the truck.

The second thought the early-morning woods were quite inviting. He said he would crawl under a pine tree and take a nap until someone came along to pull them out.

The third man, left alone, grabbed an ax and a saw and began cutting wood to slide under the wheels. Within an hour he managed to pull the truck out of the mud, and soon he was on his way.

We can choose how we respond to any problem. Just like these three men, our response may be to curse and give up, to sit back and wait for someone to help us, or to work fearlessly to overcome our obstacles. The event itself isn't important; *it's what we do about our challenges that makes the difference.*

When I'm stuck in the mud, I will act!

A Good Track Record

"The pain means there's feeling there."
—DARRYL STINGLEY, ACTIVIST FOR THE PHYSICALLY
CHALLENGED

Olympic gold medalist Carl Lewis's first exposure to track and field began in the eighth grade. Uncoordinated and barely trained, he suffered defeat after defeat. One evening he told his parents, both track coaches, that he was tired of losing. His father replied, "The successful person is easy to start and tough to stop."

Life's pathways are chock full of obstacles only overcome by persistence. By persistence the snail reached the ark. By persistence the great pyramids of Egypt were built, offering civilization a springboard to even greater knowledge. By persistence African missionaries were able to survive long, trying periods before ever obtaining a convert. There has never been a successful man or woman who hasn't known the tough answers that only come through the hard lessons of persistence.

But is there success without persistence? Yes, it's possible to achieve without persisting, but it is something like being a student who will not go to school. A soldier who will not join an army. A salesman without a customer. A sailor without a ship. A writer without a reader. A teacher without a pupil. A preacher without a prayer. A musician without an instrument. A doctor without a patient or a bee without a hive. If you are to succeed, you must persist!

A teenager had decided to quit school, saying he was bored by his lessons. His father desperately tried to convince him to stay with it. "Son," he said, "you just can't quit. History is loaded with examples of great leaders who are remembered because they didn't quit. Martin Luther King didn't quit. Booker T. Washington didn't quit. George Washington Carver didn't quit. And Willie Johnson didn't quit."

"Who?" the son burst in. "Who in the world is Willie Johnson?"

"See," the father replied, "you don't remember him. He quit!" We only remember those who persist.

When it comes to my goals, I will be easy to start and tough to stop.

Thankful for Little

"He enjoys much who is thankful for little."
——JEWEL DIAMOND TAYLOR, MOTIVATIONAL SPEAKER

After entering a department store a woman was startled when a band began to play, cameras started flashing, and a dignified executive pinned an orchid on her dress and handed her ten crisp thousand-dollar bills. She was the store's millionth customer, and the owner and staff celebrated the occasion. Television cameras were focused on her, and reporters began firing questions. "Tell me," a reporter shouted, "just what did you come to the store for today?"

The woman, somewhat miffed, hesitated for a minute then grumbled, "I'm on my way to the complaint department!" The woman revealed how she had purchased a scarf from the same store the previous day but got upset when the clerk failed to hand her a receipt.

This poor soul is an example of one of life's real tragedies: She fails to place circumstances within their proper perspective. Reflect for a moment. Ours is a history synonymous with burden. As slaves, and later as domestics and servants, we gathered, picked, chopped, planted, plowed, cooked, fetched, cleaned, bathed, built, dug, nursed, and sweat so that others could enjoy creature comforts that we could only imagine.

Today's world, by comparison, is one of opportunity, one that our forebears could only envision. Our world should be one of gratitude. Gratitude is prayer. Gratitude is strength. Gratitude is love. The best way to show our gratitude is to accept life with joy.

Today I will approach life with a grateful heart.

Working it Out

"The successful man will look for work even after he has found a job."
—JOSHUA I. SMITH, FOUNDER, THE MAXIMA CORPORATION

Have you ever noticed that the longer you put something off, the more difficult it is to get started? Ironically we deliberately add to the frustration and unhappiness in our lives that we could so clearly avoid.

A person carrying heavy burdens can manage as long as he keeps marching forward. The moment he stops and sits down to rest, his burden becomes heavier. The distance to be traveled seems greater, and the work becomes much more unpleasant. It's moments like these that lead us to believe there's just no way of overcoming our circumstances, of digging out. But there is!

Pick the task that seems most difficult and crucial to your goals and simply begin. Just by plugging in you'll feel better, and you will find that your obstacles are not as insurmountable as you imagined. Keep at it, and before long that pile of tasks that at one time seemed so overwhelming is now behind you. It isn't the struggle itself that overtakes us, it's dwelling on how difficult the task is going to be. The process of fretting over our dilemma drains us emotionally. We delay making decisions hoping that somehow, through some miracle, our problems will disappear.

All growth depends on activity. There is no personal growth without effort, and effort means *work*. Effort is not a curse; it is the prerequisite of success, the true measure of civilization. The Creator didn't burden us with work. He blessed us with it.

Today I will engage in my work and thereby ease my burden.

Again I Rise

"I'd continue to teach my children what I had been taught: that they needn't see a black become president or win the Indy 500 on television before they could do it in real life."
—ERIC V. COPAGE, WRITER

Researchers have observed a predictable and strange habit of fleas while training the tiny insects. When fleas are first placed in a jar, they try to jump out. When the lid is placed on the jar, the fleas continue to jump, and they repeatedly hit their heads on the lid. But even fleas aren't crazy. As they continue to beat their brains out, they finally catch on and no longer jump high enough to hit the lid of the jar. The scientist can then remove the lid with no fear of the fleas leaping out of the jar. Why? Because they have conditioned themselves to only jump just so high—that's all they can do!

Are you like a flea? Have you been conditioned to jump only so high? Achievers always rise to the top, especially in tough times. They're like beans in a can of peas. When you place peas and beans in a can and vigorously shake them up, the peas always settle at the bottom while the beans rise to the top. So it is with achievers. They can never be held down even when shaken up. If you truly have leadership abilities and are determined to hit your mark, you'll always rise to the top.

I may have been conditioned to only jump so high, but I refuse to be held down any longer.

Act on It

"The secret of getting things done is to act!"
—BENJAMIN O. DAVID, FIRST AFRICAN AMERICAN TO
COMMAND A U.S. ARMY AIR FORCE BASE

A familiar song tells us to whistle a happy tune so no one will know we're afraid. Unlikely as it may seem, there's a lot of truth to that. Acting the way we would like to feel really does help us feel that way.

In a university experiment psychological researchers asked student volunteers to make six different facial expressions. The six emotions to be expressed were fear, surprise, disgust, sadness, anger, and happiness. The findings were surprising. When the volunteers looked afraid, their bodies reacted as if they really were afraid; their heart rates speeded up and their skin temperatures dropped. For the most part, appropriate physical reactions also occurred when the other emotions were portrayed.

"Act as if . . ." is an important coping technique in many self-help programs. If you are fearful, act as if you are the bravest person you know. If you're having a down day, act as if it is your job to cheer everybody else up. The point of course is not to fool yourself about how you really feel. Acting successful is a prerequisite to success.

I can accelerate my positive results by acting out my objectives.

You're in Good Hands

"The tragedy of life doesn't lie in not reaching your goal. The tragedy lies in having no goal to reach."
—BENJAMIN E. MAYS, EDUCATOR

A fortune-teller studied the hand of a young man and said, "You will be poor and very unhappy until you are forty years old."

The young man responded, "Well, after that, what will happen? Will I be rich and happy?" The fortune-teller said, "No, you'll still be poor, but you'll be used to it after that."

I receive numerous letters from people across the country who say they truly wish to be successful, but don't know how. They claim to have tried all sorts of programs and involved rules supposedly leading to success and prosperity. Having met and conversed with scores of achievers, I have found the only necessary requirement of achievement is to adhere to five simple steps:

· Focus on that which you desire most—*goals*.
· Develop a gratitude attitude—*thanks*.
· Emulate someone you admire—*mentorship*.
· Recognize that strength grows out of struggle—*perseverance*.
· Dedicate yourself to lifelong learning—*study*.

Herein lies your answer. Only you know whether you adhere to these rules. *It is you, and you alone, who can predict with startling accuracy whether you will reach your goals.* The person who makes up his or her mind to reach some grand ideal must follow many steps. None are more important than these tried-and-true keys.

Today I will set aside time to apply these five keys in every area of my life.

•

Just When You Thought It Was Safe to Go Back into the Water

"It's not what you get in life, but what you give. Our Creator teaches us that by saving the life of another, we save our own."

—GREG WILLIAMS, RESCUED A KOREAN AMERICAN FROM A VIGILANTE MOB DURING THE L.A. RIOTS

What is important to you? What do you *really* value most? When asked this question writer and poet laureate Maya Angelou left no doubt as to what she considers important in her life. She wrote, "To those who would try to diminish me, I say you cannot cripple my spirit. You cannot do that, it is not yours to cripple. I alone am responsible to my God for my spirit. Not you, unless I give it to you. And I would be a fool. That is all I've got. I have nothing but my spirit, and I will not allow anyone to have or trample on it."

A frightened woman found her place in a lifeboat that was about to be lowered into the raging North Atlantic. She suddenly thought of something she needed, so she asked permission to return to her stateroom before the overcrowded lifeboat was cast off. The woman was granted three minutes by the commanding officer and then they would have to leave without her. Frantically she ran across the deck that was already slanted at a dangerous angle. Next she raced through the gambling room with all the money that had rolled to one side, ankle deep. She came to her quarters and quickly pushed aside her diamond rings and expensive jewelry as she reached to the shelf above her bed and grabbed three small oranges. She quickly found her way back to the lifeboat and settled in the back.

Thirty minutes earlier this woman would not have chosen a handful of oranges over the smallest diamond. But death had boarded the *Titanic*. One blast of its awful breath had transformed all values. Instantaneously, priceless possessions had become worthless. And in that brief moment this woman preferred three small oranges to a handful of diamonds.

The relative value of health and wealth depends on which one you have left. There's nothing wrong if you possess riches. The error arises *when riches possess you.*

I value my spirit more than any material possession or gift.

Open the Door

"I would just like to get on with my life."
—ANITA HILL, LAW PROFESSOR

A middle-aged businessman approached the entrance of the office building where he worked. As a smartly dressed young woman arrived at the same moment, he stepped back and held the door open for her. She looked at him and said with annoyance, "Don't hold the door for me just because I'm a lady."

To her surprise he looked right back and replied, "I'm not. I'm holding the door open because I'm a gentleman." As human beings, we must act toward each other with an open heart of gratitude and not on the basis of how someone else may respond.

The people who are successful are those who express sincere gratitude for their gifts. Giving thanks for "any and every little thing" always opens the door for more to come. Likewise, the more we appreciate, the more we will find to appreciate. We do not need to create anything new; we need only to see the whole picture of what we already have.

I like to start and end my day with thoughts of praise and appreciation. Throughout the course of the day I engage in self-talk, no matter the outward conditions. My favorite affirmations are "Thank you, Father," and "Something fantastic is going to happen to me today!" I like to close my day in the same manner. As I lie in bed before dozing off, I quietly reflect upon the events of the day and mentally give blessings for that which has been given to me. I live in a realm of thanksgiving.

I will develop the ability to be thankful for what I have. This is the cornerstone to wealth.

Sugar Free

"All over the world, nobody has a God who doesn't resemble them. Except black Americans. They can't even see they're worshipping someone else's God, because they want so badly to assimilate."
—AUGUST WILSON, PLAYWRIGHT

One day, a young warrior sat on a rock by a stream chewing a stalk of sugarcane. Suddenly, as if a flash of lightning burst forth in his head, he saw the Truth. He realized his divinity; he saw the marvelous perfection of the great plan of the universe. The warrior was filled with a sense of ease that brought peace and harmony to his being. He returned to his village to share his wondrous insight, and before long, crowds began to gather. His fellow villagers realized that he knew something special, and they yearned to share this gift. When he told them of his wholeness and of their perfection, someone asked, "How did you find this inner peace?"

"I'm not so sure," he admitted. "All I know is that one morning I was sitting on a rock by the stream nibbling on sugarcane, and all of a sudden the Truth was revealed to me!"

The next morning the man awoke to find his village empty. Puzzled, he began to look for his brothers and sisters. After hours of searching across dusty back roads, he gave up and decided to rest for a moment by the stream where he had embraced his wholeness. There, to his amazement, he found the entire village huddled together on that rock, all eating sugarcane!

Does this story sound familiar? Too often we mistake the form of our experience for its essence. We worship the physical manifestation—the doctrine, the dogma, the tradition—instead of the spirit itself. We confuse the circumstances of our enlightenment with enlightenment itself. We can all find inner peace, but we need only to let go of the idea that there is "something"—some church, some structure, some cloth, some water, some bead, some chant, some rite, some ritual, or somebody—that we must engage in first to find God! The way to peace is through spirit.

I will place my trust in spirit, the source of all wisdom and inspiration.

Get Real

"I figured that if I said it enough, I would convince the world that I really was the greatest."
—MUHAMMAD ALI, FORMER BOXING GREAT

A young college student preparing for his first job interview was advised by friends to be serious, dour, sophisticated, and a lot of other things that he was not. When he arrived for the interview, he was escorted to the office by a cordial and engaging woman he assumed was a secretary. Because she seemed so open and friendly, he decided he could find out what the job involved by asking her questions. The conversation went smoothly, and after an hour fear and trepidation had been replaced by enthusiasm about the position. The young student was about to ask some questions regarding the coming interview when the woman informed him that the job was his. It turned out that this pleasant conversation had been an interview. The young man had learned an important lesson: *Be yourself.*

Over the years we have shielded ourselves from the destruction we feared by covering our true self with plates of protection, masks of bravado, and stone walls of defenses. Layer by layer we overlaid our original nature with illusions and untruths about who we are. At first our intention was to protect ourselves from pain, but in the bargain we kept up an image expected of us by the outer world, but our adaptation has been at the dear cost of our inner life. Ironically, in our attempt to make others believe we are something we are not, we have fooled ourselves. If you tell a lie long enough, you begin to believe it; ultimately deceptions entrap even the liar. Accepting ourselves as we are and where we are is the first step to success.

Today I will release any thoughts of self-delusion and embrace honesty.

I'm All Ears

"Leadership begins with sound, verbal communication skills."
—TERRIE WILLIAMS, PRESIDENT,
THE TERRIE WILLIAMS AGENCY

Listening is more than remaining silent while looking attentive. Listening is making the effort to hear. It is paying attention. It is both hearing words and sensing meaning. Listening is discovering the feeling of what others are trying to convey. Celebrated entertainer Pearl Bailey said, "To talk to someone who does not listen is enough to tease the devil." We all know what she means.

A story is told of an elderly grandfather who was convinced he was losing his hearing. He visited his doctor, who gave him a thorough check-up. His physician pulled out a gold watch and asked, "Can you hear this ticking?"

"Of course," the man said.

The doctor walked toward the door and held up the watch again. "Now can you hear it?" The old man concentrated and said, "Yes, I can hear it clearly."

The doctor then walked out the door into the next room and said, "Can you hear it now?" Again the man said, "Yes."

The doctor approached the old man and said, "Sir, there's nothing wrong with your hearing. You just don't listen."

Those on the fast track to success take care to fully understand what others are saying. For even if they choose to disagree, they want to be sure what they're disagreeing with. The act of listening can change the attitude of both the listener and the speaker. When someone truly listens to us, then we, too, may come to hear what we are actually saying—and in that hearing come to change our position without the listener speaking a word.

Today I will be patient enough to listen.

The Highest Form of Love

"To love the world is no big chore. It's that miserable guy next door who's the problem."
—GARDNER TAYLOR, PASTOR, CONCORD BAPTIST CHURCH

Acts of courage may be spontaneous. But when it means sacrificing for another, this becomes the highest form of love. For example, a small child lived with his grandmother. One night their house caught fire. The grandmother, trying to rescue the little boy asleep upstairs, perished in the smoke and flames. A crowd gathered around the burning house. No one knew what to do, for the front of the house was a mass of flames. Suddenly a stranger rushed from the crowd and circled to the back, where he spotted an iron pipe that reached an upstairs window. He disappeared for a minute, then triumphantly reappeared with the boy in his arms.

Weeks later a public hearing was held to determine in whose custody the child would be placed. Each person wanting the boy was allowed to speak briefly. The first man who hoped to receive custody of the child responded, "I have a large farm; he would enjoy the outdoors." A second man told of the advantages he could provide: "I'm a teacher. I have a vast library. He could get a good education." Finally, the richest man in the county spoke: "I'm wealthy. I could give the boy his heart's desire."

The judge then asked, "Does anyone else care to step forward?" From a seat in the rear rose a stranger who had slipped in unnoticed. As he walked toward the front of the room, deep suffering showed on his face. He stopped directly in front of the child. Slowly the stranger removed his hands from his pockets. They were terribly scarred. Here was the man who had saved the boy's life. With a leap the child threw himself around the man's neck and once again held on for life.

Love like this is the highest kind of love. It comes without strings attached or any form of repayment.

I am worthy of giving and receiving selfless love.

Out on a Limb

"We learn from failure much more than from success."
—JOHN H. JOHNSON, FOUNDER,
JOHNSON PUBLISHING COMPANY

To achieve any goal, risk is always involved. Someone might say, "Well, I'm not taking any risks. I'm not going out on a limb." What this ignorant soul doesn't realize is that out on a limb is where the fruit is. This is where the fruit has always been—*out on a limb*. There's a law working within the universe that ensures that rewards come after risk and not before.

Most of us start our lives with a healthy attitude toward risk. As children we can't wait to attempt something new. A healthy, happy child, like a healthy, happy adult, loves to test and stretch himself. We are taking risks when we take those first faltering steps. Yet somehow, between the ages of two and twenty-two, many of us undergo a dramatic change of attitude. We become preoccupied with being "safe and secure." As a result there are very few people in the world who think originally. Most people act like puppets, mimicking the latest trends, voicing popular opinions, and repeating the same process day after day, year after year.

The spice of life is in doing new things, surfacing new ideas, forging something from our substance. The search for security and safety stifles our life force. Safe and secure—free from all worries—is akin to lying in a box buried six feet under. The few people who do think originally and have the courage to act on their inspiration are hailed as geniuses, trendsetters, and saints. We are all geniuses when we take risks.

I will take well-calculated risks.

Faith Is the Answer

"If your faith can't move mountains, it should at least climb them."
—QUEEN MOTHER MOORE, ACTIVIST

When life seems to bring nothing but a string of defeats and disappointments, we've got to have faith that something good is still in store for us. With this faith we can forge ahead and continue to put forth our best effort. Without it we give up and accept what comes our way. Our dreams turn to dust.

Are you troubled or confused? Faith is the answer. Are you burdened with grief or sorrow? Faith is the answer. Faith makes the difference between begging and praising, between crawling and leaping. No matter the problem—*faith is the answer!*

Indulgence may say, "Drink your way out." Science says, "Invent your way out." Industry says, "Work your way out." The military says. "Fight your way out." The world says, "Entertain your way out." Philosophy says, "Think your way out." But our Creator teaches us to "Pray your way out."

The world answers back to our faith. It trusts when we trust. It believes when we believe. It responds to our confidence. It says to the farmer, "Sow your seed." It says to the pilot, "Spread your wings." It says to the prospector, "Keep drilling." It says to the sailor, "Hoist your sail." It says to the infant, "Keep walking." It says to the newlyweds, "Walk together." It says to the downtrodden, "Lift your head up." It says to the surgeon, "Place your hand in mine." It says to the author, "Keep writing." It says to the Olympian, "Keep training." It says to the achiever, "Keep believing!"

Today I will maintain my faith.

These Chains Are Heavy

"Freedom is lost unless it is continually fought for."
—P. B. S. PINCHBACK, FIRST AFRICAN-AMERICAN UNION
ARMY OFFICER

Personal freedom is something we all long for. Far too often we passively stand by and hope that someone or something will take action that will set us free. We wait for a situation to change or an event to occur that will bring more freedom into our life. If we only understood that many times we are confined in mind only.

Once a wild baby elephant is captured, hunters tie the end of a long chain around the elephant's foot. The other end is tied to a huge rubber tree. The elephant will pull with all its strength, but it can't budge the tree. Finally, after struggling for weeks, the elephant surrenders to the chain. At this point the hunters take the elephant and chain it to a little iron stake by a circus tent. The elephant never attempts to pull away because it still thinks it's chained to a rubber tree. It never realizes how easily it could break away. It has given up and surrendered to its circumstances.

In many respects we resemble the elephant. We all have moments when we are shackled by disappointments, by unfilled expectations, and by dead-end careers. When these challenges occur, our immediate reaction is to struggle and pull and to do anything to free ourselves from these undesirable circumstances, often to no avail. Later, when we take our mind off our problems, and we encounter opportunities to break free—we meet new people, surface new ideas—we remain chained to our unwanted conditions because we are still bound to the past.

Past limitations notwithstanding, the reality is that we have far more choice in self-liberation than we may realize. Personal freedom comes not from outer conditions or external events falling into place but entirely from our own beliefs, attitudes, choices, and actions. Each of us has the strength to break free.

My past does not predict my future. My chains stem from negative beliefs, and I will break free.

Where Are You Running?

*"Some people change jobs, spouses, and friends—
but never think of changing themselves."*
—PAULA GIDDINGS, WRITER

Oh, to just escape and get away from it all! Negative relationships, problems at work, unresolved issues at home—these are just a few of the demanding situations we live with day in and day out.

But before we go running off, change our name, and start over again someplace else, we'd better think about the common denominator in all our problems. Most of those thorny situations have a lot more to do with us than they do with "them." Our unfair boss doesn't know our irritating neighbor, and neither of them knows my landlord. The only common element in all those relational problems is me.

When we take the time to search inward for change, we see everything in a different light. What we previously thought vital, becomes trivial. We delightedly perceive that we can truly choose to change from victim to victor. Many people spend their entire lives hoping their circumstances will change for the better. *Circumstances only get better as we get better.* Things change when we change. A wise man has said, "Unless you change what you think, you will always get what you've got!"

Resolving the issues that face us almost always means changing something in ourselves. Much of the hurt that stems from all of them is self-inflicted, whether actively or passively. Even if we ran from those situations, we would likely re-create them in a new setting. When even a part of the problem is us, the solution is ours as well. We can't run far enough to escape ourselves.

Today I will take a few minutes to look in the mirror. I won't ask others to change until I change first.

Have You Earned Your X?

"Power never takes a back step—only in the face of more power."
—MALCOLM X, PAN-AFRICANIST AND HUMAN RIGHTS
ACTIVIST

The above quote is indicative of the sheer magnetism and level of commitment that Malcolm X was known for. Each of us could benefit from developing Malcolm's level of passion as we pursue our goals.

Malcolm Little's boyhood was one long struggle with poverty and alienation. His father was murdered by vigilantes, and his mother suffered the indignity of life in a mental institution. Life on the streets became the only life he knew. At seventeen he hustled in New York, drowning in a sea of crime—drugs, prostitution, and gambling. Three years later he was caught and sentenced to ten years in prison.

"I was the personification of evil," Malcolm said of his first months in prison. He hurled obscenities at every white in authority and cursed God so much that inmates named him Satan. But it was here that Malcolm was exposed to a growing sect known as the Nation of Islam, who claimed they could turn his life around. This philosophy struck Malcolm like "a blinding light," and he mended his ways. For his loyalty and hard work he was rewarded with the letter *X*, which symbolized the replacement of his "slave name"—Little—with the African family name he never knew. From this platform as religious spokesman and newly crowned leader of a hope-filled people, Malcolm's life would come full circle. He had truly earned his *X*—from an *ex*-convict to an *ex*ample, from an *ex*-drug addict to personal *ex*cellence.

Our community could benefit from his example. *Black America must earn its X!* Where it applies, we must become *ex*-drug abusers, *ex*-dropouts, *ex*-alcoholics, *ex*-thieves, and *ex*-offenders, and cease to offer any *ex*cuses for our shortcomings. Instead we must strive to *ex*cel, *ex*-cite, and *ex*ceed; to become *ex*ceptional as we *ex*amine our values, and *ex*claim to the world that we *ex*pect success and *expel* any thoughts of poverty or failure. *It's time that we earn our X!*

Today I will set aside some time to talk with our youth and help them earn their X.

Red, Black, and Green

"Lift up your head, you mighty race!"
——MARCUS GARVEY, PAN-AFRICANIST

Pride is important to our self-development. Pride uplifts us. Pride encourages us. Pride takes our minds off our burdens.

We are a proud race—*prideful*! When other groups watch us walk or see us shake hands or "slap each other five," they mistakenly call it soul. But you and I know that it's really *pride*. We are proud to see another brother or sister who has made it through the struggle. Ours is a proud family.

Afrocentricity, the culmination of our efforts to reclaim our cultural past, has been healing and instructive. Today our exterior expressions of cultural pride—kente-cloth garments; red, black, and green T-shirts; and braided hair—can be seen on any street corner throughout inner-city America. We've begun to partake of a healthy pride that feeds our consciousness and empowers our spirit.

Whenever Joe Louis knocked someone out, or when Jackie Robinson stole home, or when Henry Aaron blasted another one, or Marcus Garvey stood up, or Martin Luther King, Jr., dreamed, or Malcolm X refused to back down, or Thurgood Marshall debated, or Paul Robeson recited, or Benjamin Mays read, or Mary McLeod Bethune led, or Charles Drew healed, or George Washington Carver calculated, or Marva Collins motivated, or Clara Hale loved, or Wilma Rudolph ran, or Barbara Jordan spoke, or Jesse Jackson preached, or Johnetta Cole taught, or Colin Powell saluted, or Marian Anderson sang, or Sidney Poitier acted, or Sammy Davis, Jr., danced, or Debi Thomas skated, or Warren Moon threw, or Michael Jordan slam-dunked, or Arthur Ashe broke serve, or Maya Angelou encouraged, or whenever my grandmother walked down the street, I had cause to stick out my chest and be proud!

Today I will recount all the things my race has done, and I will be proud!

Soul Survivors

*"The only reason why I am here is because
somebody held on!"*
—CHANCELLOR WILLIAMS, AUTHOR AND HISTORIAN

A thirty-year-old mother was told she was in the advanced stage of terminal cancer. One doctor advised her to spend her remaining days enjoying herself on the beaches of southern Florida. A second physician offered her the hope of living two to four years with the grueling side effects of chemotherapy and radiation treatment. She made her decision and then notified her three small children in a moving letter:

> I've chosen to try to survive for you. This choice will have some horrible costs, including pain, loss of my sense of humor, and moods I won't be able to control. But I must try to bear this, if only on the outside chance that I might live one minute longer. And that minute could be the one in which you might need me the most. For this I intend to struggle, tooth and nail, so help me God.

Like the preceding story, you are here because someone chose to survive for you. Someone struggled tooth and nail, kept alive only by the grace of God. Maybe it was your mother or father, an aunt or an uncle, your grandmother or grandfather, or even a great-grandparent—but someone, somewhere chose to survive for you. Someone chose to endure the beatings, withstand the lynchings, undergo the hardships, swallow their pride, turn a cheek to the degradation, sustain the poverty, put up with the indecencies, tolerate the inequities, look past the injustice, and withstand the oppression to *SURVIVE for YOU*!

You owe it to yourself as well as the next generation to continue your struggle forward.

Today I will thank my family for surviving on my behalf.

I Dare You!

"The collapse of character begins with compromise."
—FREDERICK DOUGLASS, ABOLITIONIST

It has been one year. Three hundred and sixty-four days of inspiration, motivation, empowerment, and wisdom from some of your best and brightest. Now it is time to place all that you have read into action. This is my challenge.

It is difficult to put a challenge on paper. I would rather look you straight in the eye and say, "I dare you!" But in my mind I have imagined that I am on one side of a table and you are on the other. I am looking across and saying, "I dare you!"

I dare you to develop the enduring qualities of Booker T. Washington and Madame Walker.

I dare you to see the bigger picture as did Benjamin Mays, to study and read, and to pay the price to secure an education.

I dare you to make your home a centerpiece for love and spiritual values as did Clara "Mother" Hale and Fannie Lou Hamer.

I dare you to step out boldly in spite of the odds to build a profitable enterprise, one that your race can be proud of, as did John Johnson and Earl Graves.

I dare you to light the fire of young, imaginative minds as did Mary McLeod Bethune and Niara Sudarkasa.

I dare you to turn a deaf ear to any possible excuses and make a name for yourself as did Bonnie St. John.

I dare you to write from the heart and stir the consciousness of a people as did Alice Walker and Toni Morrison.

I dare you to return to your roots and share with others the fruits of your daring, as did Alex Haley. I dare you to become involved. I dare you to become strong. I dare you to become rejuvenated. I dare you to become alive with possibilities. *"I dare you!"*

Today I accept the dare.